THE UNITED NAT

The United Nations in the 1990s

Peter R. Baehr
Professor of Human Rights
Leiden University and Utrecht University
The Netherlands

and

Leon Gordenker
Professor Emeritus of Politics
Princeton University, New Jersey, USA

Written under the auspices of the
Center of International Studies
Princeton University

Second Edition

MACMILLAN

First edition 1992
Second edition 1994

Published by
THE MACMILLAN PRESS LTD
Houndmills, Basingstoke, Hampshire RG21 2XS
and London
Companies and representatives
throughout the world

ISBN 0–333–60649–3 hardcover
ISBN 0–333–51034–8 paperback

A catalogue record for this book is available
from the British Library.

Printed in Great Britain by
Mackays of Chatham PLC
Chatham, Kent

To the memory of
Belia Emilie Gordenker-Strootman
Felix Baehr

Contents

Preface to the Second Edition

As this revision of *The United Nations in the 1990s* is completed, it is obvious, if it were not before, that the organization now constitutes an integral part of international politics. Whether it will maintain that position – or decline or grow yet more – remains anyone's guess. As international politics probably will not freeze in place, it seems likely that the fortunes of the United Nations will, as before, reflect dynamic factors outside of its control or purview.

Those varied and largely unpredictable activities of governments and other actors that we include in the term international politics have during the last three years deepened and broadened the agenda of the United Nations. This revised edition tries to sum up some of those additions and to show how they relate to earlier practice. As developments within the UN, especially with regard to peace and security, have so quickly and un-expectedly burst into the news, we cannot pretend to set out the last word on the organization. We have tried here, however, to sketch some of the most important changes since the last edition.

These changes include the far-reaching intervention of the organization in Iraq after its attack on Kuwait, the mounting of peace-keeping in Yugoslavia and Somalia and the apparent emergence of a new sense of international responsibility with regard to humanitarian disasters. But as with almost everything else in the experience of the United Nations, one decision or programme soon leads to supplements, complements, withdrawals or other changes. We have revised the first edition in order to take into account changes wherever they could be observed. Some errors were also corrected.

We wish to acknowledge the assistance with this revision of Ms Saskia Bal and Ms Francine van Lenthe of the Netherlands Institute of Human Rights, Ambassador N. Biegman of the Netherlands Permanent Mission to the United Nations, and Ms Sally Morphet of the Foreign and Commonwealth Office.

May 1993
PETER R. BAEHR
Heemstede, Netherlands

LEON GORDENKER
Princeton, NJ

Preface

While the last lines of this book were written in mid-1991, the usefulness, the promise and the fragility of the United Nations seemed evident. The great crisis in the Middle East, caused by the seizure of Kuwait by Iraq in August 1990, at once pulled the world organization into the central decision-making vortex. The Security Council provided the legal basis for international coercion to force Iraq to withdraw from Kuwait. It demonstrated a broad consensus among governments in every part of the world that Iraq's invasion of Kuwait was unacceptable. In the background, some parts of the UN system dealt with the needs of people who fled from Iraq to the neighbouring countries. Still other parts monitored the economic sanctions ordained by the Security Council and investigated Iraq's compliance with the complex terms of a cease-fire.

Decision-making in the Security Council was led by the United States government. The United Nations was used to define the aggression in the Persian Gulf but hardly to coordinate the military and political actions. Unlike the initial response to the attack on Korea in 1950, for the Persian Gulf in 1991, no unified military command was established. In both cases, the United States and its allies engaged the United Nations to establish legal and political reference points and to emphasize the breadth of international approval for their actions.

Both the quality of the public discussion of the Persian Gulf crisis and the role of the United Nations more generally relate to the origins of this book. The work reflects the beliefs of its authors that the United Nations is important enough in world politics to deserve an accurately informed public opinion. Our hope is that a clearly sketched introduction to the United Nations would help fill some of the recurrent gaps in understanding in public and classroom discussion. This book does not pretend to develop new knowledge, but it does attempt to set out the essential elements of forty-five years of experience with the UN system. It deliberately emphasizes historical development and legal institutional aspects, for some acquaintance with these is essential to informed judgement.

The framework of the book is formed by those principal topics which the United Nations Charter defines and which, barring cataclysmic change, can be expected to preoccupy the UN system into the twenty-first century. It attempts to avoid illusions about the role of the United Nations in international politics and about the benefits or costs it may have in terms of the foreign policies of its members. Finally, it is necessarily selective in the face of an enormous amount of UN activity.

Our transnational collaboration bridges the Atlantic Ocean. This, we hope, helps to discourage nationalistic partisanship and to encourage a cosmopolitan point of view. While we avoid policy recommendations, we do offer occasional judgements as to whether the United Nations has developed according to plans and expectations for it. The book concentrates on the UN system while attempting to remain sensitive to the world political context that conditions it. At the same time, we neither explain nor assay the world scene at every juncture, nor do we offer a general theory to cover everything that has or could happen to the United Nations.

Although we attempt objectivity, we bring to this work convictions about the value of international cooperation. Cooperation among governments, we hold – as did the founders of the United Nations – is essential to a peaceful world. That may be an unattainable goal. A great deal of cooperation nevertheless remains an unmistakable daily practice, a stable foundation, for the way governments relate to each other much of the time. Not all international cooperation works out to the benefit of all or is necessarily productive of a peaceful world in the long term. But the concept that international relations need to be organized and that institutions are useful in encouraging and supervising cooperation seems unassailable, especially after the end of the Cold War and the astonishingly quick reorganization of East and Central Europe.

Our collaboration began while we were fellows in the early 1970s at the Netherlands Institute of Advanced Study in the Humanities and Social Sciences (NIAS) at Wassenaar. A forerunner of this book was then developing. With another fellow at NIAS, P. J. G. Kapteyn, then Professor of International Law at Utrecht University, Baehr was drafting parts of what became *De Verenigde Naties: ideaal en werkelijkheid,* published in 1976 by Het Spectrum. Gordenker read the original manuscript and offered his comments. From the ensuing discussion came the first English language cousin of this book, *The United Nations: Reality and Ideal,* published in 1984 by Praeger. A revised Dutch version with the earlier title was published in 1985 by Boom.

Our confidence that this book may prove useful was bolstered by the willing help that we received from scholars, international civil servants, diplomats and national civil servants. They, as well as students in universities in the many countries where we have lectured, all deserve our thanks, although not all of them can be named here. Among those who can are Professor Theo van Boven of the Rijksuniversiteit in Limburg, who kindly read the chapter on human rights; Dr Johan Kaufmann, whose own writings have enlightened students of international organization and his fellow diplomats; and Mr Gerben Rignalda, a veteran official of the Netherlands Ministry of Foreign Affairs, who commented on the chapter on international cooperation and development. Gordenker owes specific thanks to the Rockefeller Foundation and the Ford Foundation for support for his research and to the Center of International Studies at Princeton University for its many services over the years, including those that made possible his continuing contact with the Netherlands and its scholarly community; and to the Graduate Institute of International Studies at Geneva for its many kindnesses while he taught there.

It is hardly necessary to say that we accept personal responsibility for the interpretations and errors of this book.

LEON GORDENKER
Princeton, NJ

PETER R. BAEHR
Heemstede, Netherlands

List of Abbreviations

ACC	Administrative Committee on Coordination
ECLA	Economic Commission for Latin America
ECOSOC	Economic and Social Council
EPTA	Expanded Programme of Technical Assistance
FAO	Food and Agriculture Organization
GATT	General Agreement on Tariffs and Trade
IAEA	International Atomic Energy Agency
IBRD	International Bank for Reconstruction and Development (later the World Bank)
ICAO	International Civil Aviation Organization
ICJ	International Court of Justice
IDA	International Development Association
IFAD	International Fund for Agricultural Development
IFC	International Finance Corporation
ILO	International Labour Organization
IMF	International Monetary Fund
IMO	International Maritime Organization
ITU	International Telecommunication Union
NATO	North Atlantic Treaty Organization
NIEO	New International Economic Order
OAS	Organization of American States
OAU	Organization for African Unity
ONUC	Opération des Nations Unies au Congo
OPEC	Organization of Petroleum Exporting Countries
PLO	Palestine Liberation Organization
SWAPO	South West African People's Organization
UDI	Unilateral Declaration of Independence
UNBRO	United Nations Border Relief Operation
UNCDF	United Nations Capital Development Fund
UNCTAD	United Nations Conference on Trade and Development
UNDOF	United Nations Disengagement Observer Force
UNDP	United Nations Development Programme
UNDRO	United Nations Disaster Relief Office
UNEF	United Nations Emergency Force
UNEP	United Nations Environment Programme

UNESCO	United Nations Educational, Scientific and Cultural Organization
UNFICYP	United Nations Force in Cyprus
UNFPA	United Nations Population Fund
UNHCR	United Nations High Commissioner for Refugees
UNICEF	United Nations Children's Fund
UNIDO	United Nations Industrial Development Organization
UNIFIL	United Nations Interim Force in Lebanon
UNIIMOG	United Nations Iran-Iraq Military Observer Group
UNIKOM	United Nations Iran-Kuwait Observation Mission
UNOSOM	United Nations Operation in Somalia
UNPROFOR	United Nations Protection Force (in Yugoslavia)
UNRRA	United Nations Relief and Rehabilitation Administration
UNRWA	United Nations Relief and Works Agency (for Palestine Refugees)
UNTAC	United Nations Transitional Authority in Cambodia
UNTAG	United Nations Transition Assistance Group
UNTEA	United Nations Temporary Executive Authority
UNTSO	United Nations Truce Supervision Organization
UNU	United Nations University
UNV	United Nations Volunteers
UPU	Universal Postal Union
WFP	World Food Programme
WHO	World Health Organization
WIPO	World Intellectual Property Organization
WMO	World Meteorological Organization
WTO	Warsaw Treaty Organization

1 Introduction

Representatives of 50 countries met on 25 April 1945 in San Francisco to write a document that, it was hoped, would guide the world to an era of peace and well-being. As the United Nations Conference on International Organization opened, the reek of war was fresh but hope for the future surged among the people of the nearly victorious Allied states. The Conference debated and eventually approved the Charter of the United Nations and thus the creation of a new world organization.

However novel the statesmen at San Francisco may have wanted their handiwork to appear, they faced a series of familiar difficulties and carried with them specific historical baggage. During the next four-and-a-half decades, these difficulties remained and new ones arose. Yet the San Francisco Charter has endured almost as it was drafted, while the organization based on it bent, rebounded and adjusted to the turbulent political currents that are characteristic of international relations. This book deals mainly with the fate of the organization created at San Francisco. But the United Nations, if it is to be clearly understood, must be set against the background of international politics and the history of international organization.

INDEPENDENT STATES

Although the San Francisco Conference claimed to speak in the name of 'We, the peoples of the United Nations', its participants acted on behalf of governments. In turn, those governments represented states, those legal and political abstractions within which people are governed. In some states, the people or their elected representatives can change the government or even the national constitution. Within others, woe befalls those who even breathe a criticism of governmental policy. In treating with each other, most governments pretend that they rule in their states without the slightest responsibility to others unless they specifically undertake it. Each state is said to be sovereign and independent. The UN Charter faithfully reflects this view.

If each state is sovereign and independent, then the new world organization could not be a government. Nor did the San Francisco

1

Conference leave any doubt on this point. Yet the new United Nations was mandated to produce and supervise some order in the world, to foster welfare and very specifically to maintain peace and security. How to do so raises a central issue in international politics: how to govern the ungovernable states? Despite earlier attempts to cope with this issue and despite nearly 50 years of practice by the United Nations, it remains unresolved.

INTERDEPENDENT SOCIETIES

The concept of sovereignty describes no set of facts or behaviour, especially during our time when societies daily become more closely linked. Interdependence among societies, manifested by such visible activity as commerce or transportation, reaches back to the beginning of human history. But during the last century, it has extended to the whole globe. Never before has communication among individuals and organizations within distinct societies taken place so quickly and so penetratingly.

Examples of the depth of interdependence abound. The oil boycott in 1973, ordered as a weapon against Israel by governments of Arab oil-producing lands, almost strangled automobile traffic in Western Europe and North America. An increase in interest rates, ordered by the government of the United Kingdom, raises the price of the British pound to foreigners, reducing their purchases of British goods. That slows the whole economy of the United Kingdom. In turn, workers in factories abroad, who make goods that importers in the United Kingdom bought, lose business. A flood in the grain-producing regions of China contributes to a price increase for American wheat, the stocks of which had declined under the impact of drought. In the late 1970s the Cambodian government brutally moved its population out of the cities, starving the people, killing millions and causing survivors to flood into Thailand. There refugee camps were supported mainly by funds from North America, Western Europe and Japan. Elsewhere, popular music devotees beat out the same rhythms. Scientists claimed in the 1980s that the use of fluorocarbon gas in spray cans and refrigerators was damaging the atmospheric blanket and endangering the whole earth. Other scientists predicted that an epidemic of AIDS would eventually cost millions of lives.

In a world so interconnected that these and other transnational phenomena appear, metamorphose and turn up again, regulation and international responses seem imperative. Interdependence involves all with all but not equally and not always with desired effects. Yet no government in a world of states can seize the initiative to wipe out evil or to benefit all. It would seem that only cooperative behaviour – or else a world government and the end of the national states – can lead to regulation and order in a situation of interdependence. But how can we ensure cooperation or even acceptance that some human activity is a threat to all?

Without ever using the term 'interdependence', the San Francisco Conference tried to create an institution to cope with its effects. It did do by trying to channel and encourage cooperative behaviour by governments through standing institutions. These would seek out common interests and recommend common policies which governments could then carry out. The permanent institutions could assume a perspective which extended beyond the horizons of any one government.

INTERNATIONAL LAW

The UN Charter consists of rules for an organization of states and for the limits of action on the part of their governments. These rules are cast in the form of legal obligations, binding on states and accepted as such by their governments. The UN Charter itself is described by jurists as a multilateral convention, a treaty that makes binding law. Moreover, the new organization received the task of progressively developing international law. The UN Charter thus unmistakably had the nature of public law, which serves to organize polities: in form, it resembled such documents as the United States Constitution. Yet this compact was intended to apply in a world of independent sovereign states whose very existence implies the absence of general rules.

Thus the UN Charter poses the issue of whether law can be applied to states and raises again one of the hoary issues of international relations. In fact, governments had for some 300 years recognized the existence of legal obligations, most of which were explicitly undertaken in the form of treaties. Others were attributed to custom recognized by all governments. No one questioned the ability of governments to take on legal obligations, even if their desirability could cause debate.

On the whole, the body of international law is usually applied without challenge. Thousands of treaties and negotiations and thousands of judicial settlements of disputes give evidence of the application of international law. Just as in domestic law, however, violations take place. In the national jurisdictions, examples would include breaches of contract, damage to others by negligence, embezzlements, murders or narcotic smuggling and sale. Generally, they are quickly dealt with in a court without fundamentally disturbing the society or implying a challenge to the validity of law. But at the international level, a violation need not lead to a judicial decision. A breach of law could result in a crisis, deprivation of important advantages to one or more countries or even a devastating war.

The San Francisco Conference tried to adjust to the issue of applying and extending international law by seeking a consensus among governments. Presumably, if they agreed to the rules of the Charter, then they could be depended on to cooperate in settling disputes and promoting cooperation. But the governments represented in San Francisco in no sense sought to legislate compulsory rules as a national parliament might do. Only in one instance did they approve a coercive mechanism for the new organization. This, as will be explained in detail in Chapter 4, could be used only in case of a blatant violation of the peace and thus of the rules of the Charter. Aside from that, international law was to be applied and developed on the basis of a freely-reached consensus of governments.

REFORMING WORLD POLITICS

Recurring, progressively more devastating war among states had, long before San Francisco, led to the notion that the manner in which international relations was conducted needed reform. A long list of normative thinkers, including Immanuel Kant, Jean-Jacques Rousseau, the Quaker leader William Penn, the American President Woodrow Wilson, and hundreds of others had turned their minds to redesigning international politics. However much or little their notions penetrated the thinking of the mass of people and their governors, no one could remain unaffected by the destruction that modern military technology had made possible. The deaths of 800 000 young men in the Battle of the Somme in the First World War and of whole cities in one blow in the nuclear bombings of Hiroshima and Nagasaki raised an issue that could not be ignored. In the wake of the Second World War, during which untold numbers of civilians had suffered along with the military forces, the question of whether the nature of international politics was at fault figured high on an unacknowledged agenda at San Francisco.

The query as to whether and how much the international political system could be reformed linked to the difficulty of controlling a collection of sovereign states. It was out of the question somehow to abolish sovereignty and to form a world government. None of the victorious governments, headed by such redoubtable figures as Churchill, Roosevelt and Stalin, would entertain such a notion for an instant. Yet all three of these seasoned political leaders specifically endorsed a new approach to organizing world politics. So did the mass of people wherever they could express themselves. In the United States in 1945, for instance, some 90 per cent of a representative sample of the population polled in surveys favoured joining the United Nations. Forty years later, incidentally, more than 70 per cent of those polled favoured continuing that membership.

To some extent, the tension between the rejection of old-style international politics and retention of the idea of the sovereign, national state was resolved by giving extraordinary roles to the greatest of them. Thus, the United States, the Soviet Union, the United Kingdom, France and China were expected to exercise special responsibilities for maintaining peace. The first three of this quintet had taken the lead in developing the ideas for a new international organization and had written the drafts placed before the San Francisco Conference. Together, the 'Big Five' would form a governing directorate with narrowly-defined emergency powers: Roosevelt thought of them as the policemen of the world. They would further be expected to use their prestige in the service of peace.

These ideas, resting on experience with power politics, became a keystone of the new UN Charter. But the finished document went much deeper in a reformist direction wherever the emphasis was not on short-term settlement of specific disputes. The reforms, it was thought, would help promote international peace and security. Partly they involved institutional devices and partly novel subject matter for international cooperation.

As any 'peace-loving' state could become a member of the new organization, the ultimate aim was universal membership. The initial test of 'peace-loving', ironically, was whether a state had declared war on Germany and Japan. The members would have votes in the various deliberative organs. They would make decisions, which usually took the form of recommendations, on the basis of debates that usually were open to any witness who entered the room. Majority voting patterns, sometimes qualified, were to replace the old diplomatic formula of consensus or nothing. At the same time, the 'Big Five' would have a weighted vote in matters of peace and security. Both the universality of membership and the provisions for voting might be called novel.

For the first time, an international organization was charged with promoting the international protection of human rights. This mandate could not avoid touching sensitive political nerves in many countries. Yet in the world of 1945, when the murderous behaviour of the Nazi regime in Germany became clear, protection of human rights answered a need felt by many people and leaders. But it was also an idea with revolutionary content, as will be explained in Chapter 5.

The Charter implies a theory that the conditions in which wars are bred have to do with economic deprivation and shortcomings in society, including violations of human rights. Consequently international cooperation was to seek to create conditions in which peace would flourish. Such cooperation could cope with economic and social problems that ignored national front-iers. Thus, the new United Nations would have to find a way to deal with sweeping issues of interdependence in a world of sovereigns.

In the colonial world, still very extensive in 1945, both economic and social problems and issues of human rights, such as the right to participate in government, visibly merged. The new organization included an instruc-tion to improve the conditions of colonial peoples, to bring some of them to self-government or independence and to make all colonies open to some measure of international scrutiny. Were this not done, the Charter implicitly assumes, it might become impossible to keep the peace.

The reformist goals set out by the Charter would obviously involve more than a few quick decisions. They implied eliminating social evils and changing the scope and depth of international cooperation beyond all precedent. Thus, they can be understood as reflecting a strong current of dissatisfaction with a past that comprised so much strife and suffering.

CONFERENCES AND DECISIONS

Despite the lofty aims of the San Francisco Conference, it proceeded in a time-honoured manner. The delegates represented governments and there-fore were bound to follow instructions from their capitals. This followed diplomatic practice and also the decision-making mode of confederations, such as the original Swiss state, the first version of the United States of America, and the Dutch Republic of the seventeenth century.

The diplomatic model of instructed delegates reigned in the League of Nations as well as in two sorts of early forerunners of the United Nations. As for the League of Nations, which had many tasks that resembled those of the new organization, it was decided even before the San Francisco meeting to start afresh. That would allow the governments to distance themselves from an organization that had a reputation as a failure.

The other forerunners included the international conferences to organize the peace at the end of European wars and a varied collection of functional organizations. The peace conferences did not constitute permanent organ-izations, but the functional agencies had a continuing existence. Their task was to regulate specific, specialized relationships among governments, such as navigation on the Rhine River, and to administer and supervise agreements among governments.

The first of the great postwar conferences was the Congress of Westphalia (1648), which marked the end of the Thirty Years War and the emergence of the modern concept of the sovereign state as a basis for international relations. In a 'world' that was limited to Europe, almost every state, however minor, was represented. Other examples were the Congress of Utrecht (1713) and the crucial Congress of Vienna (1815) which reorganized Europe after the Napoleonic Wars. The governments represented in Vienna gave conclusive legitimacy to the modern sovereign state and worked out many lasting rules for international conferences. Among the most important of these was the notion of equality among sovereigns; it meant that no state could claim special privileges in rank or in making decisions. This rule of equality underlies the one-nation, one-vote principle used in the League of Nations and the United Nations. The Congress of Vienna encouraged the formation of the first of the international functional organizations.

FUNCTIONAL COOPERATION IN THE NINETEENTH CENTURY

A pioneer functional organization involved the Rhine River, which flowed through and touched on the claims of several states affected by the Napoleonic wars. Negotiations stemming from the Congress of Vienna resulted in the establishment of the Central Commission for Navigation on the Rhine in 1832. All the riparian states except Switzerland joined it. It successfully organized cooperative governmental action to maintain the river channels and supervise traffic. Its success led to the creation of a similar commission for the Danube in 1856. It had delegated power to collect tolls and dredge the river channels.

By the second half of the nineteenth century, technological advances offered benefits that no government could obtain alone. This was true of postal and telegraphic traffic, weather-reporting and transport generally. In order to promote international cooperation on such matters, standing institutions were required. With a permanent secretariat and a regular schedule of meetings, instead of occasional conferences, such institutions could develop and oversee international standards. The secretariats could carefully prepare studies and expert advice for the periodic meetings of governmental delegates. This pattern of meetings, preparations and a permanent bureau offered a model and experience for later, more ambitious organizations.

The new mode of organizing international relations was employed for no less than 33 international public unions, as this form of international institution was then called, between 1865 and 1914. Some of the most important of the new agencies were the International Telegraphic Union (1868), the early version of the contemporary International Telecommunication Union (ITU); the Universal Postal Union (UPU) (1878); the International Bureau for Weights and Measures; and the International Institute of Agriculture (1905). Founding governments narrowly defined the tasks undertaken by the international public unions. Unlike the peace conferences, the delegates to the meetings of the unions were usually experts and technical personnel. They were nevertheless subject to instructions from their governments. While the secretariats assured continuity, governments provided for supervision by manning small executive committees elected by larger general conferences.

Parallel to the intergovernmental agencies, private individuals also formed agencies that extended across national frontiers. The organizations strove to coordinate work carried out at the national level. As early as 1864 in his native Switzerland, Henri Dunant formed the Red Cross movement. In 1868, the Interparliamentary Union was established. The International Olympic Committee began meeting in 1894 and in 1899 the International Bureau for Prevention of Traffic in Women and Children began to operate. These private agencies are merely examples of some of the 182 international non-governmental organizations that existed between 1865 and 1914. They frequently stimulated the growth of intergovernmental agencies. Their personnel sometimes joined delegations or staffs of the official bodies.

THE CONCERT OF EUROPE

A series of international conferences through the nineteenth and early twentieth centuries followed the lead given by the Congress of Vienna. Bringing together the European sovereigns, these gatherings served to some degree to regulate political relationships and make adjustments after relatively small armed conflicts. This practice of conferring constituted the Concert of Europe which helped to prevent a general European war for a century.

The Congress of Vienna had produced a rudimentary political organization of Europe in the so-called Grand Alliance. This was an agreement among England, Prussia, Austria-Hungary, Russia and, later, France to ensure that the decisions of the Congress were carried out. Its political aim was the maintenance of the status quo. England, however, set as its primary goal limiting the influence of the defeated France, while the other powers showed more interest in suppressing political and social change. In

1822, England withdrew from the alliance in protest against its conservative intervention in Spain. Nevertheless, all of the governments in the Grand Alliance continued the policy of conferring about political issues in Europe. They dealt with such questions as Greek independence from the Ottoman Empire (1827), the separation of Belgium from the Netherlands (1831), peace after the Crimean War, developments in the Ottoman Empire, and the tension between the Austro-Hungarian and Russian empires. The last major gathering of the Concert, the London Conference of 1912–13, again involved the Balkan area and foreshadowed the antagonisms that set off the First World War.

Even if the governments that hewed the Concert process had their own ends in mind, they laid down principles that were important for the later development of international organization. They met periodically. They used the end of international conflicts, especially the Napoleonic Wars, as a means for reorganizing their relationships. They avoided punishing the defeated, especially France, in such a way as to exclude its future cooperation. They relied on the leadership of great powers. They sought to avoid war by conferring in advance of using military power. They limited the scope of military activity. But they did not create formal permanent institutions, fixed rules of procedure, formal agendas or periodic meetings. Nor did they establish a permanent secretariat. These features were to be found in the public international unions.

THE HAGUE PEACE CONFERENCES

The experience with conferring, periodic meetings, international law and technical preparations, as well as pursuit of national foreign policy goals, all underlay an unusual initiative by the Russian emperor. He sought to protect his land from its own weakness by using the customary organizational techniques to promote disarmament. This resulted in the summoning of the Hague Peace Conferences of 1899 and 1907.

The first of these conferences developed rules for making the conduct of war more humane. They still have some application. Furthermore, rules were discussed to bring about pacific settlement of international disputes. From that beginning, the second conference created the Permanent Court of Arbitration, which in fact was a list of eminent jurists available to form international tribunals whose decisions would have binding effect, plus a permanent international secretariat. Governments had specifically to agree in advance to submit their disputes to such arbitration. This, too, still exists.

A noticeable increase in interest in the Hague Peace Conference rapidly developed. The first meeting in 1899 included representatives of 26 governments. The second in 1907 enjoyed the participation of 44 governments, including, for the first time, some from Latin America. Although the First World War nullified the plan for continuing meetings, a definite trend towards universal participation in international law-making and the creation of means to settle disputes had become clear.

THE LEAGUE OF NATIONS

Far and away the most important twentieth-century embodiment of the nineteenth-century experience with international cooperation was the League of Nations. It was equally the direct forerunner of the United Nations, whose Charter borrowed heavily from the League Covenant. It served as a testing laboratory for the ideas of its time.

The central idea underlying the League was formulated by President Woodrow Wilson of the United States in the last of the famous Fourteen Points that set out the war aims of his government:

> A general association must be formed under specific covenants for the purpose of affording mutual guarantees of political independence and territorial integrity to great and small states alike.

While that statement proposed no fundamental change of the system of sovereign states, it projected a new legal contract among governments, the creation of a permanent institution of universal membership and a system of guarantees intended to maintain international peace and security.

Wilson's fourteenth point initiated planning efforts in Great Britain and France, as well as the United States, and a vast public discussion. Fed into negotiations at the Versailles Peace Conference, this activity resulted in agreement on the Covenant of the League of Nations. As a formal part of the treaty intended legally to end the First World War, the Covenant predictably was aimed at preventing the recurrence of another such disaster.

A novel political commitment – collective security – provided the foundation of the peace-keeping system in the Covenant. It relied on the notion that governments would honour their legal obligations and their repeated declarations after wars that they did not want another – at least at once. Collective security thus assumes a common interest in peace. It also assumes a rudimentary community of states. If any one government orders an attack on another, then all of the rest view this anti-social action as an attack on them. They have the legal obligation to resist by individual and joint means. Thus, the notion of self-defence, long accepted as a sovereign right, is broadened to all in the community. Neutrality is excluded. As the community includes all states, including those with great military power, an agreement on collective security would effectively deter armed aggression.

The assumption of a community of states draws on the nineteenth-century experience with developing international law and with the functioning of the Concert of Europe. The League institutionalized the *ad hoc* conferences of the Concert. Now they would meet according to a regular calendar. For specialized purposes, including maintenance of peace, smaller bodies would meet periodically. A headquarters was established at Geneva, where a permanent secretariat, headed by the Secretary-General, was appointed.

The commitments needed to make collective security effective were set out in the League Covenant. Conflicts among members were to be solved without war. The organs of the League were available to help find such solutions. Some would be legally binding. This approach to peace through negotiation or legal judgement incorporated the diplomatic experience of the nineteenth century. Only after all other means were tried was the use of force permissible. Only if the commitments were disregarded would the penalties implied by collective security be involved automatically and legally.

The two main representative organs of the League, the Assembly and the Council, shared the responsibility for the political handling of disputes as well as other matters within the competence of the organization. All members were represented in the Assembly, which met annually, and the great powers were always members of the smaller Council which met more frequently and could be summoned on short notice. The Council usually took up disputes which might threaten peace although some came before the Assembly. The voting arrangements clearly reflected the customary practices of international conferences which could not force sovereigns to submit to the will of the majority. Therefore voting in the League was by unanimity. That meant that each member state had the veto. Formally, the League thus faced narrow limits in the face of resistance by a government.

Nevertheless, the carefully elaborated procedures for settling disputes had the backing of two centuries of diplomatic experience. The League system institutionalized the practices that had often served well. Members were expected to try to settle disputes themselves. If they could not, the Council was open for political handling, including mediation and investigation. If the parties consented, the Council could arbitrate a dispute. Or alternatively, they could submit it for a binding decision to the new Permanent Court of International Justice.

If the Council could not settle a dispute after a serious effort, it then had the duty of reporting on the facts and making recommendations for ending it. After that report or arbitral, or judicial proceedings, the members undertook not to resort to war during a three-month cooling-off period. If they did, all members were to treat it as a breach of the Covenant, invoking automatic sanctions.

The procedure by which the principle of collective security would be brought into play derived from the conception of a balance of power among the European powers. This device meant that no single power could dominate the area and that the rest of the governments would rather fight to restore the balance than let that happen. Thus, expansion would be deterred and independence of states preserved. But the League system envisaged regulating disputes through a standing institution.

That institution would have duties much beyond merely serving as a framework for automatic reaction. If any government broke the rules, the Council could organize the sanctions and even supply armed forces to check the transgressor. In order to act against aggression, members of the League declared themselves ready to offer mutual financial support. They also would permit armed forces to pass through their territory to act against the aggressor.

If the League created a new form of guiding political relationships, it also established a novel judicial organ in the Permanent Court of International Justice. This was more than the directory of experts of the Permanent Court of Arbitration. The new body consisted of a bench of 15 independent judges, appointed by the Council and the Assembly of the League acting jointly. That guaranteed the prestige of this new body, the first of its kind. It could draw upon the substantial body of international rules already respected most of the time by most governments.

The first decade of the League's short life comprised institutional construction, including the first international civil service, and several promising attempts at dispute settlement. The latter involved hostilities between Bulgaria and Greece and the judicial settlement of quarrels between Sweden and Finland over the Aaland Islands. During the 1930s, however, the lack of community, the limited membership of the League and the unwillingness to renounce war or to treat its use as an attack on all sapped its capacities.

The assumption of universal membership almost immediately proved unwarranted. The government of the United States, the originator of so much that went into the Covenant, was the first to abandon it. President Wilson failed to get the advice and consent of the Senate for ratification of the Treaty of Versailles; his successor campaigned on, and applied, a policy of hostility to the League. The new Soviet Union, isolated as it consolidated the revolution that replaced the Russian empire, joined only in 1934. That left only France and Great Britain as the great powers and, as Japan was the only non-European member of general importance, emphasized the European character of the League. Japan quit after having been condemned for swallowing Manchuria in 1931. Italy, soon to have a Fascist government, became an uncomfortable member and withdrew in 1937 after breaking the Covenant by conquering Ethiopia (then called Abyssinia). Germany joined in 1926 but its new Nazi government abandoned membership in 1933.

An unmistakable sign of retreat from the Versailles order came with Japan's disregard of demands by the League to end its expansion into China. Soon thereafter Mussolini's Italy secretly began preparing to attack Ethiopia. The League responded to the aggression in 1935 with economic sanctions, excluding oil and military steps, but that did not prevent the conquest of a weak African country. After that, the League no longer had much political significance. Although Italy, Germany and the Soviet Union all intervened in the Spanish Civil War, the League barely reacted. Hitler's successful pressure for the cession of Czechoslovakia in 1938 was handled outside the League. Finland got little help from the expulsion from the League of the Soviet attacker. The League did not take up the German attack on Poland in 1939, which began the Second World War. The formal dissolution of the organization took place in 1946 in Geneva.

Had they been faithfully used, the admittedly imperfect means at the disposal of the League for settling disputes could perhaps have made important differences in international politics. At least they would have complicated matters for an aggressor as they did for Italy when sanctions were applied at the end of 1935. Yet chroniclers of the League have left little doubt that because the major powers – only Britain and France throughout its life – declined to use its devices, what was left of the collective security system was doomed. In fact, the absence of the United States and for most of the period, the Soviet Union, Germany and Japan, gave evidence of even more lack of agreement than did the hesitancy of Britain and France. The lack of commitment was only compounded by the unanimity rule for voting. Even so, when the conflicts involved small states and limited aims, useful effects came from the League. But whether any institution depending on cooperation could have resisted deliberate aggression from such sources as Japan, Italy, Germany and the Soviet Union can be doubted.

THE SECOND WORLD WAR AND THE UN

Long before victory in the Second World War was on the horizon, the idea took root among the leaders of the allied powers that the postwar world would require a general international organization. It would help to maintain the re-established peace and much more. As Woodrow Wilson made the creation of the League of Nations an aim of the war, so too did Franklin Roosevelt and Winston Churchill.

Four months before the United States joined the war, the British Prime Minister and the American President discussed war aims in August 1941 aboard an American cruiser off the Canadian shore. The result was the Atlantic Charter, the first open statement of principles about the postwar world. Supporting FDR's Four Freedoms which he had set forth earlier, Churchill and Roosevelt favoured restoration of independence to those states that had lost it to German aggression. They rejected territorial gains for their own countries. They mentioned that 'pending the establishment of a wider and more permanent system of general security', governments that threatened aggression should be disarmed. Although Churchill preferred a clear statement that an effective international organization was desirable, Roosevelt was held back by the fear of a negative reaction from the United States Senate. Nevertheless, the message was clear. The Soviet Union, the British Dominions and the Western European governments-in-exile approved the Atlantic Charter a month later.

In the succeeding months, winning the war preoccupied the leaders, but a series of conferences and intense planning, especially in the United States and the United Kingdom, gave shape to a postwar world organization. On 1 January 1942, less than a month after the Japanese attack that brought the United States into the war, 26 governments signed the 'Declaration of the United Nations', which set out principles for a 'wider and more permanent system of general security'. In it, the originators of the Atlantic Charter were joined by China, Poland, Czechoslovakia, Yugoslavia and some Latin American states. They viewed the Atlantic Charter as a common programme for the allied states and pledged mutual support in the war effort and rejected any separate peace or armistice.

At that stage, even the term, 'United Nations' was tentative. The memoirs of Cordell Hull, then US Secretary of State, relate that Roosevelt suggested the title, 'Declaration by United Nations' to Churchill, who lay in his bathtub. 'The distinguished bather', Hull recalled, 'agreed and thus the term "United Nations" came into being.'

The planning for a postwar organization quickly evolved in 1943 from bathtub to professional diplomacy. Planning began in earnest in the foreign ministries of several governments and, above all, in Washington. The foreign ministers of the three leading allied powers, the United Kingdom, the United States, and the Soviet Union, convened in Moscow to draft the 'Declaration of Moscow' and later got a Chinese signature. It sought a general international organization as soon as possible. Aimed at maintaining international peace and security, it would be based on the sovereign equality of member states.

A further, brief glimpse of the progress towards an international organization came with the Teheran Conference of 1943, attended by Churchill, Roosevelt and Stalin. This was followed by the Dumbarton Oaks Conference in a mansion in Washington from August to October 1944. This was the most concerted, detailed international effort so far. The discussion was based on drafts set out by the American State Department.

At Dumbarton Oaks, representatives of China, the Soviet Union, the United Kingdom, and the United States formulated the governing principles of the United Nations. Among them was the name, 'United Nations', to proclaim the intention of continuing peacetime cooperation on the basis of the common purposes of the war. All the sovereign members would be represented in the General Assembly, which would have a broad agenda. The Security Council members (originally 11, now 15) would have the specialized task of keeping the peace. This distinction compromised the Soviet preference for separate organizations for peace and for economic and social cooperation. Other differences, such as the Soviet demand for 16 votes for the component republics of the USSR and the British opposition to any treatment of colonial territories, could not be settled. The remaining points at issue at Dumbarton Oaks were passed to the Yalta Conference of February 1945, where Churchill, Roosevelt and Stalin found formulae for them.

The disagreement over membership and the Soviet demand for 16 votes yielded when Roosevelt proposed giving a vote to each of the then 48 United States. Yet the Ukrainian and Byelorussian Soviet Socialist Republics, never before identified as sovereign states, did get votes. Stalin argued that this advantage was offset by Washington's influence in Latin America. The list of 'sponsoring powers' of the United Nations would be expanded from the Big Three of Yalta to include China and France, both to have permanent places on the Security Council. Invitees to the founding conference at San Francisco would include all states whose governments had declared war on the Axis powers before 1 March 1945, and that had signed the Declaration of the United Nations of 1 January 1942.

Related to membership was the question of voting, a principal agenda item at Yalta. Except on procedural matters, the five Great Powers had to agree unanimously in the Security Council in order that a resolution be adopted. That meant that any of them had a veto. Procedural resolutions and those to which the Great Powers agreed required a seven-member majority in the 11-member council. The earlier Soviet opposition to the Anglo-American proposal that a party to a dispute should not vote on it in the Council was overcome by treating pacific settlement differently from enforcement action. In the former, a party to a dispute could not vote but could in the latter.

As for colonies, Churchill was assured at Yalta that no part of the empire would be put under the control of the United Nations without British consent. Great Britain, or any country, could put a colony under the supervision of a trusteeship system that would extend only to territories voluntarily put into it; to former mandates of the League of Nations (that had been seized from Germany and Turkey after the First World War) which had not gained independence; and to additional territories that might be taken from Germany and Japan. Administration of other colonial territories would remain as before.

Within an hour of taking office after Roosevelt's sudden death on 12 April 1945, President Harry Truman announced that the founding conference for the United Nations would be held as planned. Accordingly, the United Nations Conference on International Organization opened on 25 April 1945, in San Francisco.

THE SAN FRANCISCO CONFERENCE

In what may have been the most public diplomatic conference in history, 260 representatives of 50 states attended the conference that met in the San Francisco Opera House. More than 2500 press and radio correspondents churned out the news. More than 40 citizens' organizations, encouraged by the United States, sent representatives. The intergovernmental agencies that had survived the war despatched their spokesmen. All were served by a staff of more than 1000, organized by the Department of State.

As with earlier diplomatic conferences, each governmental delegation had an equal vote. But as in the past, everyone understood that without the concurrence of the Great Powers no real results could be achieved. The debates took place in a plenary session, four main committees, and 12 subcommittees, all of them aiming at finding ways to resolve issues.

Issues there still were, despite the long preparation at Dumbarton Oaks and the subsequent agreements at Yalta. At the same time, the San Francisco Conference had solid, careful drafts on which to base its deliberations.

In addition to the never quite vanished differences among the Great Powers, two cleavages that sometimes involved overlapping groupings of states appeared at San Francisco. One of these was between small and large states; the other between colonial and non-colonial states. The small powers gained persuasiveness when the major powers drew apart. The non-colonial powers usually sought to make the colonial powers, some of which were small states, more accountable for their policies. Generally the smaller states tried to strengthen the powers of the General Assembly, in which they had the advantage of numbers and equality, against the more exclusive Security Council with its veto for the Great Powers. Strong interest in economic and social cooperation through the United Nations also was characteristic of the smaller powers.

Nowhere did the divergent tendencies among the great and small surface more visibly than in committee sessions that dealt with the Security Council. The smaller states resisted the provision for Great Power unanimity in the Council. The Great Powers responded that no Council would ever be established without the veto. The small powers won provisions to ensure that the best contributors to peace from their ranks, as well as an 'equitable' geographical representation, would be elected to the Council.

As for the colonial issue, two categories of territories were defined for different treatment. The implications of the Yalta agreement were made clear. The new drafts distinguished territories placed under UN supervision or trusteeship from the rest of the colonial world. All colonies except those placed under trusteeship were to be known as non-self-governing territories. For them, the administering states had duties of advancing the people but not granting them independence; self-government was retained as a goal. Administering states would be obliged to report to the General Assembly.

The trusteeship system was less controversial, because it was familiar from the League of Nations mandates system and because it extended only to old mandates or new ones identified voluntarily. Even so, the American navy insisted that a special category of strategic trust territories be created for the Pacific islands that the United States had extracted from Japanese control. These supposedly had strategic value; their supervision was therefore made a duty of the Security Council, not the Trusteeship Council and the General Assembly. The general aim of the Trusteeship System, unlike that of the other colonies, was independence.

No procedure for withdrawal from the new organization entered its constitution, but obviously any state that wished would do so. This most transparent of conferences formally named the new organization the United Nations, despite misgivings of French-speaking delegates who noted that the acronym 'NU' in their tongue meant 'naked'.

The vote of approval for the completed Charter of the United Nations came on 25 June 1945. Representatives of 50 states formally signed it on the next day. After the five Great Powers and a majority of the signatories ratified it, it came into force on 24 October 1945, the first United Nations Day. The new General Assembly met for the first time on 10 January 1946, in London.

2 Charter and Structure of the United Nations

The structure and some of the most important procedures of the United Nations are set forth in its Charter (for the full text see the Appendix). This constitutional document emerged from the San Francisco Conference and has remained formally unchanged, except for the enlargement of the Security Council and the Economic and Social Council. It provides the institutional framework for the organization. Examining its main features can help in understanding the UN's success in reaching its main goal: the maintenance of international peace and security. Moreover, knowledge of the constitutional structure is essential for the discussion of possible reforms, later in this book.

The aims of the organization are introduced in both soaring and sober language, as was doubtless appropriate at the end of a terrible war. The preamble, which has no strict legal application, contains a well-known, inspirational example:

> WE, THE PEOPLES OF THE UNITED NATIONS DETERMINED to save succeeding generations from the scourge of war, which twice in our lifetime has brought untold sorrow to mankind...

It is followed by two articles which describe the concrete purposes of the institution and the means provided to meet its lofty ends.

Among its broad range of activities, the central purpose is the maintenance of peace and security, the first aim set out in Article 1 of the Charter. Listed next are a series of related purposes, including friendly relations among nations, achieving cooperation to solve international problems of an economic, social, cultural or humanitarian character, and harmonization of the action of members so as to attain these ends. Implicit in this set of aims is the assumption that broad cooperation would prevent war.

Two of the most elaborate chapters of the Charter contain the provisions for activities intended to maintain peace. Yet this term is nowhere explicitly defined. It may be taken to mean an absence of international violence and the protection of the territorial status quo from forceful alteration. Chapter VI of the Charter deals with the peaceful settlement of disputes which, if continued, might lead to a breakdown of peace. Chapter VII authorizes coercive 'action with respect to threats to the peace, breaches of the peace, and acts of aggression'.

Arrangements for international economic and social cooperation intended to underpin a peaceful international order make up Chapters IX and X of the Charter. They include a wide-ranging declaration of principles that extend the scope of international organization beyond precedents. That prominent feature of international politics in 1945, the colonial empires, is treated in Chapters XI and XII. Chapter XI consists of a 'declaration regarding non-self-governing territories' in which members that administer territories that have not yet attained a full measure of self-government accept a set of regulating principles. To the people of such territories, the Charter promises self-government but not necessarily independence.

A Trusteeship System that includes closer UN supervision of a special set of non-self-governing territories is set out in Chapter XII. These lands were to be brought at least to self-government and perhaps independence. Included in the system were at least the territories taken from the vanquished in the two world wars. Thus, it succeeded the League of Nations mandates system. All but one of the territories, South West Africa (now called Namibia), that the League supervised were made Trust Territories. Other colonies could have been placed under the system, but none ever were.

CLOSE RELATIVES

Whatever the wishes of the wartime planners who framed the UN Charter, it closely resembles the Covenant of the League of Nations. The drafting committees that worked on the Charter sought to start with a clean slate in order to scotch fears that the new organization merely revived a failure. They developed significantly different features for the United Nations but nevertheless were bound by basic facts of international politics.

As with the League, only sovereign states could join the UN. In both cases, the purpose was to prevent a breakdown of international stability as defined after a war. Formal organs to reach decisions consonant with the organizational purposes were established for both organizations. Both created an assembly with all members represented and with broad concerns. Both set up a limited-membership council that met more often than the assembly. Both established international secretariats, headed by a secretary-general. Both organized an international court legally to settle disputes. Both sought to coordinate the operations of related organizations that dealt with functional issues, such as social welfare or health.

Yet the new organization departed significantly from the old pattern along lines intended to strengthen political power and broaden and deepen the scope of international cooperation. Perhaps the boldest change was intended to provide the Security Council with military power to stop deeds of aggression. It was to have at its disposal armed forces regulated by special agreements with governments, and ready for action when the Council decided to use them. This new approach, far more substantial than the provisions for coercion under the League, never resulted, however, in the creation of the envisaged force.

The Security Council itself represented a new degree of specialization for the established organs. It had specific responsibility for maintaining the peace, unlike the League Council which had general supervisory duties over the entire agenda. Furthermore, the UN General Assembly was not to deal with disputes under consideration in the Security Council. The principle of specialization was extended to other forms of cooperation through the creation of an Economic and Social Council and a Trusteeship Council.

In the case of the Trusteeship Council, the specialized subject matter was matched with a broader scope of supervision and was intended to have a higher level of governmental representation than the analogous organ in the League. Moreover, going well beyond the limits imposed on the League, the General Assembly was given limited tasks with regard to colonial territories not brought under the Trusteeship System.

The UN Secretary-General, like his predecessor in the League, would serve the entire organization. But in the new organization, he was given the independent power under Article 99 of the Charter to bring any matter before the Security Council that in his opinion threatened or breached the peace. Such explicit political powers go far beyond the earlier model.

While the League used the time-honoured diplomatic technique of making decisions on the basis of a unanimous vote, the UN replaced it with qualified majorities. For important matters in the General Assembly, a two-thirds majority is required, while committees, which frame resolutions, make their decisions on the basis of a majority present and voting. Voting in the Security Council is somewhat more complex, as all matters of substance require the concurrence of the five permanent members. Procedural decisions may be taken by a majority of all members, whether permanent or not. Thus, at least nine votes in the present 15-member Council (seven in the original 11-member Council) must be cast in favour of any successful resolution.

The design approved at San Francisco only partly predicted the actual operation of the UN, which turned out not very different in many respects from its predecessor. Over most of the history of the UN, fundamental disagreements among the permanent members of the Security Council, especially the United States and the Soviet Union, prevented quick, coercive intervention in international conflicts. The organization could not coordinate related international institutions with a strong hand any more than the League Council could in its time. Nor did the UN often serve even as well as the League at its best as an economic and social 'think-tank'. As for managing change in the colonial world, it did not smoothly and slowly proceed towards independence with the UN making the crucial decisions. But the organization certainly did reflect, preside over and influence the process.

The decline of empires related to the universal membership of the United Nations. The League membership never included any recently-independent former colonial territory. At no time were all of the great powers represented. From the beginning of the UN, all great powers were members, even if a long quarrel preceded changing the representation of China from the government in Taipei to that in Beijing. As each colonial holding became independent, the successor government promptly joined the UN. The membership is well-high universal with only a few absentees, such as Switzerland and some European mini-states, staying away.

The six main organs of the UN – the General Assembly, the Security Council, the Economic and Social Council, the Trusteeship Council, the Secretariat and the International Court of Justice – bear immediate responsibility for the policies and much of the activity of the organization. These organs will be examined in the following sections.

THE GENERAL ASSEMBLY

Each UN member is entitled to a seat in the General Assembly and to cast one vote. The usual annual session takes place between September and mid-December. Special or emergency sessions may be summoned at other times.

As the most representative of the UN organs, the General Assembly takes up an agenda that covers almost every international issue brought by the members or emerging from the work of the Secretariat and associated organizations. With so much to do and so many members, it follows a rather formal procedural pattern. This always includes a lengthy general debate that in fact is neither a genuine debate nor a discussion, but rather a series of speeches by senior governmental representatives who set out national positions. As they include foreign ministers and even heads of governments, and sometimes personalities such as the Pope or the head of the Palestine Liberation Organization, new proposals may emerge in this unique setting.

The detailed discussion of reports on earlier work and new proposals takes place in the seven permanent committees of the General Assembly. The committees are: the First (political); the Second (economic); Third (social); Fourth (non-self-governing territories); Fifth (budget); Sixth (legal); and the Special Political. When these committees end their debate and agree on recommendations, these go to the plenary session of the General Assembly, where usually debate is cursory. The plenary session may, however, take up a question without prior committee consideration.

The scope of General Assembly concern is as wide as the Charter itself and that is almost as broad as an inventory of international issues. It may take up under Article 10 of the Charter any matter within the scope of the Charter or related to the powers and functions of another organ. Although this allows discussion of matters of peace and security, the Charter nevertheless sets apart specific disputes on which action, including conciliation and coercion, may be necessary. These are reserved under Article 11 (2) of the Charter to the Security Council. Logical though this may be in terms of specialized organs taking up their appointed tasks, the General Assembly tends to discuss whatever its members wish at any given time.

The hollowing-out of the Security Council's reserved territory even has the support of an informal amendment of the UN Charter. This is the 'Uniting for Peace' resolution (UN General Assembly Res. 377 [V]), adopted by the General Assembly in 1950, during the Korean war, at the behest of the United States. It provides that if the Security Council fails to carry out its responsibility as the result of a veto by a permanent member, the General Assembly may deal with a situation threatening or involving a breach of the peace. This procedural shift occurs if a majority of the Council decides to hand over the matter to an emergency special session of the General Assembly. The larger organ may only recommend measures to deal with the situation, but these may include coercion, even including the use of armed force. Even such voluntary steps could have a substantial impact on a violator of the peace.

Although the then-cohesive Soviet group denounced the Uniting for Peace procedure as illegal, they nevertheless acquiesced in its use as early as the Suez crisis of 1956 and again during the Congo conflict in 1960. Since then, the resolution has opened the way to call the General Assembly into session to deal with the continuing conflicts around Israel and with South Africa's long occupation of Namibia (earlier known as Southwest Africa), the only remaining League of Nations mandated territory that did not reach independence before 1990. As it can no longer count on a majority of votes for its proposals in the General Assembly, the United States now regards the Uniting for Peace procedure with some reserve.

The agenda of the annual General Assembly session now includes more than 150 items. These reflect the troubles of the world and hopes of coping with them. A large number of items, such as apartheid in South Africa, the conflicts in the Middle East, economic development, protection of the world environment and promotion of human rights, recur repeatedly. Each session ends with a thick file of resolutions, some of them almost impenetrably complex. These are adopted by a variety of procedures that include majority votes, consensus, acclamation, and adoption without a vote. Among them each year is the budget of the organization, which is prepared by the Secretary-General and closely scrutinized. Unlike almost all of the other resolutions, the budget represents a formal legal obligation placed on the members.

THE SECURITY COUNCIL

The crucial point about both membership and voting in the Security Council is the special position of the five permanent members who were taken to be the Great Powers by the founders of the United Nations. Their presence and membership has remained constant, although the Council membership was increased in 1965 from 11 to 15 in the hope of improving representation by offering more places to be filled by election for two-year terms. In 1991, after the demise of the Soviet Union, its Council seat was taken over by the Russian Federation, which was admitted to UN membership. Selection of non-permanent members by the General Assembly follows a geographical formula: three African, two Asian, one Eastern European, two Latin American and two from Western Europe and other states. As for voting, only on procedural matters may a majority of 10 take decisions: on other matters, the majority must include all of the permanent members (see Chapter 3 for a more detailed discussion of voting).

Unlike the General Assembly, the Security Council is designed always to be ready to meet on a problem of peace and security. It has both conciliatory and coercive powers, which are to be exercised only after the parties to a dispute have tried to find their own solution. The Charter lists means for settlement of disputes: negotiation; enquiry; mediation; conciliation; arbitration; judgement by a court; proceeding through regional agencies; and other means parties may choose. The Council may take the initiative in a dispute which, if continued, would threaten the peace, or may wait for it to be brought to it. It can recommend means of settlement or offer conciliatory services or a plan for settlement. Under Chapter VI of the Charter, what it cannot do is employ coercion. It is legally limited to persuasion.

The legal limits on Council action expand if a direct threat or breach of the peace occurs. In such a case, it has the right to take stronger action under Chapter VII of the Charter. The first step is a decision that the matter before it does in fact threaten the peace (Article 39). If so, it may recommend provisional measures. Or it may call at once on member governments to apply diplomatic and economic sanctions (Articles 40 and 41). If the Council does so, a legal obligation to act is placed on the members. Furthermore, the Council was given the legal capacity to use armed forces placed at its disposal by members (Articles 42 and 43). In making decisions on enforcement action under Chapter VII, a member who is a party to a dispute may vote, but under Chapter VI a disputant must abstain.

THE ECONOMIC AND SOCIAL COUNCIL

Although the United Nations structure separates the organs dealing with maintenance of peace from those of economic and social cooperation, the Economic and Social Council (ECOSOC) deals with political issues, such as the creation and supervision of a system to protect human rights that may be closely related to international conflict. Moreover, the creation of a specialized organ does not ensure that governments will be represented by persons with special knowledge of the subject matter.

Election to ECOSOC, as with other organs with limited tasks, was supposed to foster representation of a broad segment of organizational membership. It began with 18 members, but formal amendment of the Charter raised membership first in 1965, to 27 and in 1973, to 54. The five Great Powers of the Security Council invariably are elected, as befits high prestige and economic capacity, while other members are chosen proportionally for three-year terms from the main geographical groups.

Fostering general welfare, in the belief that this will create conditions for peace, constitutes the main task of ECOSOC. It depends primarily on member governments to carry out recommendations, which it may make directly or, more usually, via the General Assembly; therefore it has no operating tasks. Its main work includes making and initiating studies and reports with respect to international economic, social, cultural, educational, health and related matters.

ECOSOC works out agreements for coordination and cooperation with the specialized agencies associated with the UN and receives regular reports from them. Agency representatives also participate in ECOSOC meetings. This activity is intended to coordinate the work of the specialized agencies, some of which antedate even the League of Nations. The

Council also may initiate the formation of new international organizations, as it did with such members of the UN family as the World Health Organization (WHO) and the World Intellectual Property Organization (WIPO). The Council prepares draft conventions (law-making multilateral treaties) on matters within its competence and submits them to the General Assembly for reference to governments. It summons special international conferences on matters within its wide jurisdiction.

THE TRUSTEESHIP COUNCIL

Its task now a mere shadow of what it once was, the Trusteeship Council has a complex composition intended to insure impartiality in administering the Trust Territories. It always included the permanent members of the Security Council and balanced the members that administered colonies with others that did not. It reports annually to the General Assembly, except in the case of so-called strategic Trust Territories for the welfare of which the Security Council is responsible. The supervisory methods of the Trusteeship Council have included examination of annual reports from the territories and the dispatch of visiting missions to them. It can also accept petitions from groups and individuals.

Some of the important Trust Territories that once were supervised by the Council were a legacy from the League mandate system. Examples are Tanganyika, administered by the United Kingdom; Ruanda-Urundi, administered by Belgium; and Togo and Cameroon, administered by France. All of these territories and others, except for a part of the Trust Territory of the Pacific, administered by the United States as a strategic territory, have exercised self-determination to the satisfaction of the Council.

THE INTERNATIONAL COURT OF JUSTICE

In most respects a carbon copy of the Permanent Court of International Justice which was founded with, but functioned outside the structure of, the League of Nations, the International Court of Justice (ICJ) is a main organ of the United Nations. All UN members must be parties to the ICJ statute. The court is composed of 15 independent justices, serving nine-year terms. They are elected by an absolute majority of both the General Assembly and the Security Council.

Non-members of the United Nations may become party to the statute upon recommendation of the Security Council and on conditions determined in each case by the General Assembly. South Korea, Switzerland and the Holy See have availed themselves of this possibility.

The jurisdiction of the court covers all questions that states refer to it and its decision are binding in a dispute. States can refer cases in two ways. The first is by way of a prior agreement. An existing treaty between the parties may provide for reference. Or a special agreement, setting out the dispute and providing for reference, may be reached between the parties.

The second way of referring cases to the court involves advance agreement on compulsory jurisdiction, as specified in Article 36 of the Statute of the court. A signatory to the optional clause declares that, in relation to any other state accepting the same obligation, the ICJ has jurisdiction over a case that either of them submits concerning:

(a) the interpretation of a treaty;
(b) any question of international law;
(c) the existence of any fact which, if established, would constitute a breach of an international obligation;
(d) the nature or extent of the reparation to be made for the breach of an international obligation.

In 1990, compulsory jurisdiction had been accepted by 56 states, but their declarations often contain reservations excluding certain kinds of disputes or disputes with certain states. Thus, for many years, the United States accepted compulsory jurisdiction, except in cases falling under the jurisdiction of US courts. President Reagan withdrew even from this commitment in 1986, after Nicaragua won a judgement against the United States for mining its harbours and aiding the 'Contra' rebels.

Apart from adversary proceedings, the ICJ may give an advisory opinion, requested by another UN organ or by a specialized agency, on any legal question. One such advisory opinion, for example, concerned the question of whether expenses of UN peace-keeping activities were to be considered 'expenses of the Organization' under Article 17 of the Charter and thus to be apportioned by the General Assembly as a charge on the members. (The answer was 'yes'.) It has also issued a series of influential advisory opinions in the matter of the status of Namibia.

The Court has had little effect on peace and security. In almost 70 years of existence of the ICJ and its predecessor, the average yearly number of decisions has not been more than two. None of these concerned the prevention or solution of an international conflict involving serious violence. In the absence of accepted international legislation, many inter-state disputes do not so much concern the nature of the legal situation as the question as to whether the law should be developed or changed. That is beyond the competence of the ICJ.

More frequent use of the court – desirable though that may be from the perspective of the development of the rule of law – cannot be expected. Most governments tend to consider the recognition of the compulsory jurisdiction of the court as infringing their sovereignty. Many of them doubt the non-partisan character of the court. Governments in recently-independent states view it as too much dominated by Western legal thinking and too concerned with great-power interests. The Communist world in particular used to doubt the impartiality of such international organs.

THE SECRETARIAT

The Secretary-General of the United Nations is the chief administrative officer of the organization and directs the permanent staff, the Secretariat. The appointment of the Secretary-General begins with a recommendation of a candidate by the Security Council to the General Assembly, where the formal election takes place [Art. 97]. The usual term of office is five years and reappointment is possible.

The Secretariat is organized in departments which have functions related to the other principal organs, such as special political affairs, security affairs, economic and social affairs, and legal counsel, while other departments deal mainly with internal management and services. The Secretary-General is assisted by an executive office that carries out general supervisory functions.

The Secretariat is omnipresent in the functioning of the organization [Art 98]. Its officers keep the records, interpret, translate documents in the several working languages, collect statistics and prepare numerous reports and papers. The latter serve as the basis for most of the discussions in the deliberative organs. The Secretary-General usually personally attends sessions of the General Assembly, the Security Council, the ECOSOC and the Trusteeship Council. In other meetings, he is represented by designated officers.

The Charter provides that the Secretariat should be an international civil service [Art. 100]. It is appointed by the Secretary-General under regulations adopted by the General Assembly. The paramount consideration is stated as 'the necessity of securing the highest standards of efficiency, competence and integrity'. But this provision is modulated by an instruction to pay due regard to recruiting the staff 'on as wide a geographical basis as possible [Art. 101].

The standards and international character of the UN staff, as with the first international civil service in the League, have continually come under pressure. The wide geographical basis keeps the nationals of any one government from dominating the staff, but the General Assembly has often urged the Secretary-General to improve the distribution, which is tantamount to giving priority to country of origin, rather than qualifications. Furthermore, from the beginning, governments have intruded in the appointment process. This tends to weaken the effect of the oaths of office taken by international servants as well as the Charter provision [Art.100] that they may accept no instructions from national governments, their own or any other, as well as the undertaking by governments to respect the international character of the staff.

Who gets the second-level jobs, just below the rank of Secretary-General, was the subject of an informal agreement among the great powers during the earliest days of the UN. Below this so-called 'political level', many governments promote the candidacy of their own nationals. For instance, governments in Eastern Europe and the Soviet Union, certainly until 1989, submitted lists of their nationals whom they considered qualified. The United States communicates to the Secretary-General the results of security checks – that is, information as to whether they may be communist – on its nationals who are under consideration for appointment. Other governments concentrate their efforts on particular openings, putting forward candidates who sometimes, not entirely by accident, are the representatives at headquarters. As a practical matter, the Secretary-General could hardly go much beyond these 'suggestions' or, for that matter, conduct impartial searches and examinations for the best among thousands of possible candidates. Geographical distribution, agreements among the great powers, campaigning for nationals and limiting those who would be allowed to accept appointments, all tend to dilute the international character of the Secretariat.

Beyond organizing and directing the staff, the Secretary-General takes on a special, frequently difficult, political role that reaches farther than any assigned to any other international official. It derives primarily from Article 99 of the Charter, giving him the right to bring any matter that in his opinion may threaten peace and security to the attention of the Security Council. Thus, his personal judgement and readiness to take initiatives is crucial. In addition, he can state his views in his annual report and use opportunities given by his presence, or that of senior staff members, in hundreds of intergovernmental meetings. Governments may, of course, ignore his initiatives. Consequently, his influence depends on persuasiveness and good political analysis.

The use of Article 99 has been rare and restrained. Dag Hammarskjöld, the Swede who was the second Secretary-General, expressly invoked it to convene the Security Council in 1960 to deal with a crisis in the Congo (now Zaire). His predecessor, Trygve Lie, a Norwegian national, claimed that he acted in the Korea case in 1950 under Article 99. So did Kurt Waldheim, the Austrian fourth Secretary-General, who put the seizure of the United States embassy in Iran by radical student groups before the Council. But in the latter two incidents, the legal basis of the call by the Secretary-General was less explicit than in the Congo case.

Apart from the dramatic use of Article 99 to summon the Council, it offers the Secretary-General a basis for an important behind-the-scenes diplomatic role. This activity does not necessarily become visible or even the subject of discussion in the Security Council. 'Quiet diplomacy' was the way Hammarskjöld described it. He used this approach in the Suez Crisis in 1956 and four years later in the Congo affair. It received its first test in 1954, when he flew to China in his 'personal capacity' to negotiate freedom for US military airmen who had been captured during the Korean war.

The political role of the Secretary-General achieves full development when he is given instructions by a global deliberative body, such as the Security Council or the General Assembly. Typically, he has a substantial share in designing such instructions. This was the case during the Suez crisis of 1956, when Hammarskjöld improvised the first UN peace-keeping force. Similarly he was in the public eye in the Congo. Other incidents include the actions of U Thant, the Burmese third Secretary-General, in 1964 in Cyprus and Waldheim in 1975 in the Middle East and later in Lebanon. Javier Pérez de Cuéllar, the fifth Secretary-General, a Peruvian, acted in the so-called Gulf war between Iraq and Iran, helped negotiate the Soviet retreat from Afghanistan in 1988, and South Africa's withdrawal from Namibia in 1990. Boutros Boutros-Ghali, the former deputy foreign minister of Egypt, who succeeded Pérez de Cuéllar in 1992, bluntly accused the rich, northern countries of neglecting the UN operation in Somalia in favour of what was once Yugoslavia. All of these cases involved the formation and direction of a presence in the field and negotiations with the conflicting parties under rather broad authority from a UN organ. Usually, such incidents open political opportunities for the Secretary-General to seek a lasting settlement of the dispute.

The exercise of initiative easily involves the Secretary-General in controversy. After all, the states involved in a quarrel are almost always UN members and have divergent ideas about what servants of the organization should do. Both government officials and public figures nevertheless praised Hammarskjöld for his energetic, effective creation of peace-keeping forces in the Sinai Peninsula and in the Congo. Both he and U Thant retained political support when they directed the use of force by UN troops in Katanga province of the Congo.

Yet U Thant was stridently accused of giving up too quickly to Egyptian pressure to withdraw the UN Emergency Force (UNEF) from Sinai in 1967, at the beginning of the Arab–Israeli war in 1967. Both Trygve Lie, for his role in the Korean war, and Hammarskjöld, for his generally restrained policy in the Congo, were berated by the Soviet Union, which boycotted them. Chairman Khrushchev moved from demanding Hammarskjöld's resignation to an onslaught on the office itself. The Soviet Union insisted that the Secretary-General should disappear in favour of a three-member organ (a 'troika' or carriage drawn by three horses) that would represent Western, Communist and non-aligned states.

Hammarskjöld had early on both occasions assumed considerable leeway and argued in meticulous reports that both the Charter and the instructions he received would be the basis for the activities of the Secretary-General. His response to Khrushchev was made in a still-famous speech on 3 September 1960, before the General Assembly. The UN, he declared, primarily served the smaller states, not the Soviet Union or any great power. As long as the smaller states wished, he would remain in office, serving their interests. Hammarskjöld, not the Soviet Union and its allies, prevailed in the Assembly, but that did little to diminish the tension before the Secretary-General was killed in an aircraft accident in 1961 in Zambia. After that, the 'troika' remained in the barn and the Soviet Union eventually supported the election of U Thant. He soothed relations with the Soviet Union but irritated official Washington with his sharp criticism of the Vietnam war.

How the incumbent Secretary-General interprets his function obviously conditions his political role, but in the end the major powers have the strongest voice in determining how wide the limits of the office may be. Lie and Hammarskjöld sought to expand the office, their successors less directly so. Waldheim dealt with the great powers with much caution, even while inserting himself into every possible international negotiation. Any Secretary-General must be tactful and use diplomatic skill in dealing with all member country representatives and estimate carefully how far to go in taking initiatives. Lie and Hammarskjöld sometimes went beyond the limits set by one or another of the great powers and paid dearly. U Thant and Waldheim were more circumspect and less influential. During his second term, Pérez de Cuéllar showed a rising ability to make use of his opportunities to play an active role in the management of international conflicts and by 1990 was entrusted with increasing conciliation and peace-keeping assignments. By the time his first year in office had ended, Boutros-Ghali's approach visibly favoured political activism and close management of the growing number of field missions.

CLUSTER OF UN AGENCIES

Grouped around the United Nations itself are some 20 intergovernmental agencies (see Table 2.1). Each of these concentrates on particular economic, social or cultural programmes. The most independent of these bodies, formally known as 'specialized agencies', were foreseen in the UN Charter. They have memberships that overlap with the UN's but are not identical to it, sometimes including non-members of the UN. Their establishment rests on constitutional documents that, like the UN Charter, have the status of treaties among their members. Their relationship to ECOSOC is governed by special agreements [Art. 63]. Other agencies owe their existence to specific resolutions of the UN General Assembly and in principle could be dissolved by it.

Coordinating the work of these agencies is left primarily to ECOSOC [Art. 64], which is hardly endowed with more power than making recommendations and negotiating. Each agency tends to develop its own constituency in national governments and among technical specialists. Some of them date their establishment back to the middle of the nineteenth century and have steady financial support. Some have closely-defined purposes, such as the supervision of certain copyright regulations: others represent special interests, such as rapid economic and industrial development for the Third World. Yet others deal with notions as broad as the fostering of human intellectual progress generally or the protection of health everywhere. Although each of them is in touch with experts in their fields, that does not mean that firm agreement exists on how to approach particular issues. The lending agencies successfully claim special exemption from UN examination of their specific deals. As a consequence of these factors, the UN-associated agencies can sometimes compete or act as independent fiefdoms.

The system of UN agencies is as geographically decentralized as it is functionally differentiated. Six agencies are located in Geneva: the General Agreement on Tariffs and Trade (GATT); the International Labour Organization (ILO); the International Telecommunication Union (ITU); the World Health Organization (WHO); the World Intellectual Property Organization (WIPO); and the World Meteorological Organization (WMO). Two agencies are headquartered in Washington, DC: the World Bank (formally the International Bank for Reconstruction and Development) and its daughters, and the International Monetary Fund (IMF); two in Vienna, the International Atomic Energy Agency (IAEA) and the UN Industrial Development Organization (UNIDO). Paris is host to the UN Educational, Scientific and Cultural Organization (UNESCO), and Rome to the UN Food and Agriculture Organization (FAO), the World Food Programme (WFP) and the International Fund for Agricultural Development (IFAD). Other agencies are located in Montreal (the International Civil Aviation Organization – ICAO): Berne (the Universal Postal Union – UPU): London (the International Maritime Organization – IMO): and Nairobi (the UN Environment Program – UNEP). Some of the organizations which are formally part of the UN itself have headquarters in Geneva, including the UN Conference on Trade and Development (UNCTAD) and the High Commissioner for Refugees (UNHCR). The UN Children's Fund (UNICEF), the UN Development Programme (UNDP) and the UN Population Fund (UNFPA) are located in New York. The UN University operates from Tokyo and UN University for Peace from San José, Costa Rica.

For the perhaps hopeless task of coordinating this organizational tangle and interrelated activity, the UN has an intergovernmental mechanism in ECOSOC and a bureaucratic device in the Administrative Committee on Coordination (ACC). ECOSOC invites the heads of specialized agencies with which formal agreements are in effect to give oral reports. In addition, it reviews written documentation. The agencies have the right to initiate a discussion in ECOSOC and sometimes do so in order to promote their programmes.

ECOSOC has available to it studies by the UN Secretariat and its own Committee on Programme Coordination, based on a programme budgeting analysis covering the whole system, except for the World Bank and the IMF. Nevertheless, the specialized agencies make their own budgetary decisions, which may or may not reflect the priorities and guidelines set out by ECOSOC, usually after negotiations with the institutions concerned.

Those organizations responsible to the General Assembly, such as UNHCR or UNCTAD, submit their reports through ECOSOC. The review there may be very light indeed as the documentation will again be taken up in the committees of the General Assembly.

The other coordinating device, the ACC, brings together the executive directors of the specialized agencies as well as the chief officers of IAEA, GATT, UNCTAD, UNHCR and other similar agencies. Governments are not represented in this structure, which resembles a 'summit' of feudal lords who supervise the several territories of functional international cooperation under the presidency of the UN Secretary-General. He also heads the staff that serves ACC. Aside from exchanging the information that each agency offers, its result depends on the effectiveness of the Secretary-General's leadership, the independence of the executive heads of the agencies, and the demands of their constituencies.

ORGANIZATIONAL TENSION

The simultaneously elaborate and vague coordinating machinery for UN economic and social activities illustrates a general tension that runs through all international institutions. Governmental representatives repeatedly praise centralization of some sort, along with a tight programme for the general welfare. They seek efficiency, simplicity, defined priorities and directness. Yet the same governments strongly support the programmes of functional agencies, even when they diverge from the guidance offered by ECOSOC; they presume that technical cooperation inherently produces desirable benefits. At the same time, some of the same governments inject ideological issues into technical programmes, while others simply stay out of or leave organizations whose programmes contain objectionable aspects. For instance, the United States, the United Kingdom and Singapore withdrew from UNESCO; the Arab governments have often pressed for the expulsion or limitation of Israeli participation; and the Soviet Union never took part in the World Bank or the IMF, but in 1992 some of the former Soviet Republics joined both organizations. Consequently, the weak impetus towards centralization leaves parts of intergovernmental cooperation largely unaffected.

The governmental oversight of the agencies formally emanates from assemblies that resemble the deliberative organs of the UN. As a rule, each member state has one vote. Usually, a general conference or congress meets every year or every other year. Between these meetings, an elected executive committee or council supervises the programme and the work of the executive head. Like the UN Secretary-General, the agency executive directors head permanent international secretariats. These sometimes carry out large-scale programmes to assist governments and even individual persons. Only government officials represent states, except in the case of the ILO, which was deliberately built on a tri-partite base. Each member delegation in the International Labour Conference, the analogue of the UN General Assembly, consists of two governmental delegates and one each for employers and workers. For the ILO governing body, the Executive Council, members are elected from any of the three constituencies.

The IMF and the World Bank do not follow the one-state, one-vote pattern of the other agencies. They determine voting strength on the basis of capital investment in the agencies. The weighted voting principle extends to the standing executive bodies, which make principal decisions on loans. There, each large contributor sends a member, but the smaller contributors are grouped together for common representation by a joint delegate. Although these arrangements clearly apply the principle that who pays the piper calls the tune, only rarely do issues come to a vote in the two financial agencies. Most decisions are taken by consensus.

The usual organizational structure in the agencies is centralized along the lines of the UN. A permanent secretariat is housed in a central headquarters: its expert personnel controls information which gives the secretariat a powerful voice in policy decisions. WHO, however, created a unique decentralized structure. Six regional organizations, each with a regional committee of governmental representatives from the area, take responsibility for executing much of the WHO programme, which is broadly outlined through the central organization in Geneva. Other agencies maintain regional offices with much less responsibility for programmes. Taken as a whole, the UN system shows some degree of decentralization in the wide geographic distribution of the headquarters of the component agencies. That distribution also reflects the competition of governments for the international prestige and financial benefits of hosting the headquarters of an intergovernmental agency. So far, however, no agency has been invited to establish its headquarters in Eastern Europe.

Table 2.1 lists the specialized agencies, the years in which they were set up, the number of members, the headquarters location, the main purposes, and the budget. Some important organizations that are, strictly speaking, not formal specialized agencies are also included because of their similar functions. These are IAEA, GATT, the UN University, UNEP and UNHCR.

Table 2.1   The United Nations system

Organization	Founded	Member-ship 1992	Head-quarters	Purpose	Budget/ Operation (millions)
International Labour Organization (ILO)	1919	157	Geneva	To develop international minimum standards and to draft international labour conventions on subjects such as human rights, freedom of association, wages, hours of work, minimum ages for employment, conditions of work for various classes of workers, workmen's compensation, social insurance, vacation with pay, industrial safety, employment services, and labour inspection.	$406 1992–93
Food and Agricultural Organization (FAO)	1945	160	Rome	To raise levels of nutrition and standards of living; to improve the efficiency of the production and distribution of all food and agricultural products; and to improve the conditions of rural populations.	$677 1992–3
International Fund for Agricultural Development (IFAD)	1977	148	Rome	To mobilize additional resources for agricultural development in developing states by providing finances for projects and programmes to introduce, expand or improve food production systems.	$153 1992
United Nations Educational, Scientific and Cultural Organization (UNESCO)	1946	170	Paris	To promote collaboration among nations through education, science, culture, and communication in order to further universal respect for justice, for the rule of law and for	$445 1992–3

Table 2.1 (cont.)

Organization	Founded	Member-ship 1992	Head-quarters	Purpose	Budget/ Operation (millions)
				human rights and fundamental freedoms.	
World Health Organization (WHO)	1948	175	Geneva	The attainment by all peoples of the highest possible level of health (complete physical, mental, and social well-being); to stimulate the fight against epidemics and other infectious diseases; to disseminate information on the effect on human health of environmental pollutants; and to set global standards for antibiotics, vaccines, etc.	$735 1992–93
World Bank International Bank for Reconstruc-tion and Development (IBRD)	1946	161	Washington, DC	To assist in the reconstruction and development of territories of members by facilitating the investment of capital for productive purposes: to promote private foreign investment and to supplement it by providing loans for productive purposes	Authorized capital stock: $174 500
International Development Association (IDA)	1960	142	Washington, DC	To promote economic development and increase productivity, thus raising standards of living by providing its membership with finances to meet important development requirements on flexible terms.	Resources $68 900
International Finance Corporation (IFC)	1956	146	Washington, DC	To provide risk capital for productive private enterprise in association with private investors and	Authorized capital $1 300

Table 2.1   (cont.)

Organization	Founded	Member-ship 1992	Head-quarters	Purpose	Budget/ Operation (millions)
				management, to encourage the development of local capital markets and to stimulate the international flow of private capital.	
International Monetary Fund (IMF)	1945	165	Washington, DC	To promote international monetary cooperation and the expansion of international trade; to promote exchange stability; to maintain orderly exchange arrangements and to avoid competitive exchange depreciations; to assist in the establishment of a multilateral system of payments with respect to the currency transactions between members and to the elimination of the foreign exchange restrictions that hamper world trade.	$23 210 credits 1992
International Civil Aviation Organization (ICAO)	1947	168	Montreal	To facilitate the safety, regularity, and efficiency of civil air transport and to study the problems of international standards and regulation for civil aviation.	$47 1992
Universal Postal Union (UPU)	1878	168	Berne	To form a single postal territory of countries for the reciprocal exchange of letter-post items; to secure the organization and improvement of postal services; and to take part in postal technical assistance.	$41 1992

Table 2.1   (cont.)

Organization	Founded	Member ship 1992	Head quarters	Purpose	Budget/ Operation (millions)
International Telecommuni- cation Union (ITU)	1865	167	Geneva	To maintain and extend international cooperation for the improvement and rational use of telecommunication facilities in order to increase their usefulness and to make them generally available to the public; and to harmonize the actions of nations in the attainment of these common ends.	$198 1992
World Meteorological Organization (WMO)	1951	160	Geneva	To facilitate international cooperation in the establishment of networks of stations and centres to provide meteorological services and observations; to promote the establishment and maintenance of systems for the rapid exchange of meteorological and related information: and to promote standardization of meteorological observation and to ensure the uniform publication of information and statistics.	$358 1992–95
International Maritime Organization (IMO)	1958	136	London	To facilitate cooperation and exchange of information among governments on technical matters affecting shipping and, with special responsibility for the safety of life at sea, to assure that the highest possible standards of	$43 1992–93

Table 2.1 (cont.)

Organization	Founded	Member-ship 1992	Head-quarters	Purpose	Budget/ Operation (millions)
				maritime safety and efficient navigation are achieved.	
World Intellectual Property Organization (WIPO)	1970	129	Geneva	To promote the protection of intellectual property throughout the world through cooperation among states and, where appropriate, with other international organizations; and to administer the various 'unions' each founded on a multilateral treaty and dealing with different aspects of intellectual property.	$281 1992–93
United Nations Industrial Development Organization (UNIDO)	1965	155	Vienna	To promote and accelerate the industrialization of of developing countries and to coordinate the industrial development activities of the UN system.	$181 1992–93
International Atomic Energy Agency (IAEA)	1957	113	Vienna	To seek and accelerate and enlarge the contribution of atomic energy to peace, health, and prosperity throughout the world and to ensure that assistance provided by it is not used to further any military purpose.	$186 1992
General Agreement on Tariffs and Trade (GATT)	1948	103	Geneva	To provide international control over trade restrictions and thus to help expand world trade and contribute to higher living standards.	$129 1992

Table 2.1   (cont.)

Organization	Founded	Member-ship 1992	Head-quarters	Purpose	Budget/ Operation (millions)
United Nations University (UNU)	1975		Tokyo	To help solve pressing global problems of human survival, development and welfare through internationally coordinated science and scholarship.	$60 1992–93
United Nations Environment Programme (UNEP)	1972		Nairobi	To promote international cooperation in the field of the environment and to recommend policies to this end; to keep under review the world environmental situation in order to ensure that emerging environmental problems of wide international significance receive appropriate and adequate consideration by governments.	$94 1991
Office of the United Nations High Commissioner for Refugees (UNHCR)	1951		Geneva	To provide refugees with international protection and to seek permanent solutions for the problems of refugees. To promote the adoption of international minimum standards for the treatment of refugees and the effective implementation of these standards.	$370 1991

3 Membership and Decision-making

In the 45 years of its existence, membership of the United Nations has more than tripled. In 1945, at its founding, the organization had 51 members. By 1992, membership had grown to 178 and is now almost universal. Since the sixties, African and Asian states have occupied a dominant numerical position, as Table 3.1 shows.

Table 3.1 Geographical distribution of UN Membership

	1945	1992
Western Europe	8 (16%)	21 (12%)
Eastern Europe	6 (12%)	19 (11%)
Americas	22 (43%)	35 (20%)
Africa	4 (8%)	51 (28%)
Asia	9 (17%)	44 (25%)
Australia amd Pacific	2 (4%)	8 (4%)

Formal requirements for membership, listed in the Charter, require that the applicant state be 'peace-loving', accept the obligations contained in the Charter and, in the judgement of the organization, have the ability and willingness to carry out these obligations [Article 4]. Applicants for membership are admitted by the General Assembly, after having obtained the recommendation of the Security Council. During the first ten years, the process of application was anything but automatic. Repeatedly, coalitions led by the United States or vetoes cast by the Soviet Union prevented the admission of states. Between 1946 and 1955, only five states obtained membership: Pakistan and Yemen (1947), Burma (now called Myanmar, 1948), Israel (1948) and Indonesia (1950). In 1955, the United States and the Soviet Union agreed in a package deal to end their competitive blocking tactics. This led to the admittance of 16 new members. Subsequent requests – mainly by former colonies – have caused little difficulty. The largest influx took place in 1960 when 17 new members entered. In 1990, newly-independent Namibia was the 160th member to be admitted to the organization. The German Democratic Republic merged with the Federal Republic of Germany and the two Yemens also became one state. The former Soviet republics, in addition to Belarus and Ukraine, which were original members, all became UN members.

CHINESE REPRESENTATION

The Chinese revolution, which brought the Communist Party to power in Beijing in 1949, caused a long, bitter controversy about which government had the right to represent China in the United Nations. The Nationalist government of Chiang Kai-shek, which had fled to the island of Taiwan, held the seat at the time of the communist take-over. Between 1949 and 1971, the government in Beijing vainly sought the eviction of the Nationalists from the United Nations. During those two decades, a majority in the General Assembly, led by the United States, rejected the claim of Mao Ze-dong's government that it represented China.

The United States succeeded in keeping the matter of Chinese representation off the agenda of the General Assembly until 1961. Then, the United States secured the adoption of a procedural resolution calling the issue an 'important matter'. Under Article 18 of the UN Charter, an important matter requires a two-thirds vote. During the next ten years, too few votes favourable to Beijing were cast. But on 15 October 1971, after Henry Kissinger, then US national security adviser, had visited Beijing to arrange a visit for President Nixon, the General Assembly voted by 76 in favour, 35 against, and with 17 abstentions to seat the representatives of the People's Republic of China. Since then, the Nationalist Government which still reigns over Taiwan, has been excluded from the United Nations.

DIVIDED STATES

Three divided states, the results of the Second World War or receding colonialism, caused controversy in the United Nations. Of the three, one – North and South Korea – were the last to achieve UN membership. The two parts of Germany and of Vietnam had joined under different circumstances.

In the case of Germany, the Federal Republic (West Germany), awaiting reunification, opposed for a long time the admission of both parts of the country to the United Nations. Détente between East and West during the early 1970s set the conditions for the eventual admission of West Germany and the German Democratic Republic in 1973. After reunification in October 1990, the two seats became one.

Efforts to admit both North and South Vietnam to United Nations membership failed while the contending governments sought reunification on their own terms. After the unsuccessful military intervention by the United States in Indochina, each claimed to be the sole representative of Vietnam. The defeat of the Western-backed South Vietnamese government in 1975 by communist North Vietnam produced the forceful reunification of Vietnam and, in 1977, the state was admitted to the United Nations.

Korea had been the object of an effort by the United Nations between 1947 and 1950 to achieve peaceful unification. The North Korean attack on South Korea resulted in military action under United Nations auspices to restore the peace (see Chapter 4). The eventual armistice in 1954 brought the peninsula no closer to unification: it remains divided between a Western-oriented government in the South and a communist government in the North. Both governments applied for membership in mid-1991 and were unconditionally accepted.

SWITZERLAND AND NEUTRALITY

The case of Switzerland, the host of the League of Nations and the site of the European Office of the United Nations, is unique. It declined to apply for United Nations membership, because its government believed that enforcement obligations under Chapter VII of the UN Charter could violate traditional Swiss neutrality. This has not prevented Switzerland from joining many of the specialized agencies of the UN system and serving as the host to a number of them. In 1986, Swiss voters in a national referendum rejected by a 3–1 margin a government-sponsored proposal to join the United Nations. Nevertheless, Switzerland has since joined modestly in a few UN peace-keeping ventures.

MINISTATES

Although some general criteria for membership appear in Article 4 of the UN Charter, it contains no specification as to the minimum size for membership. A consequence is the problem of mini- or micro-states. Indeed, two of the founding members of the organization – Iceland with 160 000 inhabitants and Luxembourg with 300 000 – would now be considered mini-states. At the time, these exceptionally small members caused little concern. This equanimity turned into perplexity when very small colonies gained independence and began entering the United Nations as one of their first formal acts of government. As of 1992, the following members of the United Nations have fewer than 150 000 inhabitants:

Liechtenstein	26 000
Marshall Islands	46 000
St Kitts and Nevis	47 000
Seychelles	66 000
Dominica	77 000
Antigua and Barbuda	81 000
St Vincent and the Grenadines	105 000
Micronesia	108 000
San Tomé and Príncipe	110 000
St Lucia	132 000
Vanuatu	142 000

In 1992, the republic of San Marino (23 000 inhabitants) – entirely surrounded by Italy – became the smallest UN member.

In the General Assembly, mini-states each have one vote, equal to that of the larger and more powerful states. As this equality does not reflect power and influence, the larger states become irritated by some activities of the smaller fry. Furthermore, the small and micro-states pay only tiny parts of the organizational budget. Yet, through their voting strength, the tiny states can help majorities in the General Assembly to adopt expensive programmes for which the organization as a whole must pay.

Practical ways around the difficulties caused by mini-states have, so far, never been found. No one can agree on an answer to the question of what objective criteria should be used to decide the minimum effective size. Should it be one million inhabitants, as once was proposed? Or half a million? Even if it were possible to find agreement on criteria, how should the smaller states be represented?

A new type of associate membership for the mini-states was once suggested by diplomats from larger countries. An associate member would be permitted to benefit from UN activity and be allowed to speak in the General Assembly on matters relevant to it, but it would have no right to vote. The newly-independent mini-states have kept their distance from this proposal. They suspected, rightly, that several of them that now enjoy status as full members of the UN would lose their rights. As more and more mini-states joined the UN as full members, it became less likely, under the present Charter provisions, that their rights would be curtailed.

WEIGHTED VOTING

Apart from the issues posed by micro-states, proposals to create a system of weighted voting in the General Assembly have been made, primarily by scholars and political leaders but rarely by governments. According to such criteria as size of population, gross national product, military power, or a combination of these factors, some states would cast more votes than others. The International Monetary Fund and the World Bank provide living examples. In these organizations, the number of votes per member state varies according to its capital contribution. In the United Nations, the criteria proposed for weighted votes immediately produce controversy. Small and poor states strongly oppose the whole idea, for it would mean loss of their formal status of equality. Because their cooperation is needed in order to alter the UN Charter, there is little prospect for change.

At the same time, domination of the work of the United Nations by the small states poses the danger that the General Assembly may lose authority in coping with international conflicts. An Assembly led by such states as Saint Vincent and Grenada would hardly reflect the facts of world politics.

From the point of view of newly-independent states, no matter how small, membership in the United Nations has great symbolic and practical meaning. Raising the flag of a new state on the long row of poles on United Nations Plaza in New York signals self-respect and esteem in the wider world. A new delegation takes a seat in the main assembly hall with a vote equalling that of established and powerful states. The newcomers thus enhance feelings of national consciousness that have vital importance to them. This strengthening of national self-assurance paradoxically occurs in an organization founded to foster international solidarity.

The practical importance of membership derives partly from the network of permanent missions located in New York and Geneva. The new states can use their representation to the United Nations as a super-embassy. Contacts can be made there with ambassadors of every government in the world. A government can both obtain and supply information there. Many international agreements in the fields of trade and development, often of primary importance to new states, grow out of contacts first made in New York or Geneva. In both places, they can also consult the headquarters or representatives of other UN agencies.

DECISION-MAKING PROCESSES

International organizations customarily rely on defined voting procedures in decision-making organs. Proposals are put to the member states of bodies such as the General Assembly or the Security Council in the form of draft resolutions. These are adopted or rejected. Such votes may require, depending on the organ and its rules of procedure, either an ordinary or a qualified majority of some sort.

As most public bodies in democratic states now reach decisions in this manner, it may seem almost natural that international organizations should employ the same procedure. Nevertheless, the practice of democratic voting procedures in international organizations is of relatively recent origin and doubts about its usefulness have never dissipated.

The big nineteenth-century international conferences that commonly are seen as models for contemporary organizations usually arrived at decisions by consensus. This practice followed from the idea of absolute national sovereignty. No state could be committed to anything without its express consent. Thus any decision required approval by all participants. In practice, in other words, a rule of unanimity prevailed. In principle, this rule applied in the first general international organization, the League of Nations, where each member state in fact held a right of veto.

Since then, member states of international organizations have increasingly accepted decision-making by majority vote. This applies both to legally binding as well as to non-obligatory resolutions. In the case of non-binding resolutions, the choice of majority voting may not matter very much. Voting arrangements become much more important, however, when an organization deals with matters that governments consider pertinent to their national interests. Such issues frequently engage the United Nations. Consequently, the way in which decisions are reached in the Security Council and the General Assembly, where far-reaching debates on matters of peace and security take place, has unavoidable importance.

Not surprisingly, the United Nations heads the list of international organizations in which voting problems have attracted public attention and criticism. As the Charter allots serious powers to maintain the peace to the Security Council, majority rule in that body is restricted. As elsewhere in the United Nations, the principle of equality of member states applies. Yet, power politics continues to form a basis for international relations, especially when resorting to force looms as a possibility. At the founding of the United Nations, the big powers successfully claimed the right to a veto in the Security Council as a means of protecting their power positions, over the opposition of the smaller states. Furthermore, even if the permanent members favour a resolution, a qualified majority of nine out of 15 votes in the Council is required for adoption of a proposal.

In this respect, the relatively small Security Council contrasts sharply with the much larger General Assembly, where a simple majority may take most decisions. The exception comes when the Assembly votes on 'important matters', which require a two-thirds majority.

Should this process of decision-making be called 'democratic'? Only in the sense that decisions are taken by majority vote, treating each state equally. However, the system fails to satisfy on the basis of size of population. From a democratic point of view, it is obviously wrong that such countries as China, India, Russia, and the United States, each with many millions of inhabitants, have a vote equal to that of the Seychelles, with all of 66 000 people. But even if the United Nations were able to persuade all its members to adopt a weighted voting system that would better represent the elements of power and population, a great deal of difference would still remain in the degree to which governments truly represent their people. Few of the people or their elected representatives of the states gathered in New York are consulted while government delegates make up their minds. Most member governments cannot be considered even remotely democratic in the manner of the countries of Western Europe and North America. Even if the frequent argument is accepted that Western political concepts should not be applied to non-Western societies, this uncertainty remains.

From the standpoint of democratic theory or of power politics, the present voting system may stand as the least objectionable. As long as the world divides along existing political lines, there is no reason to expect that the system will be changed. The question will then remain as to how the voices of 'We, the peoples of the United Nations' to whom the Charter refers in its preamble, can make themselves heard and accurately understood.

FUNDAMENTAL CHANGES

The expansion of membership during the 1950s and 1960s wrought fundamental changes in the United Nations. The most important of these occurred in political affairs. During the first years of its existence, the organization responded to the United States and its allies: for all practical purposes, it was a Western organization. At present, it is influenced by African and Asian states. The new alignment can be seen most vividly in the General Assembly. There, the African and Asian states, whenever they reach internal agreement, can secure the adoption of any resolution. In the Security Council too, where a decision requires nine votes, the relative importance of the African and Asian states has increased. They furnish five of the 10 non-permanent members. The African, Asian and some Latin American states may meet together as the 'non-aligned', signifying their formal detachment from the former alliances sponsored by what used to be the superpowers.

The voting strength of the African and Asian governments strongly affects the decision process in the General Assembly. In order to secure adoption of their proposals, sponsors of resolutions must assemble many more votes than in the early years. Approval of even slightly controversial resolutions demands extensive lobbying. The smallest and most obscure members enter the process, for their votes count for as much as any other government's. More than one delegation has too few people to cover all meetings in progress. In those circumstances, friendly delegations that do have enough manpower take on the task of alerting their friends among the small delegations. Delegates of small states sometimes rush into a room just before a crucial vote takes place, cast their ballot, and move on to the next meeting.

VOTING GROUPS

Traditional diplomacy is carried on outside the range of the public eye. The decision-making process in the United Nations includes public debates in the deliberative organs. This style of negotiation is called 'conference diplomacy' or 'parliamentary diplomacy'.

Nevertheless, confidential meetings usually precede important decisions, which are subsequently confirmed in public. During the last few years, this has been strikingly true of the Security Council, where private conversations among the representatives of the Permanent Members now lay the basis for any important decisions. Some knowledgeable observers consider confidential consultations as important as the actual resolutions or formulae that formally record decisions. This is all the more true in the General Assembly, because of the limited legal obligation involved in most of its decisions. Pre-voting consultations offer a chance for governments to set out their positions and to learn of others so that possibilities of reaching a compromise may emerge without the embarrassing glare of publicity. The give and take of the ensuing negotiations itself becomes an important factor in regulating the behaviour of governments. Confidential consultations are most important when they lead delegations to decide that they *cannot* pursue their project because they do not have the necessary support.

Many of these negotiations take place in group meetings. Such groups, or caucuses are not mentioned in the Charter and have no official status. Yet, they are of crucial importance in the decision-making process. The main geographical groups are the African, the Asian, the East European, the Latin American, and the West European and Others which meet for electoral purposes. In addition there are groups meeting to discuss certain issues. The African, Asian and Latin American representatives also meet as the 'Group of 77' ('G-77'), a term taken over from the designation of the developing countries in UNCTAD (See Chapter 7). The 12 members of the European Community have meetings of their own.

Further analysis discloses a complexity that in itself argues against the notion that these groups somehow have iron-bound definitions. The African and Asian groups sometimes meet together. Their Arab members may meet as a separate group. The Islamic Conference, which exists outside of the United Nations, sponsors meetings of the Muslim countries on issues in the General Assembly of interest to them. Although purely geographical criteria would dictate membership in the Asian group for Israel and the African for South Africa, they have been, for obvious political reasons, excluded. For many years, the Latin American group excluded Castro's Cuba. Greece and Turkey belong to the West European and Others group for electoral purposes, while Turkey attends the meetings of the Asian group for political consultations. Cyprus belongs to the Asian group but, as a member of the Council of Europe, could conceivably join with the West European and Others. That word, 'Others', refers to Australia, Canada and New Zealand, and came into being because of the demise of the original Commonwealth group. With the latter group, the United States is an observer and in fact joins it for the purpose of proposing candidates.

Regional groups that operate at the ambassadorial level, consisting of the permanent representatives of member states meeting for electoral purposes, can be distinguished from those at committee level, where the delegates on any one of the main committees meet together. However, the latter groups are not rigid qua composition. At the ambassadorial level, representatives of the member states that make up the five geographical groups – African, Asian, East European, Latin American, and West European and Others – meet approximately once a month. Their purpose relates to elections held in the General Assembly to fill the non-permanent seats in the Security Council, all of the seats in the Economic and Social Council, and those in some other bodies. The seats in the two important councils are allotted among the five groups according to a system set out in 1963 (General Assembly Resolution 1991 [XVIII]). That resolution provides that, in the Security Council, three non-permanent seats are reserved for the African, two for the Asian states, one for the East Europeans, two for the Latin Americans, and two for West Europe and Others. The 54 seats in the Economic and Social Council are similarly distributed.

The ambassadorial groups also decide on the distribution of the offices of vice-presidents of the General Assembly and chairmen and rapporteurs of the seven main committees. Together with the permanent members of the Security Council, these officers of the General Assembly make up the important General Committee. A different geographical group each year provides the president of the General Assembly. Whoever receives the nomination of the group that has the office that year, automatically wins the acceptance of the other member states. In effect, the geographical groups, rather than the membership as a whole, elect the president on a rotating basis.

At the committee level, unlike the arrangement for ensuring geographical distribution, a large number of groups operate. These are convened whenever the members believe it politically opportune. For example, if a resolution must be drafted or if a resolution already before the Assembly requires some adjustment in order to gain approval, groups may meet. The membership of such groups varies considerably, depending on the issue and the timing. For example, Japan joins the Asian group on questions of self-determination in the Fourth Committee, but meets with the Western group on economic issues in the Second Committee. Such consultations have a rather informal organization and much flexibility of membership and procedure.

The group of West European and Other states, comprising some of the richest and most influential UN members, has never developed its consultations to the point of reaching a common point of view or group position. Nevertheless, subgroups of West Europeans have increasingly sought to present a single position. Thus, the members of the European Community or the Nordic countries often speak with one voice. In the West European and Others group as a whole, however, consultations normally are nothing more than an exchange of views on candidates.

Some governments try to build up a majority for their views across geographical groups. Building such a common point of view may produce a majority in the General Assembly. The informal procedures of group gatherings lend themselves to easy relationships. Delegates speak languages which, for reasons of national prestige, they never would use in formal public sessions. Even French delegates have been heard to speak English! Such meetings take place in private and outsiders find it difficult to know whether, where, and when they take place, let alone to attend them. The results are treated as confidential.

GROUPS AND VOTING POSITIONS

The geographical groups have no mandate to take important decisions, and whatever consensus they do reach may still fail to hold. The delegates may declare during informal sessions that they intend to vote in a particular way. When the time comes, they may act differently, not necessarily because of bad faith or duplicity. In fact, good diplomacy requires honesty and keeping commitments. Yet, external circumstances, such as pressure from outside or from domestic public opinion, can sometimes change commitments. Under such circumstances, either consensus will not be achieved in the first place or it may evaporate. The result may well be a change in position, either at the committee level or at the plenary meeting that has to decide on committee recommendations.

In the meetings of the consultative groups of delegates at the committee level, however, some decisions have a fair chance of being carried out. That is often true for decisions pertaining to tactics. These include such matters as whether and when to introduce a draft resolution, or whether to ask for a paragraph-by-paragraph or roll-call vote. A related tactical consideration is the question of whether to try to get the General Assembly to define a particular issue as 'important', requiring a two-thirds majority for adoption. Such deals can be undertaken by delegations on their own initiative, without detailed instructions from home governments.

Multilateral consultations in regional groupings indirectly contribute to making decisions at a higher, governmental level, according to some diplomats who are familiar with the process. During the consultations, numerous issues that do not have a direct bearing on the agenda of the General Assembly come to the surface. Delegates can probe each other's views for better information or understanding. Such conversations are reported to the respective governments for consideration while they are preparing for more formal deliberations. Thus, the talks relating directly to the work of the General Assembly may have broad effects on the positions of governments.

THE POLITICAL SIGNIFICANCE OF RESOLUTIONS

The very process of proposing and deciding on resolutions engages the attention of governments. One or more members of the UN organ in question may take the initiative for submission of a draft resolution. Occasionally, a draft originates within the UN Secretariat or in a specialized agency. Even so, a representative of a member state in most cases must formally introduce the draft resolution. Resolutions always aim at having the UN organ speak out on a specific issue. A resolution may welcome, condemn, or applaud any situation or development. Usually, a resolution makes recommendations to governments or directs the Secretariat to undertake specified activities.

Resolutions of the General Assembly are only rarely legally binding: they are normally recommendations to one or more actors in world politics but not legal obligations of the sort that courts can enforce. Furthermore, if the parties to whom recommendations are directed ignore them, the General Assembly has no legal capacity to correct undesired behaviour. It can, however, give direct, binding instructions to the UN Secretariat and it can underline its wishes by budgetary decisions.

If resolutions of the General Assembly have so little obligatory effect, why do the delegates of more than 180 governments spend at least three months each year polishing, promoting, and manoeuvring resolutions? The answer is that the legal significance of resolutions represents a minor part of their meaning. Rather, recommendations may have substantial political significance. If that is so, how can an observer uncover the intentions embodied in a resolution?

Most resolutions include preambles in which the drafters explain the considerations that they believe should lead to an expression of opinion by the General Assembly. In many instances, their intention is actively to seek publicity on a given issue. The operative part of the resolution, which follows the preamble, contains a precise statement of the action desired. This can ensure additional attention to the issue. In some cases, by instructing the Secretary-General to write a report on the issue for consideration at the next session, a resolution guarantees additional publicity. Another technique for achieving the same result establishes an *ad hoc* committee to deal with the item, either at once or while the General Assembly is in recess. Such continued attention and consideration can sometimes lead to the establishment of entirely new international bodies. This was the case with UNCTAD and UNEP.

Another aim pursued by the sponsors of a resolution may be the expression of sentiments about a particular situation. Such resolutions concern, for example, apartheid or the maintenance of international peace. They have little more positive result in themselves than the recording of a widespread belief. Yet governments may find it useful as a response to pressure in their domestic settings. It permits leaders to claim legitimacy for their foreign policies and to demonstrate to followers that national goals have sympathetic support elsewhere.

Resolutions also may be introduced in the hope of creating norms of behaviour in international relations. Such resolutions may eventually provide for the creation of multilateral conventions that have the force of law on governments that ratify them and can be enforced in domestic courts. Sometimes, such resolutions seek the elaboration of general principles, mentioned in the Charter, such as the prohibition of violence, or the promotion of economic development. Two well-known examples of this process are the Universal Declaration of Human Rights (See Chapter 5) and the resolution declaring the seabed the common heritage of mankind. As for the seabed, resolutions of the General Assembly led eventually to the drafting of a comprehensive Convention on the Law of the Sea. It not only codifies existing international law but also broadens its scope and sharpens its definitions.

Even when resolutions adopted in the General Assembly do not directly stimulate lawmaking, they nevertheless command a certain moral authority. This moral force grows when a resolution receives support from a large majority, is backed by representatives of several regional groups, or is favoured by states that are considered 'influential'. The latter include such countries as India, Mexico, Brazil, Nigeria, or Canada, which have special prestige as leaders or symbols of widely-favoured positions. During the 1960s, some international lawyers and other observers even argued that the moral authority of a resolution, if carried by a large majority, could be understood as demonstrating the existence of legally binding rules. Now, however, the predictability of votes on General Assembly resolutions as the result of regional caucusing has diminished their former moral force, especially in the Western states. Nevertheless, most governments will still try to avoid a direct confrontation with, or condemnation by, the General Assembly.

The actual formulation of resolutions varies a good deal. If the expression of a widely-held sentiment is the aim, strong language may be used – the more so if the parties concerned are unlikely to heed the recommendation. South Africa provides a case in point. Resolutions condemning apartheid have contained increasingly bitter language, but the South African government, for many years, simply refused to conform. When, however, some chance remains that compliance will result, more careful language may be chosen.

One way or another, however, resolutions proposed in the General Assembly force governments to take public positions on matters that they may sometimes prefer to handle privately. Even endlessly-reiterated resolutions force governments to take positions anew. In doing so, governments sometimes must take into account strong or changing opinions at home. Furthermore, governmental politics may well change substantially over time: the votes reflect such change.

When the General Assembly deals with a proposed resolution, governments have three choices: they can vote in favour, oppose or abstain. (A fourth possibility sometimes practised is to refrain from participation in the vote, while present or not. It is akin to abstention.) Each of these choices can have diplomatic consequences. For example, the Arab governments and Israel closely watch the votes on resolutions dealing with the situation in the Middle East for signs of change. Finally, governments understand that on occasion UN members find ways outside the organization to gain the ends sought by resolutions. Yet, unless the more powerful and influential governments are prepared to carry out the resolutions of the General Assembly, the verbiage of the resolutions may have no more effect than harmless blowing off steam.

SLOW DECISION-MAKING

The way in which the General Assembly proceeds on resolutions and in general causes delegates to complain about slow and cumbersome decision-making. Almost anyone who observes the process from a spectator's seat would agree. Speeches stretch from minutes into hours, the same points are repeated with differing emphasis by a series of delegates from different countries, the speeches wander from the point and often include quite extraneous comment. What is more, during the first weeks of the Assembly, many hours are consumed by the so-called general debate, which has little to do with a real debate. The suggestions made in the general debate, to no one's surprise, seem to favour the interests of the speaker. The prepared texts inexorably find their way into the record, even if they get little attention in the General Assembly and have little to do with the points made by the previous speaker. This speech-making has grown in length with the list of members of the organization.

In addition, paper descends on the desks of delegations in daily avalanches. Reports, minutes, proposals, draft proposals, amendments, texts of remarks, answers to assertions made earlier – all of which come out in six working languages: English, French, Spanish, Russian, Chinese as well as Arabic. The situation is only compounded, when the General Assembly, unable to decide on a clutch of problems, sets up new committees, names subcommittees, creates commissions, and appoints experts to try to find agreeable ways out of impasses. Complaints about this unwieldy process only stimulate the General Assembly to create yet another committee to design improvements in its working habits. Little has resulted from these efforts. Ambassadors of sovereign states do not accept limitations on their words, for that would imply denigration of the rights of a government. Consequently, they will not accept such obvious proposals as increasing the power of the presiding officers to call speakers back into line when they drift from the subject or make discourteous remarks. Furthermore, the speakers often look over the heads of the delegates, back to their own countries, when they speak; when they address home audiences from this global platform, they accept no abridgement of their remarks.

Yet slow procedures offer advantages that cannot be laughed away. While one delegate carries on interminably, repeating what has been said thrice before, other representatives busy themselves with consultations on the texts of draft resolutions, work up amendments, and recruit co-sponsors. In the lobbies important decisions can be prepared while the scheduled meetings drone along. The time can be used to maintain contact with home governments. Without instructions, some delegates have no authority to proceed, so the discussion would falter in any case. Delegates also tend politely to overlook stalling tactics, knowing that they may themselves soon need time to manoeuvre or seek instructions. An outside observer could easily conclude from the assiduous use of the delays by delegates that they really find the slow existing procedures quite satisfactory.

FINANCES

Whatever the pace of decision-making, the member governments must adopt a budget and provide for finances if there is to be an international institution at all. The General Assembly considers and approves the budget of the organization, as provided in Article 17 of the Charter. The Secretary-General submits a proposed budget to the General Assembly to cover two years of operations. This proposal undergoes running examination during its formation by experts appointed by the General Assembly to the Advisory Committee on Administrative and Budgetary Affairs. For the 1992–93 biennium, the budget to which member governments are obliged to contribute totalled some $2.4 billion. Important headings in the 1992–93 budget include international cooperation for development ($321 million), regional cooperation for development ($286 million) and political affairs ($157 million). Assessments on staff salaries in place of income taxes were expected to return $332 million and $58 million were to come from sales of postage stamps and fees for tours and similar activities.

In addition to the regular budget, based on obligatory contributions, several UN programmes depend on voluntary financing. Examples of these programmes include the UNDP, the UN Relief and Works Agency for Palestine Refugees (UNRWA), UNHCR, and UNICEF.

Apart from the activities supported by voluntary contributions, the budget is covered by assessment of the member states. The assessment depends in an approximate way on ability to pay. Every three years, the

Assembly decides how to allocate the assessments among the members. The minimum contribution was 0.04 per cent before 1973 but has been decreased first to 0.02 per cent and then to 0.01 per cent. No state pays more than 25 per cent. A large number of members pay only the minimum, and together this makes up a small fraction of the total. The sub-Sarahan African countries, including South Africa, the largest single geographical group, pay 0.86 per cent of the budget, while the stronger and more developed states each pay a substantial fraction. The following states are the largest contributors:

United States	25.0%
Japan	12.45%
Germany	8.93%
Russia	6.71%
France	6.00%
United Kingdom	5.02%
Italy	4.29%
Canada	3.11%

The precise budgetary shares are determined during negotiations in the Assembly's Committee on Contributions, according to criteria including national income, income per capita, foreign exchange available and similar factors. The developing nations have insisted that these criteria must reflect their special financial disabilities.

Some budgetary provisions have led individual states to refuse to pay their assessments. The most important instance of this refusal grew out of the peace-keeping operations in the Middle East during 1956 and 1957, when the UN Emergency Force (UNEF) served there, and in the Congo from 1960 to 1964, when an expensive peace-keeping operation took place. The Soviet Union and France claimed that expenses for these operations were not 'expenses of the organization' that had to be apportioned among the members, according to Article 17 of the Charter. This led to a 'financial crisis' with critical political implications. The crisis actually centred on the application of the provision of the UN Charter in Article 19 that a government in arrears of paying its contributions for two years shall have no vote in the General Assembly.

The Soviet Union and its allies took the position that the peace-keeping expenses should be paid by the 'aggressors', whom they identified as Great Britain, France and Israel in the Suez incident and Belgium in the Congo. Along with France, the Soviet Union also raised substantial legal objections. The Soviet Union pointed out that the relevant budgetary decisions rested, not on the Security Council acting as provided in the

Charter, but on a resolution of the General Assembly. The legal argument was sharpened when the International Court of Justice, responding to a request by the General Assembly, issued an advisory opinion in 1962 to the effect that the expenses indeed were those referred to in Article 17 and thus subject to obligatory apportionment. The refusing states maintained their attitude until, in 1964, the issue reached a climax. The Soviet Union and some other members then owed more than two years' worth of contributions. The United States appeared determined to force the issue and to secure the suspension of the Soviet Union and its allies from voting in the General Assembly. Had the General Assembly gone through with this proceeding, the Soviet group almost certainly would have withdrawn from the organization. No votes were taken during that Assembly.

Once the General Assembly was over, the United States reappraised its position. Tacitly acknowledging the failure of its attempt to force the Soviet Union and France to contribute, the United States decided that their continuing membership after all would be more important than a pyrrhic victory. France proved willing to pay at least part of its debt, but the Soviet Union continued to refuse to contribute money for the now terminated peace-keeping ventures until the Gorbachev-led policy changes. China has adopted a similar stance, refusing to pay for actions that it considers hostile or in violation of the provisions of the Charter, by which it means the response of the United Nations in Korea. Later peace-keeping operations have been financed through voluntary contributions. The United States announced after the crisis that it would also decide for itself when it was obliged to pay. This stance had little significance until the Reagan presidency, when the United States used it actively as a threat and put it into effect in minor instances.

The financial crisis deserves to be judged dispassionately, not merely on the basis of legal and moral obligations. The question should be raised as to whether it was sensible to assume that the General Assembly could force a great power to pay for an exercise that it opposed from the very beginning as legally and politically impermissible. Under a law adopted in 1979, the US Congress has forbidden its government to contribute to UN funds that in any way support the Palestine Liberation Organization. Major powers will not contribute financially to activities to which they are politically opposed.

Quite apart from the Article 19 crisis, a steady stream of criticism is directed at the level of expenses of the United Nations. In the recent past, this type of criticism has been expressed both by the United States and the Soviet Union. Superfluous administrative activities are cited. In the General Assembly, delegates insist on the need to reduce expenditures, but then vote for countless requests for studies and reports to be prepared by the Secretariat, support new study committees, and summon new conferences in many distant corners of the earth. While it is easy to raise questions about how useful much of this activity really is, to demonstrate specific waste is equally difficult. The Secretariat is required by the General Assembly to make a report on all new expenses, to set out the cost-effectiveness of old activities, to produce a programme budget, and to allow the watchdog Advisory Committee on Administrative and Budgetary Questions to give its advice. While it is not strictly germane, the perspective of judgements is improved by recalling that the total costs of the UN system fall below the costs of running even a modest military establishment.

Another criticism related to costs of the UN system calls attention to the many receptions and dinners given by the permanent mission to the United Nations in New York. The great majority of these fall exclusively within national accounts, not the UN budget, and resemble the functions that take place continually in national capitals. They are indispensable to diplomatic work. In New York, the number of these gatherings perhaps exceeds those held in any national capital; it is not unusual for a senior diplomat to appear at as many as three receptions in one evening. These occasions make it possible for diplomats to talk informally about matters that will be raised more officially later. They also use such occasions to speak with journalists and to send gestures of amity or disdain to others. This is the way some diplomatic business is normally conducted anywhere. Complaining in public and meeting later at parties is likely to remain a permanent feature at UN headquarters.

4 The Maintenance of Peace and Security

The fundamental purpose of the United Nations is the maintenance of international peace and security. The Charter of the United Nations sets out two principal, direct approaches to maintaining peace.

The first is the pacific settlement of disputes, outlined in Chapter VI of the Charter. The second comprises coercive measures against any state that threatens or breaks the peace. This is defined in Chapter VII of the Charter. Specific issues of peace and security may be handled by the General Assembly only when they are not before the Security Council or when the latter asks for the assistance of the larger body [Art. 12].

Of these two approaches, pacific settlement and its associated devices have proved far and away the most useful. This result differs little from what diplomatic experience and the League of Nations have taught, for the use of coercion is difficult to coordinate and can spur on a more serious crisis, great costs, and even more violence.

The initial responsibility for the peaceful resolution of differences rests on the parties to a dispute. They are forbidden from using violence [Art. 2(4)] but rather must try to find a pacific solution without endangering international peace and security [Art. 2(3)]. Beyond that, the UN Charter lists several specific means of settlement.

The list begins with *negotiations* to find a solution. An *enquiry* to develop better information about a tense international relationship could be set in motion. In this case, the Security Council could ask the Secretary-General to carry out this task. The Council could offer *good offices* or direct the Secretary-General to do so. Formally, this is merely provision of a location with a suitable atmosphere for negotiation. The Secretary-General could also be instructed to send out *observers*, provided the parties agreed, and would always report back on his activity. *Mediation* and *conciliation* also are listed in the Charter. These procedures, technically somewhat different, require the services of a third party that can make suggestions about the solutions to a dispute without obliging the disputants to accept them. The president of the Security Council, or the Secretary-General, or a group of persons or national representatives acceptable to the disputing governments, could serve as third parties.

Third parties also figure in *arbitration*, but here an arbitrator or a commission is specially appointed to deliver an opinion which the disputants agree in advance to accept as binding. Differences about international law or its application can be appropriately settled by arbitration or by *judicial decision*, for example by the International Court of Justice, on the basis of questions defined by the parties or in accordance with a procedure agreed in advance (see Chapter 2). Finally, the Security Council is authorized to select other pacific measures which may be useful.

If fighting has actually broken out, the Security Council usually calls on the parties to stop practices that contradict obligations assumed under the Charter and to cease fire. Such an appeal may succeed, not so much because it emanates from the Security Council but rather either because the goals of a party were achieved or else that further violence appears futile. If an appeal results in a ceasefire, the Council may dispatch international observers to ensure observance of its terms. This requires agreement from disputants.

In fact, in all of the means for pacific settlement provided in Chapter VI of the Charter, the cooperation of the parties is unmistakably required. Generally, the disputants may prove amenable to accepting the intervention of the Security Council in the hope that their own views will gain support. Whatever the tactics of the parties to a dispute, the underlying principle of pacific settlement assumes that war must be excluded as a means of conflict-resolution. Rather, peaceful settlement techniques must prevail. Another principle underlying the Charter provisions holds that most regional conflicts may lead to a danger to wider international peace and security. Although the Charter encourages the use of regional arrangements for pacific settlement, the Security Council is in principle authorized to intervene in regional conflicts. [Art. 52 (3,4)].

UN proceedings have succeeded in preventing a number of conflicts from spreading or have dulled the sharpest edges of others. The unresolved conflict over Kashmir between India and Pakistan provides an example of repeated intervention by the United Nations in order to dampen new flare-ups. The Security Council convinced both parties as long ago as 1949 to accept the presence of a small observation group which can furnish reliable information about new outbreaks of violence. Such reports help in reasserting international concern about any disturbance. The Kashmir conflict also exemplifies the fact that the United Nations seldom can put in place permanent solutions to end disputes. Rather it often brings the parties to arrest a conflict on the spot, after fighting, or else restores the pre-conflict situation. In that way the conflict is not resolved but simply checked for the time being. Such results have little to do with the merits of the case and in many respects remain unsatisfactory. Nevertheless, the most important assumption of the UN Charter insists that non-violent behaviour is always preferable to the use of force.

The Arab–Israeli conflict provides a striking example of both the successes and the limitations of the performance of the United Nations. Time after time, in outright warfare during 1948, 1949, 1956, 1967 and lastly in 1973, action by the United Nations achieved little more than a ceasefire and the temporary restoration of at least some of the pre-conflict situation. None of this eliminated the causes of the wars.

In the series of military engagements around Israel, the United Nations eventually served as a means to bring about a standstill in military action. With the consent of the parties, it provided important services to encourage the maintenance of those ceasefires and armistices. Above all, it furnished an important specific element in the form of a 'peace-keeping force' that was deployed between warring parties. (A peace-keeping force does not normally employ violence. See the discussion below.) Furthermore, the United Nations plays an important role in the Middle East by caring for the hundreds of thousands of Palestinians, who include persons who fled from what is now Israel during the 1948 conflict or are descended from them.

Although it would be difficult to claim that these activities ensure permanent peace in the Eastern Mediterranean, the UN did help to moderate the armed conflicts there. It was the only available impartial third-party available for this purpose. Its series of mediators – Folke Bernadotte, who was assassinated: Ralph Bunche, the American who won the Nobel Peace Prize for his work: and Gunnar Jarring, a Swedish ambassador – could hardly be blamed for the lack of progress in this complex situation. They could never persuade the disputants to agree on a permanent solution and abandon military means. Without the commitment of disputants, essential in any conciliatory proceedings, the third party must eventually fall short of full success.

COERCIVE MEASURES TO MAINTAIN PEACE

Aware of the limits to pacific settlement and of the failure of 'automatic sanctions' during the life of the League of Nations, the authors of the UN Charter gave the Security Council powerful means to counter aggression and threats to the peace. These provisions are found in Chapter VII of the Charter. They authorize the Security Council to go beyond recommendations and to make binding decisions to prevent or force an end to aggression. In order to do so, the Council must decide that a threat to or breach of the peace exists [Art. 39]. That finding implies that subsequent Council decisions have the quality of a legal obligation.

Before using its full array of coercion, the Council may decide on provisional measures that legally do not alter the claims or positions of the parties [Art. 40]. Or it may go directly to stronger methods. These include non-military approaches; listed in the Charter are a partial or complete end to economic relations, breaking off of rail, sea, air, postal, telegraphic, radio and other communications, and cessation of diplomatic relations. The hope that underlies these sanctions is that the attacker would suffer such unpleasant consequences that he would restore the situation before hostilities, that he would be deterred from going on. In practice, these sanctions usually appear to fall short of the desired effect. Either the party against whom they are invoked is so strong economically that the punishment can be shrugged off, or as is more often the case, the potentialities of the Charter are not fully invoked or the members do not honour the decisions of the Security Council.

After the experience of the League of Nations, the UN planners knew that economic sanctions might not deter aggression. They therefore provided the Security Council with the authority to prepare and use military pressure against violators of the Charter [Art. 43]. This would be used if other less violent or peaceful approaches failed. According to the Charter, all members of the United Nations must make armed forces available to the Security Council on its request and in line with special agreements to be drawn up. These would include rights of passage and other assistance.

Obviously this system would not operate against the permanent members of the Security Council. They could be coerced only with great difficulty and the possibility of a general war. Furthermore, for them the unanimity rule provided the possibility of arresting any decision before it was made. Nevertheless, they formed a keystone of the system, both in respect to expectations about their behaviour and the services they would provide for the Council. The expectations grew out of the benefits of wartime cooperation and President Roosevelt's notions that international peace could be guaranteed by the four policemen, the leading victorious allies. Precisely because this wartime friendship broke down in what came to be called the 'Cold War,' the other deterrent aspect of the UN system never came into being. This was a standing force, directed by the military commanders of the permanent members, which was to act at the beck and call of the Security Council [Arts 45, 47]. The Council was to be assisted by a Military Staff Committee, made up of the Chiefs of Staff of the permanent members. It would work out the details of the standing forces, to which any UN member could contribute but which clearly would rely mainly on the permanent members. The Committee met in 1946 but soon reflected the split between the Soviet Union and the other permanent members. The broader political difficulties took the form of disagreement about the composition and disposition of the military force for the Security Council. In July 1948, the Committee reported to the Security Council that it could make no further progress unless the Council itself came to an agreement on specified issues. Such agreement has never been reached, although the General Assembly has long had a committee to study the issues. The Military Staff Committee formally still exists but has never made any progress. Nevertheless, with the receding of the Cold War during the late 1980s, from time to time tentative proposals, including repeated suggestions from the Soviet Union, have been made in favour of another attempt at providing the Security Council with a ready-armed force.

That the hope for a Security Council equipped with a military arm did not succeed can be traced directly to the antagonism between the United States and the Soviet Union. Neither of the main antagonists in the Cold War wanted to hand over decisional powers to the United Nations where the response to a political issue would be unpredictable. In the early years of the United Nations, the Soviet Union showed the greatest reluctance to accept broad authority for the Security Council. It was in a minority position both there and in the General Assembly. While it could protect itself with the veto in the Security Council, this had costs in terms of negative propaganda from its opponents. By 1970, the United States increasingly adopted political positions that left it isolated and it too used the veto. Only after Mikhail Gorbachev took over leadership of the Soviet Union did its position change to favour much more use of the United Nations in issues of international peace and security. Russia, the Soviet successor on the Security Council, indicated it would follow a similar line. China, the only remaining Communist government with a permanent place on the Council, has rarely taken a leading position and generally has favoured a lower level of UN activity over a higher one.

In a sense, the designers of the UN Charter opted for a prudent approach to international peace. They showed a clear scepticism about the notion that they could simply set out binding rules for the maintenance of peace and expect them faithfully to be followed. The Charter therefore contains provisions that cover the contingency that Chapters VI and VII of the Charter might not work. Accordingly, Article 51 provides for a 'natural right' of individual and collective self-defence for all members until the Security Council has taken the necessary steps to maintain international peace. The inclusion of 'collective self-defence' opens the way for traditional military alliances.

. The collective self-defence provision offered a legal justification for the creation of the two principal alliances that grew out of the Cold War. These were the North Atlantic Treaty Organization (NATO) and the Warsaw Treaty Organization (WTO), sometimes referred to as the Warsaw Pact. The treaties on which they were based both referred to Article 51. The existence of the two organizations could be taken as evidence that collective security in the UN system had failed. It is clear that the governments involved in the Cold War put more faith in their alliances than in the United Nations. The fact that most new states in Asia and Africa took up explicitly 'non-aligned' positions demonstrated more distrust of the alliances than faith in the UN arrangements. At the same time, most of the new states had little reason to fear attacks on their territories. With the relaxation of the Cold War during the late 1980s, NATO began to look for tasks that had less military content, while the WTO simply crumbled. The consequences for the United Nations were not immediately clear, although some voices expressed the hope that the Security Council might at last realize its original purpose.

In addition to the mode of collective defence, the UN system offers its members the possibility of joining regional security arrangements. In Chapter VIII of the Charter, members are urged to use regional organizations to settle differences that come within their purview. This is supposed to take place in preference to engaging the Security Council. Examples of these regional arrangements are the Organization of American States (OAS), the Arab League and the more recently established Organization for African Unity (OAU). For the most part, these organizations have proved useful in limited local issues, such as boundary disputes. They have only very rarely produced solutions to important disputes which involved serious threats to international peace and security.

KOREA

The involvement of the United Nations with the long dispute over the division of Korea led to the first use of force by the organization. Korea also deserves attention because it is sometimes treated as a test for the collective security idea. From a legal point of view, this concept is hardly applicable. From a political point of view, it represents primarily the reaction of the United States and 15 other governments to sustain South Korea. Their military activity took place under UN auspices but was not what either the Charter or enthusiasts of collective security had envisaged.

The question of Korea was brought to the United Nations in 1947 by the United States, which occupied the part of the Korean peninsula south of the 38th parallel. The engagement of the United Nations followed the breakdown of negotiations with the Soviet Union, occupying the northern half of Korea, about the political future of the former Japanese colony.

In the General Assembly, where the United States and its allies then prevailed, a resolution calling for free elections in all Korea was adopted. It resulted in the creation of the Republic of Korea which the General Assembly declared the only lawful government in Korea. In the north, meanwhile, the Soviet Union established the Democratic Republic of Korea, which the Communist bloc recognized as the only government in the peninsula. The enmity of the claimants to authority obviated the early unification of the country.

Precisely why war broke out in Korea in June 1950 remains unclear. It is certain that on 25 June, according to the United Nations version which is accepted by all but a few 'revisionist' writers and supported by evidence recently made public in the Soviet Union, North Korean military units forced their way through the South Korean defences on the 38th parallel.

The United Nations had never before been faced with fighting that so directly touched the interests of the great powers. Immediately after the attack became known, at the request of the United States the Security Council met. On 25 June it censured North Korea, called on it to withdraw its forces to the 38th parallel and appealed to UN members to assist South Korea.

North Korea gave no sign of acquiescence. The forces of the Republic of Korea could not resist the attack. On 26 June, President Harry Truman ordered air and sea forces to support South Korea. On the following day, when at last a report from the UN Commission on Korea that confirmed that North Korea had attacked reached the Security Council, it adopted a stronger recommendation that members assist the Republic of Korea to repel the assault and to restore peace. This gave legitimacy to the earlier action by the United States. Then on 7 July, the Security Council established a unified command to coordinate the assistance to South Korea. The United States was given this responsibility and asked to name a commander. General Douglas MacArthur, then American commander in the Far East with headquarters in occupied Japan, was appointed and authorized to fly the UN flag. Altogether 53 countries, the great majority of the UN members then, offered support.

An extraordinary situation within the Security Council made possible its rapid decisions. In January 1950, the Soviet Union had withdrawn its representative in protest against the presence of the delegate of the Republic of China, that is the government that had fled from the Communist-controlled mainland to Taiwan. The USSR insisted that the government in Beijing should represent China. If the Soviet representative had been present, he certainly would have vetoed the resolutions on Korea. He returned in August, to assume the rotating presidency of the Council.

Two other extraordinary factors conditioned the work of the Council. The first was the receipt of the report from the UN Commission on Korea. This was understood as officially confirming the initial reports of the North Korean attack. The second was the presence of strong American forces in nearby Japan and the readiness of the United States government to use them.

The military action repeatedly raised issues of policy and execution. Initially, the South Korean and United States forces barely managed to hold on to a bridgehead at the southeastern tip of the peninsula. At the end of September, a successful amphibious landing on the northwest coast, not far below the 38th parallel raised the question as to whether the UN forces should halt. The United States saw a good chance to reunify Korea, now by military means. After a Soviet veto in the Security Council, the General Assembly on 7 October 1950, recommended that all necessary steps should be taken to restore stability in all of Korea.

That resolution provided justification for the UN forces to cross the 38th parallel, despite repeated warnings from well-informed Indian represent-atives that a Chinese intervention might follow. At first, the UN forces succeeded. Beijing repeated that it would not permit UN forces to deploy along its frontiers. In November, Chinese attacks almost cut off MacArthur's troops, who had precipitously to retreat. By the beginning of 1951, the original division of Korea along the 38th parallel had nearly been restored.

The military developments of course led to political responses in New York. The Western powers introduced a resolution in the Security Council on 30 November 1950, which demanded that China recall its army. It also declared that the UN troops would not violate the Chinese–Korean frontier. The Soviet Union vetoed this resolution. The Council was thus effectively locked out of any influence on the Korean case.

From a formal point of view, the deadlock in the Security Council left the Unified Command without political direction or a supervisory organ. The General Assembly then improvised a new approach in the form of the Uniting for Peace Resolution (see below and Chapter 2) but could not use it in such a way as to end the fighting. In July 1951, negotiations towards an armistice began between the two military forces. Another two years were required to bring it about. Since then, the United States has maintained a heavy military presence and gave impressive economic support in South Korea. The United States speaks on behalf of the UN Command in Korea, which consists only of American and South Korea forces, during occasional, rather nasty negotiations with the North Korean military about the armistice.

In many ways, the Korean question offered a profound lesson about what the United Nations could achieve in maintaining international peace and security. Such a case as Korea, where each party received critical support from one of the two most powerful states in the world, cannot be treated as classical collective security which requires an automatic response of all against aggression of any kind. The Security Council was able to adopt a resolution because of the fortuitous absence of the Soviet representative. What may have appeared to be the application of the UN version of collective security, in reality, was not. Rather, Korea can best be understood as an action by the Western powers that took place under UN auspices. Decisions in the Korean conflict were made under the shadow of American or Chinese successes or defeats on the battlefield.

The Korean question also perfectly illustrates how difficult it may be to bring an international dispute to resolution. The strategic relationship there was indeed returned to roughly the *status quo ante*. Forty years after the armistice little in the military standoff had changed, although some tentative political contacts between North and South took place, perhaps opening a road toward eventual unification.

KUWAIT

After Iraqi forces overran Kuwait in early August 1990, the United Nations progressively endorsed the most forceful and far-reaching enforcement actions in its history – or for that matter, in the history of international organization. These included a wide range of economic and diplomatic sanctions, intended to damage Iraq's war-making capacity and to isolate its government from possible allies. Later the Security Council authorized all governments to use 'all possible means' – meaning military measures – to end the aggression against Kuwait. While the preponderant military force was contributed by the United States, 33 other countries joined it in expelling the Iraqi forces from Kuwait in operations that began on 17 January 1991. Its military forces paralyzed by air, sea and land attacks, Iraq formally accepted a ceasefire on 6 April 1991. This followed seven weeks of military action, including five days of combat operations on the ground that ended on 28 February 1991, when the allied forces halted a few miles inside Iraq's southern border.

The forceful reaction to the invasion of Kuwait raised the question as to whether the organization at last was fulfilling the promise of its Charter.

Was it closer to the notion of collective security than in Korea? To what extent did the organization prove central to repelling what almost every government acknowledged was aggression?

Once the news arrived in New York that on 2 August 1990, Iraqi forces had invaded Kuwait, the Security Council immediately determined that a breach of the peace had occurred and demanded an unconditional withdrawal. The Permanent Members of the Council all voted in favour of the resolution along with nine other members and one (Yemen) not participating. The onslaught had been preceded by some weeks of tension during which Iraq claimed rights to certain petroleum resources exploited by Kuwait, and denied the validity of an earlier border settlement. A diplomatic encounter between the two governments had ended in failure just before the attack by the powerful Iraqi force against the tiny state. In line with the Charter procedure, the Security Council called upon the two parties to resume negotiations.

The disregard with which the government headed by Saddam Hussein met this resolution led the Security Council on 6 August to act under Chapter VII of the Charter. It decided by a vote of 13 in favour with two abstentions to begin a programme of economic and financial sanctions that would cut off Iraqi imports and exports, especially of oil; deprive it of access to resources abroad; and cut off any governmental assistance to the Baghdad government. That decision placed a legal obligation on all UN members. The Council set up a committee to oversee the application of sanctions. Meanwhile, the United States persuaded the government of Saudi Arabia, which usually bars outsiders and avoids wide political engagements, to accept military help to forestall any attack from Iraqi forces in adjacent Kuwait or in Iraq itself. American forces and those of other coalition members quickly built up.

Over the next nine months, the Council adopted 13 additional basic resolutions dealing with the situation in Kuwait. They were supplemented frequently during the next two years. The Council demanded the withdrawal of Iraqi forces from Kuwait. In a series of actions, it tightened the net of sanctions. The Council also sought the protection of civilians displaced by the war, including a group of Europeans and Americans held hostage, and cessation of violations of the standard inviolability of diplomatic premises and protection of diplomats.

Once the Security Council decided that a breach of the peace had occurred, it was legally free to authorize the use of armed force to give effect to its decisions. The series of resolutions that led to that crucial moment in fact offered the Iraqi government repeated chances to return the situation to its prewar state. It refused to do so. A trip to Baghdad by the Secretary-General, acting under Security Council instructions, gave no result. Nor did official and unofficial missions by national representatives and political personalities. On 29 November 1990, the Security Council set a deadline of 15 January 1991 for Iraq to withdraw from Kuwait. If it were not to do so, the 'Member States co-operating with the Government of Kuwait' were authorized to 'use all necessary means to uphold and implement ... all relevant resolutions and to restore international peace and security to the area'. [UN Security Council Resolution 678] The entire series of resolutions to this point had had the support of the Permanent Members; on Resolution 678 China abstained, but 12 other governments voted in favour. Cuba and Yemen, frequent abstainers on earlier decisions, voted against Resolution 678.

By then, the United States had built up an enormous force in the area. It included some 400 000 troops in Saudi Arabia, a vast fleet of naval vessels in and around the Gulf and a huge air force. It was joined by lesser, but significant, contributions from France and the United Kingdom, among the Europeans, and from Egypt, Saudi Arabia and Syria from the Middle East, as well as a mixture of contributions from the 28 other allies. The Soviet Union offered no military cooperation but strongly supported the programme adopted by the Security Council. Iraq replied contemptuously, threatening to spread any armed conflict to Israel and to use guided missiles, poison gas and, it hinted, nuclear weapons against all comers. Saddam Hussein, in a famous phrase, threatened the allies with the 'mother of all battles'.

Even then, diplomatic efforts to resolve the conflict went on. Some governments in Arab states, perhaps torn between the obligations of the UN Charter that protect the political independence of small states and the unrest caused by Saddam Hussein's strident appeals to mass opinion, tried unsuccessfully to use the Arab League, other regional agencies and direct diplomacy. There was, however, nothing like a general retreat from the position that Iraq had breached the peace in violation of the UN Charter. For its part, the Iraqi government insisted that it would never give up Kuwait and announced its annexation as a separate province of Iraq. This too brought a denunciation by the Security Council.

Although some opinion leaders, especially in the United States, explicitly pinned their hopes on sanctions as a way to peace, the government in Washington decided to begin military action on 17 January 1991. It asserted that it and the other allies acted with the authorization of the United Nations. At first only air and naval forces were engaged. Iraq tried unsuccessfully to draw Israel into the war in order to make it seem part of the old conflict between the latter and its neighbours. It used guided missiles against Israel and Saudi Arabia to little effect. The allied air force, especially American planes and missiles, systematically destroyed the Iraqi command and control system. The commanders claimed that as little damage as possible was caused to the civilian population. Then on 24 February, the allied force launched a ground attack from bases in Saudi Arabia. Despite the earlier blustering from Baghdad, Iraqi defences immediately crumbled on contact with the allies, who halted their advance five days later with the Iraqis in full retreat. The allied forces suffered extraordinarily few casualties.

In many respects, the decisions of the Security Council appeared to conform to the model of collective security under the UN Charter but in very important detail differed. On the political plane, it was clear that the actions of the Council were driven by the permanent members, strongly led by the United States. Behind the American position in the Council were President George Bush and his colleagues, who repeatedly insisted that Saddam Hussein and his government continually threatened the peace. The obvious implication, sometimes openly stated, was that Saddam's government must be driven away. While the United Kingdom from the beginning, and France later, took parallel positions, the Soviet Union and China were more circumspect about the degree of intrusion into Iraqi affairs that was needed. Yet for the next two years, the required cohesion or acquiescence of the great powers' views was never absent, even during the collapse of the Soviet Union and its replacement by Russia.

The elected members of the Council were of course consulted in advance of the presentation of resolutions but usually only after the permanent members had reached a consensus in private. This leadership by the permanent members, begun with the decline of the Cold War, now gained a new, not altogether popular, prominence. The open meetings of the Council were largely devoted to formal statements about positions already taken in private and to voting on resolutions. The open sessions gave two elected members, Cuba and Yemen, and some of their successors, a chance fruitlessly to promote a more restrained position on far-reaching resolutions; they voted against or abstained several times, reflecting Cuba's strong opposition to American leadership and, in Yemen's case, the divided views of the Arab world.

All the Council's actions were necessarily taken without the advice of the Military Staff Committee, although it met twice in private sessions. Nor had any forces been organized or ear-marked in advance of the Iraqi invasion. Thus the Council had no ready military forces at its disposal. The entire military campaign was in fact organized under the strong leadership, not to say the dominance, of the United States, as had been the case forty years earlier in Korea.

At first, reactions of the Security Council conformed to the procedures set out in the Charter: a finding was made under Article 39 that a breach of the peace had occurred. The Council sought a resumption of procedures to settle the dispute between Iraq and Kuwait peacefully. When Baghdad gave no sign of heeding the Council, sanctions followed, while diplomatic efforts continued. Only after Iraq refused to budge from Kuwait were military measures by UN members authorized. At no time, however, did the Council appoint or give political directives to a UN commander or to a joint command of the sort established in the Korean case: the United States obviously opposed any such arrangements and prevailed without open dissent. Thus rather than the centralized source for politico-military policy implied by the UN Charter, the enforcement action against Iraq was based on decentralization and coordination. At the same time, the very wide support given to the Security Council by UN member governments and the broad spectrum of military response fitted with the notion that the world must unite against governments that breach the peace.

As the Iraqi forces in Kuwait staggered under the full force of the allied attack, the government in Baghdad accepted Security Council Resolution 660, which had demanded the unconditional withdrawal of its troops and resumption of pacific settlement, and retracted its annexation of the territory. Left behind was a looted city, hungry and displaced people and more than 500 burning oil wells. The Security Council then set out far-reaching conditions for a permanent ceasefire. These were contained in Security Council resolution 686, adopted on 2 March 1991 by a vote of 11 in favour with Cuba opposed and China, India and Yemen abstaining. Iraq agreed to carry out this resolution on 3 March in a letter that claimed that the American superpower sought to dominate the resources of the world and asserted that no peace could be established in the Middle East until a Palestinian state was established. To monitor the demilitarized zone which was established along the Iraq–Kuwait border, the Security Council in Resolution 687 on 3 April 1991 created the UN Iraq–Kuwait Observation Mission (UNIKOM). After repeated violations, a peace-keeping force was sent there in early 1993.

The conditions set out in Resolutions 686 and 687 led to extraordinary penetration by an international organization into the Iraqi polity. As a direct result of the vast military buildup in Iraq before the invasion of Kuwait and the threats made by Saddam Hussein and his associates, the Security Council demanded that Iraq dispose of all its chemical and biological weapons and ballistic missiles with a range of more than 150 kilometres. A series of inspection missions, fervently denounced and sometimes harassed by Iraq and still uncompleted in mid-1993, uncovered unsuspected capacity to produce materials for such weapons, as well as violations of the International Atomic Energy Agency regulations to which Iraq had earlier agreed. Step by step, Iraq was driven under UN supervision towards full compliance with resolution 687. Iraq was also held responsible for reparations for damages in Kuwait. To pay for this, a part of its sales of petroleum would be set aside under UN supervision, but Iraq refused to sell oil for this purpose or for purchase of needed food and medicine. Iraq was also ordered to repatriate displaced people.

The end of active fighting also impelled turbulent, sometimes desperate, measures to organize humanitarian assistance for an unanticipated mass of displaced persons and forced migrants. Driven by considerable public criticism, all of the UN facilities for dealing with humanitarian disaster, as well as other transnational agencies and military units, were mobilized under the leadership of a senior UN official. After a shortlived, confused uprising, a huge flight of Kurds, an often persecuted minority people in Iraq, into Turkey and Iran heightened the emergency. The Kurds in the Turkish area were induced to return to their homes after the allies used military forces to provide a safety zone. This was, however, not explicitly authorized by the Security Council. In Iran, the attention from abroad had a less intrusive and dramatic quality, despite the large numbers of people who feared the Baghdad government too much to return home. They, as well as other Iraqis who fled in the south, received some help under international auspices. There the United States and some other allies established a 'no-fly' zone and carried out some punitive bombing after violations. All the while, Saddam Hussein's government remained in charge in Iraq, from which the allied forces had withdrawn, and proved able to mobilize enough military power to control deep agitation among parts of the country's population. Especially in south Iraq, around Basra, where a predominantly Shi'a population opposed the Baghdad government, force was used on a few occasions. Nearby in Kuwait, the burning oil wells and oil spills set off during the war inflicted enormous damage on the environment. By mid-1993, Iraqi targets had been hit from the air in restricted actions, and the United States remained nearby to enforce the UN ceasefire terms.

Tight economic sanctions were still in place three years after the initial breach of the peace. The Security Council demonstrated much reluctance to relax them beyond permission to import foodstuffs and essential civilian supplies, despite claims from Baghdad that humanitarian needs mandated exceptions, such as permission under its own terms to sell petroleum in order to import goods. At the same time, large-scale humanitarian assistance brought by the practised UN machinery reached many of the people most in the need as a result of displacement, expulsion or disappearance of jobs. This aid was complemented by efforts from governments eager to aid their own nationals and by programmes of transnational voluntary organizations. All of this, along with the sensitive political issues of the area, suggested that bringing an enforcement action to an acceptable conclusion may be as important as initiating it. In addition, by 1993, it had raised serious questions about the legal and political limits of enforcement action.

Nearly three years after the invasion of Kuwait, the Middle East was anything but a stable, pacific part of the world. The invasion itself had deeply disturbed local expectations of tranquillity. Although the Security Council strenuously avoided linking the Arab–Israeli dispute to what happened in Kuwait, nevertheless political groups and some governments in the area insisted that the two issues were bound together. The United States government, moreover, saw some possibility that the upset relationships in the area offered opportunities for new initiatives in the Arab–Israeli dispute. By the end of 1992, as a result of energetic diplomacy by the American Secretary of State, direct negotiations with Arab governments, so long sought by Israel, had begun. The United Nations had only an indirect role in these talks, still underway in mid-1993. Over the longer term, however, steady, intimate involvement of the organization with issues of the Middle East seemed likely to continue.

'UNITING FOR PEACE'

After it became obvious in the autumn of 1950 that decision-making in the Security Council could be frozen solid by a permanent member, the United States sought a way around the veto. Its solution to the problem was embodied in the 'Uniting For Peace' resolution.

In essence, Uniting for Peace substituted recommendations of the General Assembly for the directives that the Security Council was unable to adopt. The resolution provided that when the Security Council was prevented from acting because of a veto by a permanent member, any seven members or a majority of the General Assembly could summon an emergency special session of the Assembly. This could meet within 24 hours. The procedure made it possible by a two-thirds majority to label a member as an aggressor. From there, the Assembly could recommend coercive sanctions against the aggressor. The member states that could provide military forces in such circumstances were asked to set them aside for possible UN use. The use of these forces would be planned by a

Collective Measures Committee of the General Assembly which would also study other methods for maintaining peace.

Adoption of the Uniting for Peace Resolution really signified a fundamental alteration of the UN Charter, although this did not take place according to the formal provisions for amendment [Art. 108–9]. Supporters of this resolution, however, denied that it violated the Charter. They argued that even if the Security Council had 'primary' responsibility for maintaining peace, this did not mean exclusive jurisdiction. Aside from legal hair-splitting, supporters of the resolution relied on Article 1 of the Charter, which sets out the maintenance of international peace and security as the most important aim of the United Nations. If the organization does not achieve that end, then ways have to be found so that it can. In any case, it was clear that Uniting for Peace shifted important functions in maintaining peace from the Security Council to the General Assembly. There, the United States and its allies could at that time count on a permanent majority.

Uniting for Peace both arose during the Korean issue and was first used in handling it. At the end of 1950, after the People's Republic of China intervened in Korea, the General Assembly decided to place the matter on its agenda. It stated on 1 February, 1951, that China was guilty of aggression in Korea and demanded the withdrawal of its troops. This was the first time that a country was accused by the United Nations of aggression. The Assembly followed this up in May with a recommendation that all member states embargo shipments of weapons and strategic materials to North Korea and China. The Soviet Union and its allies refused to have anything to do with these proceedings on the ground that these were matters for the Security Council.

After naming China an aggressor, the General Assembly used the Uniting for Peace Resolution rather sparingly. In 1956, it censured the use of armed force by the Soviet Union in Hungary. In this case, the Security Council could not act because the Soviet Union vetoed resolutions on Hungary; Britain and France did the same with proposals on Suez. In the Congo case in 1960, after the Security Council became deadlocked, the General Assembly was summoned in September.

At that time, the Soviet Union stoutly opposed action on matters of peace and security by the General Assembly. That was one of the reasons why it refused until the late 1980s to pay for the costs of peace-keeping in the Middle East between 1956 and 1967. These operations grew out of General Assembly resolutions. Later the Soviet Union softened its position and began to accept the legality of some such activities by the General Assembly. At the same time, the United States had became more reluctant to trust the General Assembly and to pay for its activities.

Meanwhile, the non-aligned countries repeatedly demonstrated the ability to dominate the General Assembly but not a like competence to back up strong resolutions on matters of peace and security. Summoning an emergency special session also found some favour as a device to dramatize particular issues. For example, the seventh emergency special session in 1980 was convened at the behest of the Arab countries and supporters from the non-aligned group to point up the grievances of the Palestinian refugees against Israel.

The role of the General Assembly always is conditioned by the use of the Security Council, which has varied a great deal. During the early 1960s, it was kept busy, but then a long eclipse ensued. Beginning about 1987, however, it was revived by growing cooperation between the United States and the Soviet Union that followed President Gorbachev's endorsement of the value of multilateral institutions (see Chapter 8). An important symbol of its resurgence was a meeting of the Council attended by heads of state or government in January 1992, when the newly-elected Secretary-General Boutros Boutros-Ghali took office. This meeting instructed Boutros-Ghali to report on methods for strengthening the maintenance of peace and, by implication, the work of the Security Council. In unusually colourful and direct language, the Secretary-General, in his *Agenda for Peace*, pleaded for full use of the Council's capacities, more summit meetings there, the revival of the Military Staff Committee more attention to preventive diplomacy and to peace-building after conflicts, and creation of standby enforcement units.

The development of Uniting for Peace, its occasional use and the variations in the political readiness of the Security Council to act often made the separation between its jurisdiction and that of the Assembly vague and unpredictable. The Security Council remained the readiest instrument for responding at once to crises. The General Assembly could more easily deal with long, slowly maturing political issues and as the Collective Measures Committee never developed enough to direct coercive measures, the Assembly could not simply substitute for the Security Council in collective security. Proceedings in one organ, moreover, could be played off against the other. Neither could be fully reliable, whatever the tactics, in a complicated, rapidly changing world political environment.

UN PEACE-KEEPING FORCES

The Suez Crisis of 1956 led to a quite different use of military forces from what was foreseen in the Charter. This was the so-called peace-keeping force. Its primary task is to encourage comformity of the parties to a ceasefire or armistice. Important methods include interposition, that is, stationing troops between the forces of the disputants, and surveillance.

Such duties have military aspects. They are carried out by military units, but these dispose of very limited weaponry that could only serve for personal self-protection. By constant presence and the ability to move between the parties, a peace-keeping force encourages conformity to agreements. It can also negotiate on-the-spot settlements to minor violations. Thus, as it is an organized military force, usually of several thousand officers and men, it suggests greater strength than UN military observers, such as those used in Kashmir and in the UN Truce Supervision Organization (UNTSO) for the Israeli area. Observer groups usually consist of only a few officers, who usually move around a great deal in the course of their work and can only report on what they have seen.

THE UN EMERGENCY FORCE

The first UN peace-keeping force originated amidst events too complex to be set out fully here, but these bore heavily on the nature of the UN Emergency Force (UNEF). Nevertheless, the precedents set then, adapted to each situation, still provide the conceptual basis for peace-keeping.

In the background of the 1956 crisis was the armistice agreement of 1949 between Egypt and Israel. It was repeatedly violated despite the presence of UNTSO. In July 1956, Egyptian President Gamal Abdel Nasser reacted to the failure of financial negotiations for completion of the Aswan dam on the Nile by seizing the French-based company that operated the Suez Canal. That led to heavy protests by the British and French governments against what they described as violation of their national interests.

With the fedayeen, suicide squads that had raided Israel, as their declared target, Israeli troops at the end of October 1956 crossed the Egyptian border into the Sinai Peninsula. This was followed by a British–French ultimatum to Egypt and Israel. They were told to pull their troops back 15 kilometres from the Suez Canal. Israel accepted the ultimatum which Egypt promptly rejected. Subsequently, British and French aircraft bombed Egyptian targets. Meanwhile, ground forces were on their way, ostensibly to protect the canal.

In the Security Council, British and French vetoes blocked resolutions proposed by the American and Soviet representatives for a ceasefire and withdrawal of foreign troops. The majority of the Council then used the Uniting for Peace procedure to summon an emergency special session of the General Assembly. At the beginning of November, it adopted an American draft resolution which followed the lines of the version that was vetoed in the Security Council.

After several days of clumsy military operations and heavy pressure from abroad and dissidents at home, the British and French governments accepted the General Assembly resolution. It was then that UNEF, an unprecedented device, was deployed to assist with the withdrawal of troops and observe the ceasefire.

These steps followed each other with extraordinary speed. The idea of a peace-keeping force was approved by the General Assembly on 5 November as proposed by Lester Pearson, Canadian Minister of External Affairs, who had been conferring with Secretary-General Hammarskjöld. The latter was asked by the Assembly to report back in 24 hours on the organization of UNEF.

He set out the following principles:

● the peacekeeping force would be temporary;
● it would remain strictly neutral: it could not be used to change the military balance between the disputants: it would have the task of maintaining order, supervising compliance with the ceasefire, patrolling along the truce lines and observing the execution of the UN resolutions;
● troops for UNEF would not be accepted from the permanent members of the Security Council;
● the force commander would be appointed by the United Nations and would be responsible to the General Assembly or the Security Council: he would be under the immediate supervision of the Secretary-General;
● an explicit requirement was the agreement of the parties to UNEF's deployment.

The actual organization of UNEF fell to Hammarskjöld. He had to negotiate with member governments over precisely what they would contribute and under what conditions. He borrowed the commander from UNTSO and with him sketched the organization and developed rules of engagement for the force. The Secretary-General set up an advisory committee of national representatives to counsel him on the novel venture. All of this added up to a much more active role for the Secretary-General in maintaining peace. It had a great potential which would later partly be realized.

The first UNEF troops landed on 15 November in Egypt and during the next month reached full operational status in the Suez zone. From offers of troops by 24 countries, Hammarskjöld accepted units of about 500 men from Canada, Denmark, Finland, Norway, Sweden, Brazil, Colombia,

India, Indonesia and Yugoslavia. Under the UN command, these units were led by their own national officers and were not combined in an integrated force. At the high point, they totalled about 6000 men.

The operation in the Suez zone proceeded in two phases. First, UNEF concentrated on the maintenance of the ceasefire and the creation of a kind of buffer-zone between the Egyptian and the British–French forces. When the latter withdrew in December 1956, UNEF filled the vacuum and then returned the territory to the Egyptian authorities. UNEF then began patrolling the entire 273-kilometre front between the two forces but was confined to the Egyptian side, because Israel never granted permission to extend the observer and patrolling functions to its side of border. Yet, on the whole, UNEF succeeded in its assignment of impeding infiltration and watching for violations.

UNEF's work abruptly halted at the end of May 1967, when in the midst of increasing tension in the Middle East, the Egyptian government requested the Secretary-General to withdraw the peace-keepers. U Thant, who had succeeded Hammarskjöld as Secretary-General, conferred with the UNEF Advisory Committee and concluded that he had to accede to the Egyptian request. He argued that as it had always been understood that the presence of UNEF required the assent of the host government, he could not do otherwise than take out the force, which had already been surrounded by Egyptian troops. Furthermore, most of the contributing governments had decided to withdraw from UNEF. U Thant became the butt of severe criticism. Opponents of the withdrawal argued that the matter should have been brought first to the General Assembly or even the Security Council. By mid-June 1967, UNEF had left the Middle East, ending the first peace-keeping venture but without peace between Israel and Egypt.

After the October war of 1973 between Israel and its neighbours, new peace-keeping ventures came to life. The Security Council decided on 25 October 1973, to create UNEF II to watch over the ceasefire that had just come into effect. The new force was stationed this time on both sides of the Egyptian–Israeli armistice line. The General Assembly tried to avoid controversy about financing the new force by apportioning expenses among the members, assigning a higher level to the permanent members of the Council and rich countries. UNEF II formed a buffer between Egypt and Israel until July 1979, when the Security Council decided to give it up. The decision reflected growing tension between the United States and the Soviet Union about their respective influence in the Middle East.

Meanwhile, at the other end of Israel, another UN military unit took shape. This was the UN Disengagement Observer Force (UNDOF) that was given the task of watching over the Golan Heights. This strategic area, which commanded the road to the nearby Syrian capital, Damascus, had been captured by the Israelis. UNDOF, established as an autonomous part of UNTSO, includes some 1200 men who are assigned to signal violations of the peace. UNDOF's mandate must be renewed every six months by the Security Council. The force has served as an important factor in abating friction between Israel and Syria, even while dangerous fighting continued nearby in Lebanon.

Yet another peace-keeping force was assigned to Lebanon itself after the Israeli occupation of the southern part of the country in 1978. The UN Interim Force in Lebanon (UNIFIL) was created by the Security Council to observe the Israeli withdrawal from the southern Lebanon area, to help restore and sustain international peace and security and assist the Lebanese government to regain authority over the district. Troop contributors included France but not other permanent members of the Security Council nor countries with much direct interest in the area. Until 1982, UNIFIL succeeded reasonably well in helping to keep the peace. Yet it was not possible to bring the area under firm control because of the opposition of an Israeli-supported Lebanese military movement in the area. In June 1982, Israel drastically changed the situation by invading Lebanon and occupying territory as far north as Beirut. UNIFIL had no mandate to try to prevent this invasion, let alone strength to halt it. Since the Israeli withdrawal, UNIFIL's mandate has been regularly renewed by the Security Council, no doubt in the hope that some UN presence was better than none, even though its effectiveness was doubtful, especially because of Israeli resistance to its operation.

ONUC

Of the peace-keeping ventures undertaken before the 1990s, that in the Congo – the former Belgian colony that is now Zaire – had the widest scope. ONUC, as it is usually designated from the initials of its French title, differed considerably from UNEF. The Suez crisis involved definite enemies, three on one side and one on the other, in a rather defined conflict. Once agreed, UNEF went directly to operations with clear expectations and useful aid from existing governments that worked.

Like more recent peace-keeping ventures (see below), the Congo possessed little of this basic order. It involved an international conflict, caused by the military intervention of Belgium in the new state that had been its colony. It was also a domestic conflict, which greatly complicated the UN task. Furthermore, an adequate governmental structure was lacking. In such conditions, the United Nations could rarely count on the cooperation of all the parties. On the contrary, the Secretary-General repeatedly was accused by member governments of bias and failure to execute his mandate.

A few high points of the political developments in the Congo and of ONUC make clear the difficult circumstances of peace-keeping there. The Belgian government withdrew from the Congo, which was ill-prepared for independence, on 30 June 1960. Within days, units of the Congo army, garrisoned near Kinshasa (Leopoldville), mutinied against Belgian officers who had been asked to stay on. Prime Minister Patrice Lumumba failed to bring the mutiny under control. Congolese soldiers attacked some of the remaining European civilians, mostly Belgians: other took fright and fled. In the southeastern province of Katanga, Premier Moïse Tshombé called on the Belgians for help. Belgian paratroopers stationed in Lumbumbashi (Elizabethville), the capital of the rich mining province, responded. Meanwhile, the Belgian government, seeking to protect its citizens, ordered troops to the Congo to join those kept on with the agreement of the Lumumba government. On 12 July Lumumba and President Kasavubu cabled a request to the Secretary-General for military help to protect the country against aggression.

Hammarskjöld reacted under Article 99 of the Charter to put his view that a threat to the peace existed before the Security Council. It called on Belgium to pull its troops out of the Congo and instructed the Secretary-General to take the needed steps, in consultation with the Congolese government, to provide military aid. In his usual efficient way, Hammarskjöld went to work to set up ONUC. The following day, the first UN troops – Tunisians and Ghanaians – arrived in the Congo where they were to be commanded by the Swedish head of UNTSO.

The Secretary-General assumed that ONUC would have broad responsibilities to integrate political, military and technical help. This required a substantial civilian organization aimed at restoring order and providing a chance for the Congolese to decide their own policies. Initially, plans were made for a peace-keeping force of about 3000 men; it would quickly restore order, but during the last three months of 1960, some 20 000 troops were in place. They came mainly, but not exclusively, from African countries. Altogether 30 countries furnished troops, varying from one man from New Zealand to 6000 from India. ONUC also provided hundreds of advisers to keep the Congolese government functioning after a fashion.

ONUC quickly despatched its first task as the Belgian government withdrew its official forces by the beginning of September 1960. That only began the far more difficult work of trying to restore law and order in the face of a three-way domestic political contest that included the secession of Katanga province. Divisions appeared among the UN members. The Soviet Union, its allies and many non-aligned governments supported Prime Minister Lumumba and urged that the UN force put an end to the Katanga secession. The United States and its Western allies became suspicious of Lumumba's intentions and generally backed ONUC policies.

Hammarskjöld steered a very cautious course. On the one hand, ONUC then had insufficient military force to pull Katanga back under Kinshasa's authority. On the other hand, the political foundations of ONUC, set out in resolutions of the General Assembly and the Security Council, were shaky indeed. Hammarskjöld usually could obtain backing from the majority of the General Assembly. The Security Council became deadlocked in September 1960, when the Soviet Union vetoed a resolution that explicitly directed members not to intervene in Congolese domestic affairs and to send all assistance through ONUC. That would have meant ending the Soviet practice of directly assisting Lumumba. The General Assembly was at once summoned under Uniting for Peace. The majority there accepted an African–Asian resolution that really showed a lack of confidence in Hammarskjöld, for it requested him to undertake forceful action to help guarantee the territorial integrity and political independence of the Congo – in short, to force an end to the Katanga secession and support Lumumba's view of ONUC's role. In the midst of this came the Soviet attack on Hammarskjöld and the proposal of the famous 'troika' to take over his office (see Chapter 2).

Renewed criticism of Hammarskjöld arose from the tension between Kasavubu and Lumumba. The president ordered his chief minister arrested on 27 November 1960. While under arrest, in late January 1961, Lumumba was murdered in circumstances that have remained obscure. This shock promptly raised the already high political temperature in the Congo. The Security Council again became active and enlarged Hammarskjöld's mandate so that ONUC could now use force beyond mere self-defence.

The use of foreign mercenaries by the Katanga government, as well as other activities, was continually increasing the tension during the early months of 1961. The UN representative in the Congo, Conor Cruise O'Brien, in August ordered troops to take a number of strategic points out of Katangese hands. In doing so, O'Brien went further than Hammarskjöld thought wise. The Secretary-General then set in motion an attempt to deal directly with the Katangese leader, Tshombé. On his way to Ndola, in what is now Zambia, where he was to meet Tshombé, Hammarskjöld died in an aircraft accident.

The new Secretary-General, U Thant, seemed readier to use force in Katanga. In December 1961, UN troops again went into action in Katanga, even though U Thant had no express authorization from the Security Council. The Council had met during the previous month, renewed permission to use force for self-defence and strongly opposed the Katangese secession. As the UN was supposed to have freedom of movement, the new action by the Security Council could be turned into a justification for U Thant's policy in Katanga.

Nevertheless, another year would pass before Katanga really became part of the Congo again. The end of the secession came in December 1962, when UN units occupied the main cities and strong points in Katanga, putting local forces to flight. After that, the UN forces were steadily diminished and at the end of June 1964, the operation came to an end. It left a unified Congo behind but also suspicion in Africa of UN peace-keeping as well as creating a large budgetary deficit.

NEW-STYLE PEACE-KEEPING IN THE 1990s

The original concept of peace-keeping as defined by Hammarskjöld began visibly to give way to novel demands in the 1990s. These were exemplified by the UN concern with Cambodia, Yugoslavia and Somalia. Rather like the Congo 30 years earlier, the governing authorities in these countries either dramatically weakened or disappeared under the impact of civil strife. Human rights were violated in a brutal manner. Hundreds of thousands of people were displaced both by fighting and fear. Their plight brought demands from interest groups and governments for internationally-mounted assistance. The fighting was believed by some to threaten international peace. The demands for assistance to displaced people and refugees, as well as the effects on international stability, brought a variety of responses from regional groupings and from the UN system, including in all three cases the use of peace-keeping forces in conditions that gave little respect to their neutrality and that frequently threatened their safety. Nor could these conditions easily be obtained without the construction of new governments and even states, a task quite beyond the military personnel sent only to supervise shaky ceasefires and disorderly gangs.

Cambodia

Of the three peace-keeping operations, that in Cambodia loomed as until then the largest ever planned and undertaken by the United Nations. In its

Border Relief Operation (UNBRO) on the Cambodia–Thailand boundary and in some refugee camps on Thai territory where UNHCR was at work, the United Nations had an earlier role in coping with the human destruction wreaked by the Pol Pot government in Cambodia. Little progress, however, had been made by the beginning of the 1990s on the controversial, not to say fatal, issue of who would govern the country in the long term.

After years of negotiations, mostly outside the UN framework and often engaging the Association of Southeast Asian States, an agreement was reached in Paris among the four Cambodian factions that aspired to power. This provided for a massive UN operation, entitled the UN Transitional Authority in Cambodia (UNTAC) that began in November 1991. It was to eventuate in an election under UN supervision in late May 1993 and the establishment of a government to succeed the one that had been imposed by Vietnam in 1979, in order to replace the Pol Pot group. Its costs were budgeted at some $2 billion to begin with, far more than any earlier peace-keeping operation, and to be financed by assessments on a membership that already owed large amounts for earlier operations and the regular budget.

As planned by the Security Council, the spine of UNTAC was a peace-keeping force of some 20 000 members who would serve with more than 2400 civilian administrators and election observers. The main military task was to oversee the demobilization and disarmament of 70 per cent of the troops of each of the four armed factions, to regroup and secure their withdrawal to barracks and to oversee their ceasefire. UN troops, who came from Asia, Europe and the Americas, were stationed throughout the country and could mount mobile teams to help ensure that the conditions before and during the election would remain peaceful.

Whether the election could be held under peaceful conditions or whether it would have the desired effect still remained uncertain a month before the appropriate date. UNTAC was in place, a UN-supervised civil administration was trying to prepare the election and refugees were coming back to the country. Yet the Khmer Rouge faction that stood for the Pol Pot regime increasingly resisted UN supervision and flatly refused to disarm or to take part in the election. Sporadic fighting broke out under the eyes of some of the UNTAC soldiers who were increasingly attacked by the Khmer Rouge. As peacekeepers, they had neither the mandate nor the strength to force compliance with the rules. The election went ahead as planned, with support from three of the four Cambodian political factions. Afterwords, the Khmer Rouge made conciliatory gestures.

Yugoslavia

The situation in what had been Yugoslavia was even more complex than that in Cambodia. Some of the component republics of that Communist-led state had begun to break away along ethnic lines even before the 1990s began. Serious fighting broke out in the summer of 1990 and then became centred in Bosnia-Herzegovina, a province of mixed Serb, Croat, Christian and Muslim population who lived together in towns and villages. Guerrilla groups and official forces from Serbia, the biggest component of a rump Yugoslavia, from Croatia, now independent, and from the aspiring Bosnian state, were all engaged in tangled attacks, some of them directed towards 'ethnic cleansing', which involved serious violations of human rights, including murder, torture and rape. Large numbers of refugees were set on the move and turned up in neighbouring states, suffering from various deprivations.

While no military action outside the old Yugoslav territory was reported, clearly the scale of fighting and the destruction concerned neighbouring countries. The European Community sought without success to bring the parties to a political settlement. In September 1991, both West and East European governments began to urge UN action on the grounds that a threat to the peace was manifest. Responses were always reluctant and limited.

In the first of a long series of resolutions, the Security Council for the first time undertook enforcement action against a European government when in September 1991, it mandated an arms embargo for the whole of Yugoslavia. Other sanctions were applied later. Some governments of smaller and Third World countries made clear their hesitancy about what they took as interference in internal affairs. The Secretary-General was invited to try his hand, which he did by appointing Cyrus Vance, former American Secretary of State, as his personal representative. Vance was later joined by Lord Owen, former British Foreign Secretary, to represent the European Community. Vance was replaced in mid-1993 by Thorwald Stoltenberg, then Norwegian foreign minister. Vance's frustration with negotiating while the fighting raged led him to recommend creation of a peace-keeping force, which would be known as the UN Protection Force, consisting of 14 000 soldiers. The plan was accepted by the Security Council and the force, which included British and French units, was deployed early in 1992 to give special attention to fighting in Croatia. Its commanders at first set up headquarters in Sarajevo, the capital of Bosnia, where the focus would soon shift as a complex ethnic struggle in which the Muslim population became a special target soon ensued.

A peace-keeping force, UNPROFOR, could not prevent fighting. It became so embattled that Secretary-General Boutros-Ghali urged its withdrawal, but the Security Council rejected that advice and broadened sanctions. More and more voices urged using the peace-keepers as enforcers, especially when the fighting caused a disastrous human emergency under the eyes of a blockaded Sarajevo and a swarm of television news gatherers. In fact, UNHCR and other parts of the UN system found their efforts to supply food and medical help impeded at every turn, even when their convoys and depots were under UNPROFOR protection. Airborne deliveries to Sarajevo were repeatedly suspended because of artillery bombardment of the airport, even after a Canadian battalion took up its protection. By late spring 1992, Boutros-Ghali was saying publicly that the UN approach had not been a success.

Nor had it stopped the fighting, the violations of human rights and the misery nearly a year later. Gradually, in one town after another, Bosnian militias of Serbian extraction, using heavy weapons, destroyed or drove out their Muslim neighbours, who sometimes fled with help from UN relief personnel. Meanwhile, an increasing number of peace-keepers had died in the course of their duties and the British and French governments moved a substantial additional force nearby. By early 1993, the United States government had joined in directly trying to assist negotiations towards an effective ceasefire and offered the eventual use of its troops as peace-keepers. As the severe Bosnian winter gave way, Owen and Vance had negotiated a peace plan which in essence divided Bosnia into provinces based on ethnic majorities. Still the Bosnian Serbs declined to cooperate and the fighting went on. The Security Council adopted a resolution allowing the enforcement by air of a no-fly zone over Bosnia. Western European governments provided the enforcement planes, while the United States and others stationed heavy naval units nearby. Stricter control, with UN help, was set up to reduce blockade-running via the Danube River to Serbia. This was followed some weeks later by a Security Council decision that safe-haven zones for Bosnian Muslims should be created. In the background was the possibility that actual force, probably furnished through NATO, would be employed under UN auspices in the Bosnia-Herzegovina area. But reluctant governments reached no agreement on enforcement action. By mid-1993, the remaining residents of Sarajevo faced disaster. Elsewhere fighting had emptied many towns of thousands of Muslim residents who, as displaced persons, depended on UN aid.

Meanwhile, the General Assembly tried to cope with the changing political geography of Yugoslavia. It declared in September 1992 that what remained then of Yugoslavia – Serbia and Montenegro – would not automatically take over the former Yugoslav seat in the United Nations. By that time, Croatia, Slovenia and Bosnia-Herzegovina had all been admitted to UN membership.

In the former Yugoslav province of Macedonia, farther south, another experiment with peace-keeping was underway in 1993. Boutros-Ghali sent 500 peace-keepers there, even though there was neither ceasefire nor fighting. There was, however, a serious threat of disorder because of cross-cutting ethnic demands and resentment by Greece of the use of the name of Macedonia by an independent province. Boutros-Ghali explained that this use of peace-keepers fell into the category of preventive diplomacy which he sought to develop with the blessing of the Security Council. In early 1993, the General Assembly admitted the curiously-titled 'Former Yugoslavian Republic of Macedonia' to membership.

Somalia

The military government that had ruled the troubled East African state of Somalia, frequently a scene of fighting with Ethiopia and producer and receiver of masses of refugees, collapsed in 1991. Armed bands mounted by rival would-be governors took to the streets of the capital, Mogadishu, and other towns. The northern part of the country, which had once been British Somaliland, announced its secession. Within weeks, the would-be national leaders had produced disintegration of the already skimpy infrastructure, and continuing fighting.

The OAU made no progress with negotiations to end the fighting. Boutros-Ghali tried his hand early in 1991 as it became evident that the fighting was causing large-scale starvation and the flight of people to neighbouring countries. UN relief organizations and non-governmental groups were unable to work under even reasonably safe conditions, and armed bands made it impossible to deliver supplies through Mogadishu, the best port and other landing places. Boutros-Ghali dispatched negotiators to Somalia, which was becoming daily more lawless, and eventually the Security Council authorized a 500-man peace-keeping force (UNOSOM I) with special duties at the port of Mogadishu. Once on the ground, persistent gunfire tied them to their base. The people suffered more hunger while localities were ruled by armed bands that stole as much relief goods as they could.

Events took a dramatic new turn when President George Bush announced in December 1992, after increasing concern from a public agitated by ghastly television pictures, that 28 000 American troops were to be sent to Somalia. The Security Council promptly approved this action which was intended to protect delivery of relief supplies. The troops would remain under exclusive American command and began withdrawing as early as February 1993. The immediate effect of the Americans dampened the fighting and led to some disarmament of irregulars, but substantial forces remained at the disposal of the contending political chiefs. In May 1993, the US had withdrawn 20 000 members of its force and placed the rest, for the first time, under a UN Commander of non-US nationality. A UN peace-keeping force (UNOSOM II), to be built up to 30 000 persons, then took over the task of helping to maintain enough tranquility to encourage negotiations among the Somali factions for a new government. Overseeing the efforts to reconstitute Somalia and protect its people, who had given up 400 000 victims to the fighting, was an American admiral, who was appointed special representative of the Secretary-General. Yet continuing confusion and violence in the country ensured that phasing in a conventional peace-keeping presence would involve perhaps as much nation-building as diplomacy.

OTHER PEACE-KEEPING CASES

Three other peace-keeping operations by the United Nations varied from very brief and conclusive to long and uncertain as to outcome. (A fourth operation associated with the independence of Namibia is described in Chapter 6.) The most clearly defined of these took place in connection with the shift of sovereignty over West New Guinea (now called West Irian) from the Netherlands to Indonesia between October 1962 and May 1963. The atmosphere of this operation was rather uncontroversial as the Netherlands, the former colonial power, had already agreed that Indonesia, its successor, should take over this remnant of empire. The UN Temporary Executive Authority had at its disposal a force of 1500 Pakistani troops to help maintain the peace. While the force hardly operated in the tension characteristic of Suez or the Congo, it contributed to the smoothness with which the transfer of sovereignty took place.

Far longer and more complicated is the UN peace-keeping effort in Cyprus. There, the UN Force in Cyprus (UNFICYP) has been in place since March 1964, when it took up stations between Turkish and Greek forces on the island-state. Its presence grew out of serious friction between the Turkish- and Greek-speaking communities in Cyprus and has been compounded by claims and military action by both Greece and Turkey on the island, that until 1960 was a British possession. When the Security Council took up the issue at a time when Turkey threatened to intervene and Greek elements in Cyprus were encouraging unification with Greece, it was thought that the matter could be settled quickly. The first mandate for the force was three months long, but since then it has been repeatedly renewed for six-month periods. It is financed by the contributing countries, voluntary contributions and by Cyprus itself.

Until 1973, the 3000-man force held off serious conflicts, but repeated mediatory efforts could not resolve the political issues. Meanwhile, the Greek majority and the Turkish minority on Cyprus became increasingly separated, although as a state it was represented by a government of Greek-speakers. In July 1974, a *coup d'état* removed the government of Archbishop Makarios that had been in place since independence. An invasion of the northern part of the island by Turkey followed. Makarios eventually returned to a country now even more divided with UNFICYP stationed between the two halves. A separate government was formed in the Turkish-speaking north and the Turkish forces withdrew. The government in the north has only been recognized by Turkey. Special UN mediators and Secretaries-General Waldheim and Pérez de Cuéllar have taken part in negotiations between the two principal parties. Some progress has been made, but as of 1993, UNFICYP still was deployed, awaiting the elusive political settlement.

The remaining venture, not precisely the same as earlier peace-keeping but perhaps less passive than some observation missions, was undertaken as part of the UN negotiations to end the eight-year-long war between Iran and Iraq. After repeated pleas and demands by the Security Council, negotiations with the Secretary-General and pressure from the presence of Western and Soviet naval units in the Persian Gulf, Iran and Iraq finally agreed to a ceasefire in August 1988. This went into effect under the eyes of a 350-man UN Iran–Iraq Military Observer Group (UNIIMOG) assembled from contributions by 24 countries. The fighting stopped and a UN mediator set to work. The Security Council also empowered the Secretary-General to set up direct talks between the two parties. By the time that Iraq overran Kuwait during August 1990 (see Chapter 8), no definitive settlement of the Iraq–Iran war had been reached.

Beyond these rather substantial ventures, smaller peace-keeping groups were on the ground in 1992 in Mozambique, where a civil war was winding down, in Angola, where observation of an election had not been followed by peace, and in the Western Sahara where a UN-supervised plebiscite about the future of the territory had been delayed by political manoeuvres by Morocco and the Polisario liberation group.

NEGOTIATIONS AND CONCILIATORY METHODS

Peace-keeping invariably has been accompanied by encouragement to the parties to reach a settlement of their disputes. The UN record contains a long series of examples of such activities. These have varied in character from formal resolutions by the Security Council to rapid shuttling of a mediator or the Secretary-General between capitals. The underlying assumption of these efforts, as well as that of peace-keeping, is that in a world of independent states, permanent settlement of disputes depends on consensus, rather than coercion, and that third parties can help. That implies negotiations, either direct or indirect, among the parties. Unlike peace-keeping or coercive methods, these procedures usually remain in the background, seldom reported by the mass media, and often employ nothing more than conventional diplomatic methods.

As a third party in disputes, however, the United Nations has created some noteworthy variations in diplomacy. One of these, closely related to the more elaborate peace-keeping, is the use of observers. This began on the Greek borders during the civil war there in 1946 and reached a much larger scale in Kashmir and especially with UNTSO along the Arab–Israeli ceasefire lines. It has been used repeatedly not only in tense military situations but also in elections taking place under conditions that could involve violence, such as those in Nicaragua in 1990. A main purpose of observation is to establish a factual account of violations of rules. Behind that is the notion that governments will not neglect the opinions of other members of the UN. A similar line of thought underlies the work of peace-keeping forces as supervisors of truce agreements.

Multinational commissions frequently were set up in the early years of the UN to carry out conciliatory missions. Examples were to be found in Korea, where a nine-country commission watched for signs of military activity, and in the Middle East where a UN Conciliation Commission for Palestine operated. More recently, the Security Council has repeatedly asked the Secretary-General to keep a developing dispute under watch and to encourage negotiations. In turn, he appoints a mediator, usually a senior diplomat from a country not close to the disputants, to try to reach a solution. Some examples are the work of Gunnar Jarring in the Israeli–Arab disputes during the early 1970s, and UN Under-Secretary-General Diego Cordovez, who for seven years shuttled around a circuit that included the interested parties in Afghanistan. In the latter, Cordovez had the backing of a majority of the General Assembly which demanded the withdrawal of the Soviet invader in 1989. Cordovez's work supplied an important element in the procedures adopted by the Soviet Union for withdrawal from Afghanistan, which was also observed by a few military officers despatched by the Secretary-General. Fighting nevertheless continued between government troops, who had Soviet backing, and several guerrilla groups, based in Pakistan and supplied by the United States.

The Secretary-General frequently offers good offices to disputants. This has resulted in a long series of involvements by the Secretary-General in important international disputes. In some of them, he acts on his own initiative. In others, the Security Council or the General Assembly instructs him to act. Strictly speaking, good offices involves merely furnishing premises for a discussion, but the Secretaries-General over the years have often used it as an introductory step to more concerted mediation. By 1990, the Secretary-General had ample precedent for offering disputants his help; it was increasingly accepted in the new atmosphere of cooperation that followed Gorbachev's accession to the Soviet leadership.

Aside from the more cooperative approach in the Security Council, Secretary-General Pérez de Cuéllar convinced insiders with his initiatives during the Anglo-Argentine war over the Falkland Islands in 1982, of his talent for diplomacy. From then on, he became a part of a series of negotiations in which he served as an impartial intermediary and source of ideas. Aside from Afghanistan and the Iran–Iraq war, he and his close associates had an important share in the creation by the Security Council in 1989 of a UN Observer Group for Central America, which was to help with efforts to bring peace in the civil war in El Salvador and better relations between Nicaragua and its neighbours. Pérez de Cuéllar successfully took the initiative in 1988, along with the OAU, in developing a plan for ending the long-running dispute between Morocco and the insurgent Polisario front over the Western Sahara. The Secretary-General has continued negotiations intended to settle the long division of Cyprus. Other UN representatives have recently attempted to mediate in parts of the disintegrating former Soviet Union, in Angola, in Mozambique and South Africa. None of these initiatives has magically liquidated long-standing disputes, but they did indicate a renewed acceptance of the UN process and the initiative of the Secretary-General as useful in regional conflicts.

LIMITS AND POTENTIALS OF PEACE-KEEPING

More than 40 years of experience with pacific settlement of disputes and nearly that much with peace-keeping forces can be summed up in a few rather solid conclusions. The first of them consists of two generalizations that colour all the rest. First, the settlement of international disputes, and even cooling them off, remains a slow process in which the time-honoured methods of diplomacy figure large. The second is that the pacific settlement mechanism that includes Chapter VI of the UN Charter, the activities of the Secretary-General and the political atmosphere developed especially by the General Assembly, still depend mainly on the willingness of disputants to use it. Other conclusions include the following:

1. The use of peace-keeping forces links to what Hammarskjöld called 'preventive diplomacy' – using the UN and especially the Secretary-General to prevent the worsening of a dispute and its broadening into a great-power confrontation. In fact, preventive diplomacy and peace-keeping require at least some cooperation from the great powers and, during the Cold War, especially from the United States and the Soviet Union. They must define their interests in such a way as to keep their distance and also to allow the Security Council to bring the peace-keeping force into being. UNEF fulfilled these conditions. ONUC did at first, but the later discord demonstrated how damaging increasing demands for influence by the great powers, each of them backed an opposed camp in the internal strife, could become both to peace-keeping and the leadership of the Secretary-General.

2. If the United Nations actually does use force (as in Korea or during August and September 1961 in Katanga and in January 1991 in Iraq and Kuwait), it has to be strong enough to accomplish its aim quickly. If it does not, the credibility of the United Nations declines and the peace-keeping operation suffers. In case force is used, the Secretary-General may be excluded from substantial participation. If he is given substantial responsibility, he has to have acceptance of his own interpretation of his authorization either by the Council or the General Assembly. That means the Secretary-General has in some manner to maintain the confidence of the majority of members, including some with broad influence, in his decisions. This was indeed so for most of the Congo operation, despite the inimical relationship between Hammarskjöld and the Soviet Union. The principles he set out for his policies continue to guide peace-keeping. Moreover, the Secretary-General uses these principles as a basis for negotiations with the disputants and the contributing governments that resemble those of a governmental leader or a very senior diplomat. He has to assemble contributions to a military force, arrange for its safe passage, obtain permission from the disputants for its emplacement, and find a means of financing the operation. Moreover, he has to cope with the problem of selecting from offers of forces. Hammarskjöld barred the use of great-power troops. Later, however, British troops were kept on in Cyprus to help with peace-keeping, French soldiers served in UNIFIL and Russian and East European military

men have taken up UN duties in the Middle East and in Yugoslavia. Americans began for the first time to serve in peace-keeping in Somalia and Macedonia. Nevertheless, the host governments must consent to the presence of any foreign troops, the choice of which may pose a crucial issue.

3. Several important legal problems concerning peace-keeping remain unsolved. The first of these concerns the degree of obligation that rests on member states after decisions to set up a peace-keeping force are taken. Then, if a government does provide troops, it is not clear whether it has the right to withdraw them without consent from the UN responsible organ. Finally, the right of a government, on whose territory a peace-keeping force is deployed, to end its operation is not clear. An agreement between the host country and the UN defines some of these rights, but overriding political reasons easily reopen uncertainties.

4. UNEF and, even more, UNFICYP and UNIFIL illustrate how temporary arrangements in international politics have a tendency to continue so long as to seem permanent. The presence of a buffer between warring parties can help to maintain international peace but does not necessarily resolve the dispute so that further outbreaks can be avoided permanently. Thus, peace-keeping differs from peace-making.

ARMS CONTROL AND DISARMAMENT

The authors of the UN Charter thought that the creation of stable international society would reduce the need for national armament. To the degree that the Security Council could ensure international peace and security, the chances would increase for world-wide arms control. Thus, disarmament – or at least arms control – was set out as principal aim of the new organization.

Few ideas have occupied so much UN time and effort and delivered so little concrete result as arms control and disarmament. Almost all international agreements on armaments, until Gorbachev's vast alterations of Soviet policy, concerned secondary issues. Before and after that, the great powers tended to keep their negotiations outside of the UN framework. Actual control of the general level of armaments through an international organization thus remains a distant ideal. Meanwhile, the firepower of national governments, even those of poor countries, has increased as never before.

However limited the results, both the General Assembly and the Security Council have made a long series of gestures towards carrying out their duties under Articles 11 and 28 of the UN Charter. The General

Assembly may consider general principles of maintaining peace, including disarmament and arms control. The Security Council has responsibility for setting up a system of regulation of armaments.

Almost immediately after its establishment, the United Nations began exploring possibilities of arms control. Equally soon, it appeared that the Soviet Union and the United States would not accept regulations that reduced their military strength or its further development. So long as those attitudes prevailed, UN efforts would be limited to formulation of general principles, furnishing a forum for discussing the problem and striving for limited arms control agreements.

The early, tone-setting debates took place in the Atomic Energy Commission, established in 1946 by the General Assembly, and in the Commission on Conventional Armaments, set up in 1947, as the result of an initiative by the Security Council. In both these limited-membership bodies, efforts to create effective control systems were frustrated by the attitude of the major powers and the Cold War. Both organs were dissolved in 1952 and replaced with the UN Disarmament Commission, to which all UN members eventually belonged; it reported to the General Assembly. Besides, in 1961, the General Assembly set up the Eighteen-Nation Disarmament Commission with the hope that this smaller body could organize a workable system of arms control. Seven years later, it too disappeared, and all discussions were carried in a new UN Conference on Disarmament in Geneva. It reports to the General Assembly and remains the most important global forum for debating trends in arms control and disarmament. The General Assembly has summoned three special sessions, in 1978, 1982 and 1988, on disarmament. These stimulated a great deal of public attention and adopted a series of resolutions that fuelled more discussion in the General Assembly without reaching the desired goal.

By 1990, after the decline in tension between the United States and the Soviet Union, negotiations outside the UN framework had begun to produce quite real reductions in arms in Europe and in nuclear weapons. In mid-1991, after more than a decade of Strategic Arms Reduction Talks (START), the American and Soviet Presidents signed an agreement in Moscow to reduce the number and type of nuclear weapons in their arsenals. In addition to direct negotiations, European security issues, including reduction of forces, engaged the members of NATO and the WTO, in unprecedented negotiations that included real successes. In these circumstances, UN discussions may have helped keep governments that did not participate in the European talks better informed and able to submit their reactions. In this way, the UN concern with disarmament at least helped to form a political atmosphere that favoured arms reductions. In addition, it continued work on certain specialized approaches to arms control, which are discussed in the following paragraphs.

Non-Proliferation of Nuclear Weapons

Taking the position that the spread of nuclear weapons endangers the world, the General Assembly in 1968 approved the text of a treaty to limit further proliferation. The treaty had the backing of both the Soviet Union and the United States. It came into effect in 1970 for the states that ratify it. These included the superpowers, but China and France, possessors of the weapons, have declined to become party to it. So have a list of possible nuclear powers, including Israel, Brazil, Egypt, India and Pakistan. The treaty obliges nuclear states not to furnish such weapons or means of making them to non-nuclear powers. Moreover, the nuclear powers pledged to develop security guarantees for non-nuclear signatories and to negotiate on nuclear and other disarmament. This led to the SALT and later the START talks between the Soviet Union and the United States. These took on new life as the superpowers began to agree on other limitations of armaments. The non-proliferation treaty is reviewed from time to time in special conferences.

A Ban on Nuclear Testing

A treaty to ban testing of nuclear devices was for years a controversial proposal in the General Assembly. Forbidding the testing of nuclear materials or dumping nuclear waste in outer space as well as in the sea or on land was a related notion. In 1963, the Soviet Union and the United States reached agreement on a partial ban on nuclear testing in outer space, on the land and underwater. Only limited underground testing remained legal. The majority of the General Assembly never accepted this treaty as entirely satisfactory and continued to press the parties to extend the ban to all testing everywhere. Enough signatory states sought to invoke a clause providing for a review conference to extend the treaty so that the General Assembly in 1989 began preparations for it.

Demilitarized and Nuclear-Free Zones

The notion of forbidding dangerous nuclear activities in several defined places has won the support of the General Assembly. One of these areas is outer space and another Antarctica. Specific treaty provisions covering both of these were recommended by the General Assembly and have entered into force for signatories. A UN convention is also in force to prohibit the emplacement of nuclear weapons on the deep seabed. The General Assembly also has recommended treaties barring nuclear weapons in Latin America, while in 1986, 12 South Pacific states developed a treaty, endorsed by General Assembly, to limit nuclear weapons and testing activities. Similar attempts have been made with regard to the Indian Ocean, Africa and the Middle East and East Asia, although by 1993 little progress was recorded towards binding treaties.

Chemical and Biological Weapons

Since 1975, a convention approved by the General Assembly has been in force to prohibit the manufacture or use of biological weapons, although the main potential users have never acceded to it. An earlier convention, supervised by the International Committee of the Red Cross, bans the use of chemical weapons. An attempt to link the two was begun by the UN Conference on Disarmament, but negotiations between the United States and the Soviet Union collapsed as a result of the invasion of Afghanistan in 1980. Presidents Reagan and Gorbachev pledged in their 1985 summit meeting to prohibit chemical weapons and destroy stockpiles. By 1990, negotiations continued on several fronts. They were made all the more urgent by well-documented evidence that Libya had constructed a factory to make chemical weapons and that Iraq used its own in its war against Iran and against Iraqi Kurds, as well as threatening to use them after its invasion of Kuwait in August 1990. In early 1993, a convention to forbid the production, possession, stockpiling and distribution of chemical weapons was signed by 127 governments but not by Iraq.

Altogether these conventions form a web of controls on important aspects of arms control. Ratifying states accept obligations to respect these controls. Yet it is obvious that they did not extend far enough to stem an enormous arms race that continued almost without pause from the end of the Second World War to the late 1980s. Responsibility for either the arms race or the lack of control over armaments can hardly be laid at the door of the United Nations. Only national governments, acting on their own or jointly, can stop producing or buying weapons or using them. The United Nations offered a forum for negotiation and discussion. These provide reference points for national policy. If the results were modest, so were the intentions of leading governments with regard to the UN process.

CONCLUSIONS

Very soon after the establishment of the United Nations, it was clear that the system of collective security, as envisaged, failed to operate. Attempts to use the organization to maintain peace, moreover, raised the query as to whether the system could work at all or, if it did work, would produce satisfactory results.

The proximate cause of the failure of collective security – a system that calls for the use of coercion when the Charter is violated – lay in the antagonistic relationship and view of the world of the Soviet Union and the United States. These two great powers could most easily sustain the cost of ignoring the United Nations and the collectivity of states it implied. If either of them had started a war against the other, the United Nations would have been brushed aside as futile. When one or other supported a party to a conflict, the organization encountered great difficulty in delivering the promises of its Charter.

Sometimes, however, the United Nations produced useful results during violent conflicts. It sometimes used coercive methods or the suggestion of ultimate coercion. An international force was mounted in Korea, according to the decision of the Security Council and with support from the General Assembly. The United Nations did assemble the needed support for UNEF. The superpowers agreed to open the ONUC chapter; it closed with forceful measures. They and their fellow governments employed the organization in the Iran–Iraq war and in ending the Afghanistan invasion. The United Nations achieved its aim in Namibia without the use of force (see Chapter 6). It helped in the struggle over Zimbabwe (see Chapter 6). It had a role in adjusting the politics of Central America at the end of the 1980s. In fact, the UN presence was hardly ever entirely absent, and sometimes took a leading role, in a long series of international conflicts.

Yet the accent in maintaining the peace through the United Nations never was on the use of force. The entire system, rather, depended almost always on peace-making and peace-keeping by consent. No UN army ever existed and perhaps never will. Even had there been such a force at the disposal of the Security Council, its use would be intended to return the parties to the methods of pacific settlement. It seems likely to remain so as long as national governments dispose of armed forces and the doctrine that they make their own decisions.

In fact, it would be difficult to find a single member state whose government would under all circumstances respect Article 2 (4) of the UN Charter, which forbids the use of force against the territorial integrity and independence of any other state. Moreover, any government can try to defend its use of force under the self-defence provisions of Article 51. These facts ensure that maintaining peace has to depend on the cooperation and consent of governments. In case of a conflict, the best reaction, from the point of view of keeping the peace, usually would be to stop the fighting. If the disputants discern that neither can fully achieve its goal, then they can perhaps be brought to settling their dispute or at least not to spread it to other countries. Peace-keeping forces usually signal that a great majority of governments in fact supports an end to fighting and a resumption of pacific settlement. This signal gains intensity by the fact that military units may be employed for non-coercive purposes, as was the case with UNEF and with UNFICYP.

The good offices and mediation of the Secretary-General, which again in the late 1980s began to achieve the prestige of Hammarskjöld's time, relies exclusively on non-coercive approaches. One way or another, the parties to conflicts have found ways to accede to the Secretary-General's suggestions. Boutros-Ghali's active approval to his office and parts of his *Agenda for Peace* suggest that the future may include a Secretary-General more openly involved in seeking settlements of disputes.

If the fundamental conflicts remain, perhaps the time gained by peace-keeping and other methods of pacific settlement could ultimately resolve more conflicts. If not, as least in the short run, human lives have been spared and even more misery avoided.

5 Human Rights

The contemporary concern for human rights is inextricably linked to the crimes against humanity by the German National Socialist government in the period 1933–45 and the insufficient reaction from abroad. The initial inhumanity of the Nazis, as well as of the Italian Fascists before the war, culminated in an explicit programme to exterminate Jews, gypsies, homosexuals and other 'subhuman species', especially in the German-occupied territories. One of the purposes of the newly-established United Nations was to see to it that this would never happen again.

Unlike the League of Nations Covenant, the UN Charter contains specific articles on human rights. One of the principal purposes of the organization, according to Article 1, paragraph 3 of the Charter, is international cooperation to promote and encourage respect for human rights and fundamental freedoms for all without distinction as to race, sex, language or religion. In this task, the General Assembly was given the power to initiate studies and make recommendations to governments [Article 13]. This general authority was supplemented with the specific requirement that ECOSOC organize a commission for the promotion of human rights [Article 68]. ECOSOC itself can also make recommendations on human rights. Finally, one of the basic objectives of the Trusteeship System (see Chapter 6) concerns human rights and fundamental freedoms [Article 76].

For the first time in history, the United Nations formulated fundamental human rights for all mankind. Earlier efforts, which influenced the United Nations, had been only on a national scale, as in post-revolutionary France and in the newly independent United States. The ambitious new work began in 1946, when the Commission on Human Rights was created. Its presiding officer for the first few years was Eleanor Roosevelt, the widow of the US president – a powerful personality in her own right. The Economic and Social Council instructed the new commission to develop proposals for:

● an international bill of rights;
● international declarations or conventions relating to civil liberties, the status of women, freedom of information, and similar matters;
● the protection of minorities;
● the prevention of discrimination on grounds of race, sex, language, or religion;
● any other matter concerning human rights.

The Commission on Human Rights meets annually for five or six weeks. Enlarged over the years, it includes representatives of 53 states, elected for three-year terms by the General Assembly after expansion in 1992. It has a broad mandate touching on any matter relating to human rights. The Commission orders and examines studies, usually drafted by rapporteurs or by the Human Rights Centre in Geneva, which is a division of the UN Secretariat. It drafts international instruments relating to human rights for ratification by governments. It also undertakes special tasks assigned by the General Assembly or ECOSOC. It investigates allegations of violations of human rights and receives and processes communications related to such violations.

Under what is called the '1503 procedure', the Commission deals in closed meetings with confidential communications about patterns of gross and systematic violations of human rights. Private complaints are discussed first in the Sub-Commission on Prevention of Discrimination and Protection of Minorities. If that body concludes that there seems to be 'a consistent pattern of gross and reliably attested violations of human rights', it refers the complaint to the Commission, which may then investigate further. The fact that such complaints are dealt with may have a certain corrective effect, the more so because it is now common practice that the chairman of the Commission will announce, after the meeting, the names of the states that were discussed under the 1503 procedure.

In its public meetings the Commission may discuss human rights situations in all parts of the world. ECOSOC resolution 1235, adopted in 1967, allows both members and non-members of the Commission to raise violations of human rights anywhere in the world. This may lead to resolutions with recommendations to be submitted to ECOSOC and to the General Assembly. It may also lead to further study of the problem, for example by a working group or special rapporteur. The latter possibility has been widely used by the Commission with the appointment of *country rapporteurs* on such countries as Afghanistan, Bolivia, Chile, El Salvador, Guatemala, Iran and Romania. Furthermore, it has appointed *thematic rapporteurs* on summary and arbitrary executions, on torture, on religious intolerance, the abuse of children, and the use of mercenaries; working groups deal with the problem of involuntary disappearances, and with arbitrary detention. Their reports are presented in the public meetings of the Commission. It also deals with the annual report of the Sub-Commission on Prevention of Discrimination and Protection of Minorities. The 26 members of the Sub-Commission are selected in their personal capacities, although it is well known that some retain rather close relations with their governments.

Notwithstanding its name, the Sub-Commission deals with studies on a broad range of human rights, which it submits to the Commission.

The Commission may invite representatives of non-member states or liberation movements to take part in its deliberations on a non-voting basis. Specialized agencies and certain other intergovernmental organizations also may take part in discussions on topics of concern to them. Finally, a unique feature of the Commission on Human Rights is that, along with the formal members of the body, are seated a large number of non-governmental organizations with consultative status. They have the right to address the Commission, take part in its debates and to have written statements circulated as United Nations documents.

In the past, the Western states occupied a relatively large number of seats (10 out of a total of 43) in the Commission. In 1989, the General Assembly decided, supposedly as part of an effort to 'enhance' its effectiveness, on the enlargement of the membership that took place in 1992. The ten additional members were allocated to the African, Asian and Latin American states.

THE UNIVERSAL DECLARATION OF HUMAN RIGHTS

The United Nations made its first major step of practical importance in the field of human rights with the adoption of the Universal Declaration of Human Rights on 10 December 1948. Drafted by the Commission on Human Rights, it was adopted by the General Assembly by 48 votes in favour, none against and eight abstentions (the Soviet Union, Byelorussia, the Ukraine, Poland, Czechoslovakia, Yugoslavia, Saudi Arabia and South Africa). Not legally binding, its preamble proclaims it a 'common standard of achievement' for all peoples and all nations. It has become the foundation for establishing obligatory legal norms to govern international behaviour with regard to rights of individuals. It has shifted some of the emphasis of international law from its concern exclusively with the state to greater attention to individual people. It has inspired and stimulated thinking and the formation of private groups, and has served as a model for national constitutional protection for persons.

Roughly three categories of rights can be distinguished in the Universal Declaration. First, certain articles relate to the physical and spiritual integrity of the human person. These rights include that of life as well the prohibition of slavery or servitude, torture, cruel, inhuman or degrading treatment or punishment; and arbitrary arrest, detention or exile. Freedom of thought, conscience and religion are to be guaranteed. The second category concerns political life, including the right to freedom of opinion and expression; and peaceful assembly and association and participation in government, directly or through freely chosen representatives. Finally, the declaration includes social, economic and cultural rights, among which are social security; free choice of employment; just and favourable conditions of work; protection against unemployment; rest and leisure; education; and participation in the cultural life of one's community.

The rights set forth in the declaration have such deep attractiveness everywhere in the world that few political leaders would admit simply to disregarding them. Most of the individual civil and political rights are familiar as behavioural norms for Western governments, even when practice violates them. Many non-Western states tend to give more emphasis to the importance of social, economic, and cultural rights – sometimes at the expense of civil and political rights. It has been claimed that developing countries need first to provide the necessities for human survival, such as food, clothing and shelter. Until such basic needs are met, the argument goes, guaranteeing fundamental civil and political liberties is bound to take second place. Some repressive regimes even defend their violations with the claim that they cannot allow the luxury of civil and political rights so long as the population suffers from underdevelopment. This argument is patently fallacious: it has never been demonstrated that the curtailment of civil or political rights does contribute to economic development. Nor is there any reason to assume that the right not to be tortured or to have a fair trial for an alleged criminal offence interferes with economic development in Ghana or Cambodia, but does not in the United States. The curtailment of civil rights may contribute mainly to the preservation of the oppressive government itself!

From such arguments, both the strength and weakness of the declaration can be inferred. The document settles no legal obligations on the UN membership. That partly explains why the General Assembly adopted it with relative ease, although the effect of the then-recent annihilation of people by the Nazis should not be underestimated. It also helps to explain why many governments that voted for it have in fact done little to give it effectiveness.

Furthermore, in 1948, few African and Asian states were members or even independent. Had they been, perhaps other aspects of human rights would have been emphasized. An example is the right of all peoples to self-determination, mentioned as a principle (not a right) in the UN Charter but omitted from the Declaration. It is, however, contained in the two human rights covenants of 1966, which are binding as legal obligations on the governments that ratify them. At the same time, the Afro-Asian states accept the Declaration: no government has ever publicly dissociated itself from the document, and indeed the General Assembly and other UN organs have repeatedly underlined its significance. Specific reference to it is made in such important resolutions as the Declaration on the Granting of Independence to Colonial Countries and Peoples of 1960 (see Chapter 6); the Declaration on the Elimination of All Forms of Racial Discrimination of 1963; and the Declaration on the Protection of All Persons from Torture and Other Cruel, Inhuman or Degrading Treatment or Punishment of 1975. In 1968, an international conference adopted the Proclamation of Teheran in which the Universal Declaration is proclaimed as stating a common understanding of the peoples of the world concerning the inalienable and inviolable rights of all members of the human family and constituting an obligation for the members of the international community. Similarly, in the final act of the Helsinki Conference on Security and Cooperation in Europe, the 35 participating states agreed in 1975 that they would act in conformity with the provisions of the Universal Declaration.

In addition to its influence on many national constitutions and on UN policies, the Universal Declaration has inspired the creation of a wide net of new international regulations. In the form of multilateral treaties, they have been ratified by various states and give evidence of the increasing attention that international law pays to individual persons. A topic that has benefited from profound treatment is discrimination and the protection of minorities, for which the Commission on Human Rights established its Sub-Commission in 1947. In studies and special reports, the Sub-Commission laid the foundation for preparing a Convention on the Elimination of All Forms of Racial Discrimination that was adopted by the General Assembly in 1965, and to which 128 states had acceded in 1992. The convention established a committee on the elimination of racial discrimination that meets twice a year and reports annually to the General Assembly. The committee examines the information placed before it by states party to the convention. From time to time it comments upon particular situations involving racial discrimination or draws them to the attention of the General Assembly. So far, only 17 states have recognized the competence of the committee to deal with communications from individuals within the jurisdiction of those states and to prepare proposals and recommendations in regard to such communications.

THE INTERNATIONAL COVENANTS ON HUMAN RIGHTS

The most comprehensive development of the Universal Declaration can be found in the two international covenants on human rights, adopted by the General Assembly in 1966, after extended drafting exercises by the

Commission on Human Rights and consultations with governments. These two covenants deal respectively with economic, social and cultural rights, and with civil and political rights.

Like the Universal Declaration, the covenants carry the mark of the political context of their time of birth. The then-new influence of the Afro-Asian states led to an emphasis in both documents on the right of every people to self-determination. Furthermore, the covenants state that all peoples may, for their own ends, freely dispose of their natural wealth and resources without prejudice to any obligations arising from international economic cooperation that is based on the principle of mutual benefit and international law. 'In no case', the covenant on economic, social and cultural rights proclaims, 'may a people be deprived of its own means of subsistence.' Thus the former colonial countries insisted that nations should be able to govern their own political and economic destinies without imperialistic control.

The covenants further include most of the other rights mentioned in the Universal Declaration, omitting, however, the right to property, the right to nationality, and the right to seek and enjoy asylum. The rights that are mentioned are given stricter legal form and developed further than in the original document.

In the covenant on economic, social and cultural rights, articles set out the right to work and to fair wages and equal pay for work of equal value. In particular, women are guaranteed conditions of work not inferior to those enjoyed by men. The right of everyone to form labour unions and to choose which he or she will join is also guaranteed. The document spells out the right of each person to an adequate standard of living for himself and his family. This standard includes food, clothing, and housing. Other rights included in this covenant cover:

- the enjoyment of the highest standard of physical and mental health;
- the right of everyone to education;
- the right of everyone to take part in cultural life and to enjoy the benefits of scientific progress and its applications; and
- the right to social security, including social insurance.

The specific rights familiar to North Americans and West Europeans appear in the covenant on civil and political rights. These include the right to life; to liberty and security of the person; to freedom of thought, conscience and religion; to hold opinions without interference; to freedom of expression; and to peaceful assembly. The covenant specifically forbids torture or cruel, inhuman and degrading treatment or punishment. Persons arrested by the state have the right, when they are held, to be informed of any charges. A person detained on a criminal charge must be brought promptly before a judge or other authorized officer of justice and tried within a reasonable time or else released. Freedom of movement is also dealt with. Anyone lawfully within the territory of a state is entitled to liberty of movement. Everyone is entitled to leave a country, including his or her own. The covenant defines the conditions under which exceptions ('derogations') may be made to the exercise of these rights.

Each of the covenants establishes a method of supervision of compliance by governments. The economic, social and cultural covenant requires that parties periodically furnish reports to the UN Secretary-General on the measures they have adopted and progress made in achieving the observance of the included rights. These reports are submitted to the Committee for Economic, Social and Cultural Rights, a committee of 18 individual experts, which was established in 1985 by the Economic and Social Council. This Committee considers the national reports and submits its findings to the Economic and Social Council for consideration. ECOSOC may make recommendations of a general nature on these matters to the relevant organs of the organization. Under the provisions of this covenant, individuals may not complain directly to an international body about violations of these rights. The covenant serves as a standard of aspiration and means of judging progress toward a broad list of economic, social, and cultural benefits.

The covenant on civil and political rights provides for a special permanent supervisory organ. This is the Human Rights Committee (to be distinguished from the Commission on Human Rights) that consists of 18 persons of high moral character and recognized competence in the field of human rights. Nominated by governments, they serve in their personal capacity. The parties to the covenant must submit reports to the committee on any national measures to give effect to the relevant rights and on the progress made in the enjoyment of those rights. A specific authorization obliges the committee to deal with complaints by a state that another has failed to fulfil its obligations. This procedure is limited to states that have recognized in advance the competence of the committee: so far, only 40 states have done so. Finally, if it adheres to an optional protocol, a state allows its subjects to communicate to the committee that they are victims of violations by that state of any rights set out in the covenant. The committee, after determining that the communication is admissible under the protocol, must bring it to the attention of the state concerned. That state must within six months submit written explanations or statements clarifying the matter and the remedy taken. The committee then considers the communication in light of all available information and forwards its views to the state and the individual concerned. Over the years, the Committee has built up an important body of case law and it has formulated a number of general recommendations which constitute an important source of interpretation of many substantive articles of the Covenant.

Capital punishment, though not forbidden in the covenant, is limited to the most serious crimes in accordance with the law in force at the time of the commission of the crime. It may not be imposed for crimes committed by persons below 18 years of age and or carried out on pregnant women. In 1989, the General Assembly, by a vote of 59 in favour, 26 against, with 48 abstentions, adopted a second optional protocol, against the death penalty. States that become parties to it are bound not to carry out executions. Only a limited exception is permitted: states may make reservations when accepting the protocol allowing them to use the death penalty 'in time of war pursuant to a conviction for a most serious crime of a military nature committed during wartime'. The large number of votes against, including China, the United States and most Middle Eastern countries, and abstentions shows that abolition of the death penalty is still a controversial issue.

Both covenants were unanimously adopted by the General Assembly and recommended to the members for accession on 16 December 1966. Both covenants entered into force in 1976. In mid-1992, 114 governments had ratified the covenant on civil and political rights: 66 had ratified the first optional protocol. The other covenant had been ratified by 116 governments. The Soviet Union and its allies have acceded to the covenants. In 1992, the United States ratified the Covenant on Civil and Political Rights, attaching a number of 'reservations' and understandings: the other Covenant was kept pending in the Senate.

No member of the United Nations, whether a party to the covenants or not, complies with all obligations to protect human rights. A steady stream of reports from such non-governmental organizations as Amnesty International, the International Commission of Jurists, and the 'watch' committees (Helsinki Watch, Asia Watch, Africa Watch, Americas Watch) brings to light numerous violations of fundamental human rights, especially in the civil and political realm, in many countries. The UN Commission on Human Rights also deals with a full agenda of alleged violations. In recent years, it has looked into charges against, among others, Chile, Bolivia, El Salvador, and Guatemala, as well as Poland, Romania and Iran. Certain governments, such as those of Chile, Poland, Iran and Romania, failed during particular stages of the investigation, to cooperate. One of the grounds they adduced was that it intervened in their domestic affairs. Such refusal obviously hampers, but does not prevent, the gathering of evidence.

Whether parties to the covenants or not, governments usually pay lip-service to their provisions and the Universal Declaration. They also take the trouble to react to the Commission's comments, especially when they are critical. Yet such documents and recommendations do not govern all behaviour of governments, although some governments consciously try to protect at least some of the rights of their citizens. These UN documents, it can be argued, constitute an accepted normative framework of which governments are conscious and according to which their subjects sometimes seek justice.

At the same time, the reality of governmental behaviour tends to be covered with a great deal of symbolism, a strong feature of UN activity in the field of human rights in particular. For example, as early as 1950, the General Assembly declared 10 December of each year as Human Rights Day, when special attention should be paid to human rights in all countries throughout the world. The General Assembly named the period 1973–83 the 'Decade Against Racial Discrimination'. Such symbolic actions – and even the very rhetoric of the Universal Declaration itself – have some meaning, for they keep alive the consciousness of the concept and focus attention of various groups and individuals on aspects of human rights violations. The symbols cannot, of course, replace actual observance by national governments of the obligations of the covenants.

OTHER HUMAN RIGHTS ACTIVITIES

In addition to the Universal Declaration and the two covenants, which cover human rights in general, over the years the General Assembly has adopted a large number of declarations and conventions with regard to specific subjects. One of the first was a declaration that the principles, including the prohibition of crimes against humanity, applied by the Nuremberg Tribunal in trying German war-criminals after the Second World War, were a part of international law. This was followed by the adoption in 1948 by the General Assembly of the convention on the prevention and punishment of the crime of genocide (the deliberate eradication of a people or their culture) that came into force in 1951. In 1968, the General Assembly adopted a convention on the non-applicability of statutory limitations to war crimes and crimes against humanity, two of the laws enforced at Nuremberg: it came into force in 1970.

Discrimination on the basis of sex has also received significant attention. The convention on the political rights of women won the approval of the General Assembly in 1952. In 1967, it adopted a declaration calling for the abolition of all rules, laws, regulations and customs that discriminate against women, and their replacement with legal protection; states are supposed to report regularly on their progress in executing the provisions of the declaration. In addition, governments were urged in 1962 to accede to a convention regulating minimum age for, and consent to, marriage. In 1979, the General Assembly adopted the convention on the elimination of all forms of discrimination against women.

Another topic that has involved much activity by the General Assembly relates to the protection of rights of individual persons who are subject to arrest or detention. It supplemented long-standing treaty law by adopting a new convention on the abolition of slavery, the slave trade, and practices similar to slavery in 1956. In 1959, it adopted a declaration on the rights of the child, which was followed in 1988, by a binding convention on that subject. The declaration against torture or cruel, inhuman or degrading treatment or punishment, adopted in 1975, was also followed in 1984 by a binding convention. In 1979, the General Assembly adopted an eight-article code of conduct for law-enforcement officials and, in 1981, a declaration on the elimination of all forms of intolerance and of discrimination based on religion or belief. More broadly, the notion of a high commissioner for human rights, whose duties would include intervention on behalf of individuals whose rights were threatened, has been discussed in much detail but remains too controversial to win majority support. It has been argued by some that the activities of the UN thematic and country rapporteurs, taken together, cover a terrain that is already much wider than presumably would ever be allotted to a high commissioner.

The General Assembly has also increasingly emphasized the importance of applying a more structural approach to the solution of the human rights problem. In addition to the struggle against violations of human rights, ways should be found to prevent such violations. In 1977, the Assembly adopted, for instance, a resolution on alternative approaches and ways and means for improving effective enjoyment of human rights and fundamental freedoms. The United Nations has also set up a training programme in human rights in which young academics from all over the world participate. A number of studies has been undertaken, with an emphasis on the principle of non-discrimination. Through its 'Advisory Services' programme, the UN Centre for Human Rights in Geneva organizes global and regional seminars and courses on human rights. Governments, at their request, obtain the advice of the Centre. Offending governments, such as that of Guatemala, may invite the visit by an expert under the Advisory Services Programme, rather than having a special rapporteur visit them.

Since 1968, there has been a Special Committee to Investigate Israeli Practices Affecting the Human Rights of the Population of the Occupied Territories. It meets at Geneva and New York and holds hearings in cities of states close to the occupied territories that have concentrations of Palestinian refugees. Israel has so far rejected the General Assembly's request that it permit the Committee to visit the occupied territories to make on-the-spot investigations. Israel has also repeatedly been criticized by non-governmental organizations for excessive use of force by law-enforcement officers and for holding Palestinians in administrative detention without charge or trial. While there is reason for serious concern about these human rights violations, the amount of attention paid to such abuses by Israel by UN organs, as compared to alleged violations in other countries, would seem to be motivated not only by the quantity or nature of the abuses.

In addition to the instruments and activities mentioned so far, a great many recommendations and conventions bearing on human rights have been adopted by specialized agencies in the UN system. ILO and UNESCO have been especially active. Some of the more important conventions are the following:

● freedom of association and protection of the right to organize (ILO, 1948);
● equal remuneration (for men and women for work of equal value) (ILO, 1951);
● abolition of forced labour (ILO, 1957);
● discrimination in respect of employment and occupation (ILO, 1958);
● discrimination in education (UNESCO, 1960);
● employment policy (ILO, 1966);
● protection of workers' representatives (ILO, 1971);
● protection of the right to organize and procedures for determining conditions of employment in the public service (ILO, 1978);
● right to self-determination of indigenous peoples (ILO, 1957, 1989).

These conventions also involve supervision of national behaviour by relevant international organizations and, especially in the case of the ILO, violations can lead to embarrassing publicity and even painful sanctions.

APARTHEID

With the release of Nelson Mandela, the leader of the African National Congress – the main opposition group in South Africa – in 1990, after 27 years of imprisonment, and with the beginning of serious talks between the South African Government and the ANC, the racial and political situation in South Africa was subject to a change of major proportion. Whatever uncertainties remained, it seemed certain that South Africa was undergoing deep social changes.

UN bodies have spent more effort dealing with the policy of apartheid in South Africa than with any other issue of human rights. During most of its sessions since 1946, when India first lodged a complaint about discriminatory legislation directed against South Africans of Indian origin, the General Assembly has made pronouncements on the issue. It has increasingly become a concern of the specialized agencies as well. Obviously related to the General Assembly's opposition to racial discrimination generally, apartheid attracts focused international attention, because it has stood as the only deliberately created, legally based system of racial discrimination in the world.

Apartheid as such has figured on the UN agenda since 1952, following the legal codification of older South African practices of discrimination and their extension in accordance with the doctrines of the government formed by the whites-only National Party after its electoral victory in 1948. Attempts to change the apartheid system have run the gamut of UN methods, ranging from diplomacy and legal steps to coercive programmes. Until very recently, South Africa has not wavered from its resolute defence of the system as its own affair and no one else's, and as ultimately beneficial to all of its people.

At first, the General Assembly sought to deal with complaints against South Africa by diplomatic negotiations. It urged India and South Africa to negotiate. It set up a commission of good offices and another committee to study the matter and report to the General Assembly in 1952. South Africa rejected these approaches, claiming that its racial affairs were a domestic matter under Article 2 (7) of the UN Charter.

The General Assembly reacted with annual resolutions of increasingly strident character. It has strongly condemned South African behaviour and defined apartheid as 'a crime against humanity'. It has urged other UN organs to exclude South Africa from international meetings and conferences. In fact, since 1979, the South African delegation has been excluded from the General Assembly on the grounds that its credentials are invalid. South Africa has complained that this action and others represent the application of a double standard that discriminates against it. The General Assembly has denounced efforts to turn the all-black 'homelands', which South Africa claims are the centres of several cultural groups that make up the majority of its population, into independent states. Governments, the Assembly has insisted, should break off all cultural, educational, scientific and sporting contacts with South Africa. Rather, support should be given to the suppressed South African blacks and to liberation movements.

Since 1962, UN efforts have been sparked by a Special Committee against Apartheid, supported by a Centre against Apartheid in the UN Secretariat. The Commission on Human Rights, certain specialized agencies, and non-governmental organizations also lend their aid to the Special Committee. It carries out such tasks as monitoring arms trade, bank loans and foreign investments in South Africa, and holding hearings on nuclear collaboration with South Africa and its treatment of political prisoners.

Legal approaches are represented by the General Assembly's adoption of an international convention on the suppression and punishment of the crime of apartheid (1973) and a convention against apartheid in sport (1985). In mid-1992, these conventions had been ratified by 91 and 54 states, respectively. States party to the convention against the crime of apartheid undertake to adopt legislative and other measures to suppress this crime and to bring to trial in national courts or an international tribunal persons charged with such acts. States party to the sports convention are obliged to take all possible measures to prevent sporting contacts with a country practising apartheid and to act to secure the expulsion of such countries from international and regional sports bodies.

The General Assembly has demanded by large majorities that South Africa be coerced into adopting a different racial policy. The Assembly has repeatedly asked the Security Council to deal with apartheid as a threat to international peace and security and to take necessary measures, including sanctions, to force South Africa to adhere to international standards. It has also asked the Security Council to consider the expulsion of South Africa. These demands have been reiterated in lengthy texts adopted each autumn. They usually receive large majorities but are not supported by the major Western powers, the United States and Great Britain, that would have to bear the brunt of any heavy coercive measures. Yet, without their collaboration, these resolutions took on the tone of an annual ritual rather than a serious effort to build up effective leverage on South African violations of human rights.

At the same time, the Security Council showed mounting sensitivity to the disturbances and friction caused in the southern African region by policies of apartheid and supporting actions by South Africa. The Sharpeville incident, in which South African police killed 67 and wounded 186 blacks, propelled apartheid into the Security Council in 1960. Accepting part of the argument so stridently put forward by the General Assembly, the Security Council concluded that the situation in South Africa, if unchanged, might endanger international peace and security. It called on South Africa to end apartheid and instructed the Secretary-General, in consultation with the South African government, to take adequate measures to uphold the purposes and principles of the UN Charter. A visit by Secretary-General Hammarskjöld in January 1961, however, produced no result.

Two years later, the Security Council called for a voluntary arms embargo, no unimportant step, as the United States and Great Britain acceded to it. Eventually, the Security Council decided on a mandatory arms embargo that prohibited any state from providing South Africa with arms and military equipment for police use. It also banned cooperation with South Africa in nuclear development. Then, after the turbulent uprising in 1976 in the black township of Soweto, the Security Council reacted to the death of several hundred people by condemning the South African government and calling on it to end apartheid because of its effects on peace.

Since then, the Security Council has taken up South African raids on the neighbouring countries, including Lesotho, Mozambique and Angola, issuing condemnations and warnings. But the Council has never adopted proposals for stronger economic and military sanctions, because the Western countries decline to support such actions. The Soviet Union has verbally supported coercion, but it never made concrete commitments, although it gave substantial covert aid to the liberation movements. A principal source of investment in South Africa, Britain has vacillated on arms embargos as its government changed political colour. So, too, the United States approach has varied between heavy pressure such as the sanctions bill passed by the US Congress, and rather gentle negotiating tactics. In general, the major Western powers have declined to sell arms that would be useful in consolidating apartheid, but precisely which arms and materials has not been spelled out.

Aside from its legal objections under Article 2 (7), South Africa has built up its military forces throughout the years. It has stockpiled large quantities of oil and invested a great deal in creating a capable armaments industry. It recently admitted to possessing nuclear capacity. Between 1966 and 1989 South Africa made lightning military raids into the surrounding territories. However, these ended when a United States-sponsored agreement was reached in 1989, under which Cuban soldiers were withdrawn from Angola, and South Africa promised to grant independence to the territory of Namibia (see Chapter 6).

The situation inside South Africa in mid-1993 remained fluid. Although parts of the apartheid system have been removed, it remained to be seen whether this would lead to a peaceful changeover to black majority rule – the implicit or explicit aim expressed in most UN resolutions. Extreme conservatives among South African whites have announced their determination to oppose such a change with all means at their disposal.

CONCLUSIONS

Given the controversial, not to say revolutionary, aims of the human rights activities of the United Nations, it is understandable that no simple assessment of what has been done can be given. In terms of the goals set out in the UN Charter and elaborated over the years, the human rights programmes have had both successes and failures.

The most positive result of the human rights programmes is undoubtedly the creation of an international standard for the treatment of human beings all over the world. Common criteria now exist for judging whether human beings enjoy fundamental human rights. The United Nations can claim the accomplishment of making the norms sufficiently concrete so that it is possible to determine where and when they are violated. All governments accept human rights norms in principle, if not in practice. By paying at least lip-service to this idea, they also implicitly accept the assumption that a limited world community exists. Moreover, non-governmental organizations rely on these very norms to take governments to task and remind them of whatever moral or legal obligations they have assumed.

A second positive outcome can be demonstrated in the remarkable increase in information that UN organs collect and distribute on the performance by states in the field of human rights. A vast reporting network includes the Commission on Human Rights, its special rapporteurs, various committees, some of the specialized agencies, the member states themselves in their national reports, and such publications as the *Yearbook on Human Rights*, containing new national legislation. These efforts are again supplemented by extensive information-gathering on the part of non-governmental organizations.

Both the process of creating norms and the monitoring of the performance of states have encouraged the active participation of non-governmental organizations, such as Amnesty International, the International Commission of Jurists, and the various 'watch' committees. They constantly demand more effective enforcement and protection of human rights. They attempt to influence the United Nations directly through persuasion and indirectly through the member governments.

An example of successful collaboration between one such organization, Amnesty International, and the UN system, can be found in the adoption by the General Assembly in 1984 of the convention against torture and other cruel, inhuman or degrading treatment or punishment. This convention condemns acts of torture as a denial of fundamental rights and of the purposes of the UN, and urges states to take measures against such violations. Similarly, relief organizations have been active partners of UNHCR in its efforts to succour those who flee from massive denial of their rights. These private organizations, such as Catholic Relief Services or the International Rescue Committee, have helped to spread consciousness of the international norms for human rights.

Yet the performance of the United Nations in supervising and controlling the actual performance of states in the human rights field must be accounted as much less positive than the formulation of norms. Even when violations of human rights can be pinpointed as to time and place, this does not necessarily ensure that UN organs will deal with them in an objective manner. Some of the worst offenders in the field of human rights are members of the Commission on Human Rights, where their representatives make pious statements. Whether or not a case will be considered by a UN organ depends more on political factors than on the nature of the alleged violation. The apartheid policies of South Africa or human rights violations by the Israeli forces in the Occupied Territories unfailingly figure highly on the agenda, while at the same time dramatic violations taking place in such countries as China or Iraq remain unchecked by UN action. Only after Idi Amin was removed from power in Uganda were his government's murderous transgressions of human rights norms publicly taken up in UN forums. The same is true of the massive-scale killings by the regime of Pol Pot in Cambodia. Within the Commission on Human Rights, debates have a predominantly political character, as governments try to defend their behaviour and accuse others of wickedness. In fact, complaints about violations of human rights often become the vehicle for presenting political points of view. It is not completely without reason that some observers have accused the United Nations of applying a double standard.

The United Nations can, moreover, neither effectively punish nor reward governments for their degree of compliance with human rights standards. Incentives to secure compliance are, in fact, practically unavailable. The Security Council has the right to act only when it is convinced that a violation of human rights threatens international peace and security. It stated, however, in 1991, in resolution 688, relating to the repression of the Kurdish population in Iraq that 'the consequences ... threaten international peace and security'. This was widely interpreted as linking human rights violations with the possibility of action by the Security Council. Not all violations in fact can clearly be considered as endangering the peace. Furthermore, enforcement action under Chapter VII of the Charter may be too heavy an instrument to be appropriate, and in any case, the powers that command the veto in the Council have shown much reluctance to undertake sanctions. Voluntary sanctions remain an option, but these have never worked well. Finally, enforcement actions may bear more heavily on those who already suffer than on those who cause the difficulties. For example, severe economic sanctions against South Africa would seriously affect the majority population of blacks while whites might be better able to protect themselves. Nevertheless, African nationalists strongly favoured sanctions for want of more effective means for ending apartheid.

Despite the difficulty of securing a high level of compliance with human rights norms, the importance of UN activities in this field should not be underestimated. The ideas on which such work are based may take on a life of their own, just as did the French Declaration on the Rights of Man and the US Declaration of Independence. They matured over decades, slowly entered law and practice, and eventually became the actual limit on the behaviour of governments. A similar development should not be excluded for the human rights norms developed within the framework of the United Nations.

6 From Colonialism to Independence

Most of the present members of the United Nations are former colonies that gained political independence through direct or indirect involvement of the United Nations. In 1945, more than 750 million people lived in non-self-governing territories of various kinds: by 1990, after Namibia gained its independence in a world that had undergone rapid growth of its population, fewer than two million lived in the remaining 18 dependent territories.

At its 1988 session, the General Assembly declared the 1990s the International Decade for the Eradication of Colonialism. It seems likely that this goal, in the sense of overseas territories gaining their independence from their West European administrators, will be met before the beginning of the twenty-first century. Perhaps the colonies would have gained their independence during the past 45 years in any case, but UN involvement helped to keep the process relatively peaceful and maintain its explicit legitimacy.

In a sense, the replacement of dependent relationships between metropolitan lands and overseas territories began with the League of Nations. Then, for the first time in history, an international institution had to oversee changes in the colonial system. The League operated a mandates system to deal with colonies that had been detached from Germany and Turkey as a result of the First World War. Divided into three classes, according to the degree of international supervision, the territories were put under the administration of League members as a 'sacred trust of civilization'. Class A mandates, including Palestine, Iraq, Syria and Lebanon, were taken from Turkey: they were expected to gain independence before long. Class B mandates, comprising former German territories in East and West Central Africa, were handed over to mandatory states for direct administration. The remaining class C mandates, including German holdings in Southwest Africa (the present Namibia) and islands in the Pacific Ocean, were administered by the mandatory powers as integral parts of their own possessions. Under special agreements covering the administration of each territory, the mandatory powers reported periodically to the League Council, which set up a Permanent Mandates Commission. Its members were independent experts who examined the reports. This commission at least encouraged clear reporting on the progress, or lack of it, in the territories and sometimes succeeded in influencing the administrators to provide better conditions for the inhabitants.

Despite this modest step towards international responsibility for the non-self-governing territories, the purview of the League of Nations was strictly limited to the colonies of the defeated. The future of the colonial empires held after the First World War by the victors remained their business. Even during the Second World War, many leaders regarded as totally unacceptable the idea that some international supervision should apply to all colonies. During the early stages of drafting the UN Charter, the British government in particular stoutly opposed the idea that the new organization should deal with the future of colonies. Prime Minister Winston Churchill exclaimed that he would never consent to the 'fumbling fingers' of 40 or 50 governments prying into the life of the British Empire. He had not become prime minister, he insisted, for the purpose of presiding over the dissolution of the empire.

Nevertheless, the spirit of the times proved contrary to the colonial empires. The UN Charter sets out self-determination of peoples as a principle [Article 2 (1)]. Other sections seek to promote the welfare of non-self-governing people and to move the former League of Nations mandates along to eventual independence [Chapters XI and XII]. In 1945, however, few people envisaged the pace at which the colonial empires were to be almost dissolved in a little over two decades.

DECLARATION ON NON-SELF-GOVERNING TERRITORIES

At the insistence of the United States and the Soviet Union, the San Francisco Conference inserted a 'declaration regarding non-self-governing territories' into the UN Charter as Chapter XI. This declaration laid on administering states the duty of ensuring the political, economic and social advancement of the territories they administered. Moreover, the administering powers were enjoined to develop self-government, to take due account of the political aspirations of the people, and to assist them in the progressive development of their free political institutions. An effort to include political data in the reports was turned down. This was, then, not an actual declaration of independence: the goal was self-government.

THE TRUSTEESHIP SYSTEM

The UN Trusteeship System took over from the League of Nations mandate system, assuming responsibility for the remaining territories that had not reached independence. To the former League mandates were added colonies taken from Italy and Japan after the Second World War. States also had the right to place other territories under the supervision of the system, but none were added by this means. In practice, the system became a stepping-stone to independence. Before that time, it was intended to promote the political, economic, social, and educational advancement of the inhabitants of the trust territories. Beyond the aims of the League system, the new one also was charged with progressive development toward self-government or independence, as appropriate to the situation in the lands, based on the freely-expressed wishes of the people concerned.

In the postwar period, the following former trust territories gained independence: British and French Togoland; British and French Cameroons; Somaliland; Tanganyika; Ruanda-Urundi; Western Samoa; Nauru; and New Guinea. By 1992, only one trust territory, the US-administered trust territory of the Pacific Islands, remained. In 1986, the Trusteeship Council had recommended that the trusteeship agreement be terminated on the entry into force of the Compacts of Free Association for the Marshall Islands, Palau, and the Federated States of Micronesia and the Commonwealth Covenant for the Northern Mariana Islands. Lacking the required three-quarters majority among the Palaun population, the compacts of free association with Palau have not yet entered into force.

Supervision over ordinary trust territories was exercised by the Trusteeship Council, which reported ultimately to the General Assembly. Its reports on the strategic trust territories, all administered by the United States, go to the Security Council.

Two of the former mandated territories of the days of the League of Nations never became part of the Trusteeship System. The British mandate of Palestine was excluded because of the dispute between the Jewish and Arab populations that eventuated in the establishment of Israel in 1948. The other territory, Southwest Africa, was long administered by South Africa as an integral part of its territory. It remained the subject of continuing dispute between that country and the United Nations until it finally was granted independence in 1990 as the state of Namibia (see below).

Because the ordinary trust territories reached independence, the role of the Trusteeship Council as a supervisory organ is now almost a thing of the past. It used to consist of an equal number of administering and non-administering powers, always including the permanent members of the Security Council. It considered reports submitted by the administering states, accepted and examined petitions from the inhabitants of the trust territories, and decided on whether progress had been made toward the goals of the system. It sent missions to the territories, which observed the situation and interviewed officials and inhabitants about every three years.

DECLARATION ON GRANTING OF INDEPENDENCE

Altogether, 30 former non-self-governing and trust territories became independent between 1945 and 1960. Yet, the African and Asian states became increasingly impatient with regard to setting dates for the independence of the remaining territories. They turned their attitudes into action when the General Assembly in 1960 adopted a 'Declaration on the Granting of Independence to Colonial Countries and People' [Resolution 1514 (XV)]. This document proclaimed the need to end colonialism quickly. It claimed that alien subjugation of a people denied human rights and violated the UN Charter. It demanded immediate steps to tranfer power to the people of non-self-governing territories on the basis of the right to self-determination. It also directed its fire against any attempt to disrupt the national unity of the territories, by which was meant a policy of 'divide and rule' by colonial powers.

THE SPECIAL COMMITTEE ON DECOLONIZATION

The declaration on decolonization provided a framework for closer attention by the General Assembly to progress towards an end to alien subjugation of peoples. A body whose long title – Special Committee on the Situation with Regard to the Implementation of the Declaration on the Granting of Independence to Colonial Countries and Peoples – led to its being called the Committee of 24 for the number of its members, was set up to examine the implementation of the declaration on decolonization. It has become the main body concerned with self-determination and still busies itself with the few remaining non-self-governing areas.

From the beginning, non-administering governments have dominated the Committee of 24. Administering powers, showered with criticism, gradually left the body, increasing its anti-colonial tone. Since 1971, not one administering state has belonged to the Committee of 24. As the number of dependent territories declined, the demeanour of the committee and the tone of its debates have increasingly sharpened. It took an especially hard line on the last remaining major colonial areas, such as Rhodesia, the Portuguese

colonies in Africa, and Namibia. It also has demanded full independence
for the dozens of dependent islands and archipelagos in many parts of the
world, no matter how small their territories or how benign their governors.

To carry out its tasks, the Committee of 24 has taken some cues from
the provisions of the trusteeship system and added some of its own
inventions. It receives petitions and offers forums to people from the non-
self-governing territories. It tries to send visiting missions to the
territories, but the administering authorities do not always allow them to
enter. The committee issues periodic reports and makes recommendations
to the administering states. These recommendations sometimes stridently
criticize administering governments and demand the adoption of specific
methods that always are intended to fix a date for independence. For the
most part, the committee has a tense relationship with the administrators.
They regard some of its recommendations as ignorant meddling and think
of its meetings in many parts of the world as a travelling circus. But it is
also hard to deny that the committee includes matters that influence the
maintenance of peace. This has been the case with the last remnants of
colonialism in southern Africa, especially Namibia.

NAMIBIA

The year 1990 finally brought a successful end to 44 years of pressure by
the United Nations to achieve independence for the former German colony
of Southwest Africa, more recently called Namibia. A Class C mandated
territory, administered by South Africa under the League of Nations, it has
figured on the UN agenda since 1946, when the General Assembly
rejected the mandatory's request to incorporate the territory. The positions
taken subsequently by South Africa and the majority of the General
Assembly led to the use of almost every possible means of pacific
settlement of disputes. The fierceness of the General Assembly's position
can be explained by the resentment that the South African policy of
apartheid has caused in most of the world.

When the General Assembly declined in 1946 to allow South Africa
simply to make Southwest Africa (which came to be called by the
nationalist name of Namibia) part of its realm, the government of General
Jan Christian Smuts, a founder of both the League of Nations and the
United Nations, was dealt a heavy blow. The Smuts government re-
nounced plans for annexation but declared it would administer the territory
in the spirit of the mandate from the League. At the same time, it rejected
requests from the General Assembly that Namibia be made a trust

territory. The Nationalist government of David Malan, who took over from Smuts in 1948, announced that the mandate had ended with the demise of the League and that the United Nations had no authority in the matter; it ceased reporting to the United Nations. As the new government began to install features of the apartheid system in Southwest Africa, the two issues were inseparably joined from that point onwards.

Initial responses in the United Nations sought to settle the dispute by judicial means. The General Assembly requested an advisory opinion by the International Court of Justice as to South African obligations. The court reported in 1950 that South Africa could not arbitrarily change the status of Namibia without UN consent and that it must continue to report on the territory. But South Africa had no legal obligation to conclude a trusteeship agreement. The General Assembly concurred with the advisory opinion; it was rejected by the South African government. In subsequent years, the UN tried in vain to persuade South Africa to agree to a trusteeship for Namibia.

An important legal step began in 1960, when Ethiopia and Liberia, both former members of the League of Nations, brought a suit against South Africa in the ICJ. The two governments claimed that South Africa had failed to carry out its obligations under the League mandate, complaining among other things that it violated the human rights of the inhabitants. Somewhat to the surprise of many observers, South Africa appeared in court to answer the charges, thus implicitly acknowledging that it would be bound by the decision. After long consideration and argument on the merits of the case, the court issued a divided opinion that held that the two complainants could not be considered to have established a legal right to bring a case with respect to their claims. Therefore, the court could not pass judgement and dismissed the case. The result was disillusionment among Third World countries with respect to the ICJ. A consequent attempt to heighten political pressure through the General Assembly began.

Political means to free Namibia from South African rule had already started in the General Assembly. In 1961, by a large majority, it proclaimed the inalienable right of the people of Namibia to independence and national sovereignty. As it has done repeatedly since then, the General Assembly set the following goals for the territory: repeal of apartheid laws; preparation as soon as possible of general elections for a territorial legislature based on universal suffrage; UN supervision for such elections; and preparation, with advice and assistance of the resulting government, for independence. But South Africa remained unmoved.

The General Assembly tried to organize voluntary coercive measures against South Africa. Since 1963, it and the Committee of 24 have repeatedly urged UN members not to supply South Africa with arms, military equipment, oil and oil products or do anything that would hamper the application of resolutions on Namibia. Some of the most influential governments have complied in significant ways with these recommendations. In the face of this pressure, about which the South African government expressed resentment, that government acted in Namibia contrary to the spirit and letter of the wishes of the UN majority. In 1964, it decided in principle to apply the system of 'homelands' for each ethnic group of blacks in the territory and in other respects it applied the measures of racial separation used in South Africa itself. Many governments regarded this policy as openly provocative at a time when the rest of Africa was moving toward independence and the elimination of racial discrimination in society.

The next strategem employed by the General Assembly relied on its powers as a rule-maker at the international level. It decided in 1963 to terminate the League of Nations mandate for Southwest Africa on the grounds that South Africa had failed to fulfil its obligations there. The United Nations assumed direct responsibility for Namibia. It organized an 11-member UN Council for Southwest Africa to administer the territory until it became independent. The new council was instructed to do everything in its power to bring the territory to independence by 1968 through discussions with the South African authorities. Those authorities flatly refused any contact. Thereupon, the General Assembly in 1967 called upon South Africa to withdraw its military and police from the territory and, in April 1968, the Council for Southwest Africa (thenceforth to be called Namibia) tried unsuccessfully to enter the territory.

Various kinds of pressures exerted by UN bodies, including a visit by Secretary-General Waldheim in 1973, were to no avail. The General Assembly then decided that the Southwest African People's Organization (SWAPO) was the authentic representative of the Namibian people and supported its efforts to strengthen national unity. Five years later, in 1978, the General Assembly met in special session to adopt a declaration and programme of action on national independence for Namibia. This session expressed full support for the armed liberation struggle led by SWAPO and insisted that any negotiated settlement would have both to be agreed to by the national liberation group and conform to the resolutions of the United Nations. Thus, by 1978, the United Nations had tried diplomacy, law, voluntary sanctions, and support of a guerrilla movement to set Namibia free from South Africa.

Another effort that in the end turned out to be successful began in 1978, when discussions took place on the future of Namibia among the five Western members of the Security Council – then Canada, France, the

Federal Republic of Germany, the United Kingdom and the United States. Consulting SWAPO and the governments of states bordering South Africa, they developed a programme based on free elections for the whole of Namibia as one political entity. In July 1978, the Security Council noted their proposal, thus giving it legitimacy [Security Council resolution 435]. The plan called for the appointment of a representative of the Secretary-General in the territory for a transitional period. The United Nations would supervise and control elections there and guard tranquillity with a peacekeeping force. The South African government agreed to the plan in 1978. It envisaged a UN Transition Assistance Group (UNTAG) consisting of military and civilian personnel.

Disputes soon arose over the details of the plan, with South Africa insisting that it had not agreed to permit SWAPO bases in Namibia. Furthermore, with the backing of the United States, South Africa made withdrawal of Cuban troops from Angola a condition for its cooperation. A visit by Secretary-General Pérez de Cuéllar in 1983 left the situation unchanged, although South Africa began to raid Angolan bases of SWAPO and gave support to UNITA, a dissident movement inside Angola.

Over the years, the fight in Angola turned out to be a heavy military burden for South Africa. Its forces got bogged down in engagements with SWAPO guerrilla fighters who avoided direct battle contact with the technically superior South African military. It never became quite clear whether the South Africans planned an outright attack on Angola, but in that event they would have had to engage the 50 000 well-trained Cuban forces stationed in that country. Also the financial aspects of the war became a substantial cost to the South African economy. Finally, the brunt of the war effort was carried by the relatively small white South African population, numbering not more than five million people.

These factors may help to explain why South Africa showed itself willing in 1988 to enter into serious negotiations about Namibian independence. At the initiative of the United States, meetings were held of representatives of Angola, Cuba, South Africa and the United States. These finally resulted in an agreement, signed in New York on 22 December 1988. It provided for South African withdrawal from Namibia and independence in accordance with Resolution 435 as well as the withdrawal of the Cuban military from Angola. The latter factor – linking Namibian independence to Cuban withdrawal, though never explicitly mentioned in UN resolutions – was clearly important in obtaining South African consent to Namibian independence. An even more important background factor was the improved United States-Soviet relations, which opened the way to having the 'Cuban factor' included in the agreement.

After some initial dispute about the precise size of the UN contingent to oversee the transition to independence, agreement was reached on an UNTAG force numbering 4650 men, plus some 600 policemen and nearly 1000 civilians and UN personnel. It was the largest UN force since the Congo operation. During 1989 and part of the following year, UNTAG fulfilled a successful function in overseeing the holding of the first free elections in Namibia, the repatriation of an estimated 80 000 refugees, and the maintenance of law and order. Elections were held in November 1989, which resulted in clear victory for Sam Nujoma's SWAPO movement. In April 1990, Namibia gained formal independence and shortly thereafter it was admitted as the 160th member of the United Nations.

The case of Namibia illustrates both the weakness and the strength of the United Nations in managing political change. Though in the end the goal desired by the international community – Namibian independence – was reached, this was only marginally due to activities of the UN. Forty-two years of UN dealing with the future of Namibia produced few concrete results, although it kept the issue on the international agenda. The crucial breakthrough in the negotiations occurred outside the formal UN process in the context of the improved relations between the United States and the Soviet Union. Once agreement in principle had been reached, the United Nations, through UNTAG, provided a useful channel to help to carry out the agreement.

THE IMPOSITION OF ECONOMIC SANCTIONS

The case of Rhodesia/Zimbabwe deserves to be recalled, not merely as an instance of decolonization, but also because the Security Council for the first time in UN history ordered limited economic sanctions under Chapter VII of the UN Charter. This was in reaction to the Unilateral Declaration of Independence (UDI) from the United Kingdom, the formal sovereign, proclaimed the year before by the white minority government of Ian Smith.

The Security Council characterized the situation in Rhodesia as a threat to peace, requiring correction. When limited sanctions failed to dislodge the Smith government, the Council extended them in 1968, to include all exports and imports, except for educational and medical supplies and, in special circumstances, foodstuffs. Most members of the United Nations complied with the order of the Security Council, except for Portuguese Mozambique and South Africa, both of which bordered Rhodesia. Moreover, traders in Western countries evaded the boycotts, sometimes by putting false labels on Rhodesian tobacco, the most lucrative export.

The Committee of 24 and the General Assembly repeatedly urged the Security Council to strengthen the sanctions system by extending it to the two non-complying regimes. The Council refused to do so or to employ military means, for political reasons and because of the great cost and the huge effort of blockading the coastlines and scattered ports of the two territories that gave access to the sea to landlocked Rhodesia.

The sanctions against Rhodesia exacted costs from the white minority government. But it endured for 18 years and contrived to evade some of the effect of the boycotts. Its own high-cost industry thrived, in trying to replace missing imports. The non-compliance and half-hearted measures on the part of some UN members hardly contributed to the prestige of the Security Council. The establishment of independent Zimbabwe in 1979, under a government with a majority of black ministers, was more due to the success of the struggle of black guerrilla fighters than to that of UN-imposed economic sanctions.

REMAINING COLONIAL ISSUES

One of the remaining colonial issues is the territory of Western Sahara, a former Spanish colony on the west coast of Africa. The former Spanish colonial administrator left long ago, but the future of the territory has remained in dispute between the Kingdom of Morocco on the one hand, and the Polisario movement, supported by Algeria, on the other. Polisario claims independence for the territory, which is largely held by the Moroccan army. Sporadic fighting has not helped to solve the issue. In 1988, the Security Council passed a resolution which led to the appointment of a special UN representative for Western Sahara. Efforts to have the parties start negotiations for establishing a ceasefire and holding a referendum on self-determination have so far not been successful.

In the case of the Falkland Islands (Malvinas), the question of whether it is a colonial issue, is itself a matter of dispute. The islands have been governed by the United Kingdom since 1833, but Argentina claims that they are part of its national territory. The United Kingdom placed the islands on the United Nations' list of Non-Self-Governing Territories in 1946, while Argentina expressed its reservations regarding sovereignty. At the invitation of the Committee of 24, negotiations took place between 1965 and 1982 between the United Kingdom and Argentina, which, however, did not solve the matter of sovereignty.

Argentinian armed forces invaded and occupied the islands in April 1982. The Security Council demanded an immediate end to the hostilities, the immediate withdrawal of Argentine forces, and urged that negotiations take place in order to find a diplomatic solution to the dispute. The Secretary-General was asked to offer his good offices, but in the end a military confrontation led to the defeat of Argentina. The British Government has taken the position that the wishes of the two thousand inhabitants, mainly of British descent, who want to retain their ties to the United Kingdom, should prevail. The General Assembly has repeatedly urged Argentina and the United Kingdom to resume direct negotiations on all aspects of the future of the islands.

The case of Gibraltar, which is also governed by the United Kingdom, is somewhat similar to that of the Falkland Islands, but Spain has been less insistent in recent years in its demand for transfer of sovereignty.

East Timor, a former Portuguese possession, was annexed by Indonesia in 1976. In this case, the major problem is the allegation of widespread human rights abuses by the Indonesian armed forces. The UN still regards Portugal as the administering power in East Timor. The General Assembly has asked Indonesia and Portugal to resume talks under UN auspices.

The General Assembly continues to pay attention to the future of six territories administered by the United Kingdom: Anguilla, the Cayman Islands, Montserrat, Bermuda, the Turks and Caicos Islands, and the British Virgin Islands. It has also adopted resolutions on the territory of New Caledonia in the western Pacific Ocean, in response to disturbances that have taken place on that island, which is formally part of metropolitan France. With regard to Guam, a territory held by the United States, the General Assembly has declared that the military bases on the island could become an impediment to decolonization.

CONCLUSIONS

The United Nations has been a major channel through which independence for former colonial territories has been effected. In many cases, such as Indonesia, Libya, Algeria, Angola, Mozambique and Guinea Bissau, the role of the UN has been significant in facilitating the decolonization process. As the decolonization process in its classic sense has been virtually completed, most of this is now a matter of history.

Yet the remaining situations that have colonial overtones can cause international concern, as in the cases of the Falkland Islands and New Caledonia. The answer to the question of 'what constitutes a nation' is important for the way in which the struggle for national self-determination presents itself. Many ethnic minorities view themselves as actual or potential nations. Illustrations are offered by secessions, such as Biafra, which tried unsuccessfully to secede from Nigeria in 1967, and Bangladesh which broke off from Pakistan in 1971. More recently, ethnic minorities in such diverse countries as Ethiopia, Sudan, the Soviet Union, Yugoslavia, India (Sikhs), Spain (Basques), Turkey and Iraq (Kurds) and the Palestinians have based their claims for independence on the right to self-determination.

In the 1990s, the fight for national self-determination is likely to continue in a form somewhat different from that of earlier years. As there are only a few overseas territories still governed by Western European or North American rulers, the issue of self-determination is increasingly faced by governments from inside their own territories. Most governments are aware of this danger to the territorial integrity of their states. The classic form of colonialism may be over by the end of this century, but a related, new form has developed: the actual or perceived oppression of ethnic minorities. This may well become one of the dominant problems the world is going to face toward the end of the century.

7 Cooperation for Economic and Social Progress

In the UN system, far more time, effort and money go into cooperation to promote economic and social progress than into any other endeavour. More than 80 per cent of the personnel of the global agencies, including the United Nations itself, work on issues concerning a higher level of general welfare for the world's people. A huge list of programmes covers practically every human preoccupation, from the condition of the world environment, down to better methods of drying dishes in outdoor tropical kitchens. The vast scope of these programmes has generated an organizational tangle so complex that, some observers have concluded, it is beyond either understanding or management. Yet all of it is intended to contribute, and arguably to some extent does, to 'the creation of conditions of stability and well-being which are necessary for peaceful and friendly relations among nations...' [Art. 55, UN Charter]. If so, its slow course contrasts sharply with the crisis atmosphere of the conflicts taken up in the Security Council, but the issues may be no less important to the long-run future of mankind.

The UN system approaches economic and social problems through four main avenues:

- collection and distribution of information about the economic and social situation in the world;
- the adoption of non-binding resolutions, declarations, and recommendations to guide member states in their policies so that the results of cooperation may be maximized;
- the establishment of practical programmes of assistance to governments and through them to their people;
- the negotiation of binding international conventions or agreements, such as the 1988 UN Convention against Illicit Traffic in Narcotic Drugs and Psychotropic Substances.

The United Nations has devoted much effort to the elaboration of operational programmes for economic development. The UN system mounted nearly 20 000 development projects, aside from loans, during 1988. Reaching to more than 130 countries, these programmes, like so much that the United Nations system undertakes, assist governments and only occasionally reach without intermediaries to the people who are intended ultimately to benefit. At the same time, they involve commitments of money, people's work, and hope on a scale never before reached by international agencies.

GLOBAL CONFERENCES

Although the notion of international conferences to deal with common problems can be traced back at least to the public international unions of the nineteenth century (See Chapter 1), as well as to smaller networks of scientific and intellectual collaborators, the technique of concentrating the attention of governments on specific issues gradually became a keener instrument. Most of the gatherings originate in discussions carried on in the normal machinery of the UN system and are then prepared by special committees. The outcome has further added to the conceptual equipment and organizational devices available for global cooperation. A list of some of the most important recent conferences makes clear their salience to contemporary global issues:

1963 – UN Conference on the Application of Science and Technology to Developing Countries, in Geneva.

1964 – the First UN Conference on Trade and Development, which led to the establishment by the General Assembly of UNCTAD as a permanent body, in Geneva.

1971 – the First Conference on Industrial Development, in Vienna.

1972 – conference on the physical environment, which set up the UN Environment Programme, in Stockholm.

1974 – conference on world food issues, which set up the International Fund for Agricultural Development and the World Food Council, in Rome.

1974 – conference on world population issues, in Bucharest.

1976 – conference on human settlements, which established the Nairobi-based Habitat, a UN body, in Vancouver.

1976 – conference on employment, income distribution, social progress, and the international division of labour, in Geneva.

1977 – conference on water, in Mar del Plata, Argentina.

1977 – conference on desertification, in Nairobi.

1978 – conference on primary health care, in Alma Ata, Soviet Union.

1979 – conference on agrarian reform and rural development, in Rome.

1979 – conference on refugees in South East Asia, in Geneva.

1980 – conference on UN decade for women, in Copenhagen.

1981 – conference on the development of the least developed countries, in Paris.

1981 – conference on new and renewable sources of energy, in Nairobi.

1981 – conference on international assistance to refugees in Africa, in Geneva.

1981 – conference on Kampuchea (Cambodia), in Geneva.

1982 – conference on the exploration and peaceful uses of outer space, in Vienna.

1984 – conference on population, in Mexico City.

1987 – conference on cooperation for peaceful uses of nuclear energy, in Geneva.

1987 – conference on drug abuse and illicit traffic, in Vienna.

1990 – summit conference on children, in New York.

1992 – conference on environment and development, in Rio de Janeiro.

1993 – world conference on human rights, in Vienna.

Such meetings end with the adoption of a programme of action, which sets out goals and programmes for both the UN system and member governments. Increasingly, too, such conferences are attended by representatives of transnational, non-governmental organizations. Along with government representatives, they become active publics. Follow-up sessions to assess the results are frequently summoned.

A comprehensive list of conferences would also include those called for the purpose of approving the text of international conventions, such as that on the law of the sea. A related device is the proclamation of years or decades dedicated to a particular cause, such as an international year of youth.

In all cases, the subject matter of the conferences also forms part of the agenda of the General Assembly and often of the Economic and Social Council. While the conference method presumably promotes the awareness of government officials and interested publics and stimulates the work of the UN system, critics suggest that it results in one-time spectacles that raise false expectations and that programmes of action often remain dead letters.

ECONOMIC AND SOCIAL DATA

All the organizations in the UN system collect, process and publish masses of data on the economic and social situation in member countries and in the world generally. They also assist in improving the quality of available material. Generally speaking, data are furnished by member governments. This is especially the case with statistics. It could hardly be otherwise, for a national census, for example, involves great costs and a large organization of collectors. Such costs could not be paid by an intergovernmental organization, even though it may offer technical assistance. Other kinds of data, such as descriptions of natural resources, may result from development projects supported by the UN system. The UN Secretariat, as well as those of other agencies, includes a statistical office to deal with the constant flow of data that reaches it.

Statistical and survey material provide an essential basis for programming any kind of development or discerning trends. Without such information, cooperative programmes would simply be stabs in the dark. Moreover, governments depend on such publications in order to keep track of the context of important transactions, such as international trade in commodities or the transport of goods. The data also provide important raw material for academic analysis of economic processes and social evolution. Increasingly, statistics and other survey materials have been subjected to standardization and, in some instances, correction.

Among the annual surveys published by the United Nations is the World Economic Survey. From their own vantage points, three other agencies of the UN system, the World Bank, the IMF and UNCTAD, publish analogous documents: the Bank's annual World Development Report has been especially influential. The UN produces a Report on the World Social Situation and UNICEF its own analysis of the state of the world's children. UNDP has begun to turn its data into a report on human development. They are complemented by and based on periodical statistical collections, such as the *UN Statistical Yearbook* and the monthly *Statistical Bulletin.* Some of these publications of the UN system unfortunately appear only after considerable delays.

Although the analytical reports may err on the side of caution, they nevertheless sometimes create controversy because one national governmental bureau or another disagrees with their conclusions or has serious doubts about their quality. Further, the fact that governments provide most statistical data published by the UN system means that reporting is sometimes open to manipulation for nationalistic purposes or is based on dubious methodology or deficient collection facilities. Correction of such distortion lies beyond the modest capacity of the UN system. Nevertheless, the publications from the UN system constitute the most reliable global social and economic data.

ECONOMIC DEVELOPMENT AND REDUCTION OF POVERTY

Although, from its earliest conception, the United Nations has been associated with encouraging economic development, this took on new dimensions with a growing realization that not only were large parts of the world's population poor but that they were growing poorer. The incidence and consequences of poverty were underlined repeatedly by the General Assembly and in studies carried out by the secretariats of organizations in the UN system. Although development activities grew rapidly, they have never breached the rather narrow limits imposed on them both by major financial donors and by the conditions under which recipient governments would accept aid. Moreover, neither experts nor governments have been able to mark out highly reliable paths to development. Consequently, both economic theories of development and practical measures still generate controversy.

The activity within the development apparatus put together by the General Assembly reflects changing approaches and time periods. Some of it began early in UN history, while other pieces were added as styles changed. It included a phase of anti-capitalism, favoured by many of the new governments in the former colonies: by the early 1980s, this had much diminished. All of the activity, too, connects in some manner with the broader UN system that includes the World Bank, the IMF, the World Food Programme (WFP), and the specialized agencies. All parts of this system compete for scarce financial, intellectual and other resources. Member governments collaborate with different agencies for specific purposes and are both agents and objects of competition. In no case, however, do member governments receive unrestricted financial grants or supplies: every agency in the UN system insists on defined programmes and projects worked out jointly with the recipient government. Nor does the total cost of development programmes begin to approach in value the military aid programmes that have been offered by various national governments.

TECHNICAL ASSISTANCE

During the Second World War, the main sponsoring governments of the United Nations organized the UN Relief and Rehabilitation Administration (UNRRA) to meet some of the most urgent human needs in the allied territories that were liberated from German and Japanese forces. In order to stimulate war-damaged economies, UNRRA offered advice on reconstruction along with foodstuffs and relief supplies. This advice was a precursor of technical assistance offered later by the United Nations. In fact, as early as 1948, it responded to a request from a government for advice on modernizing its whole economy.

The UNRRA and initial UN experiences joined both governments of poor and rich states. The poor wanted help, while the rich held that a secure world required productive economies. This led to the creation in 1948 of the UN Expanded Programme of Technical Assistance (EPTA) by the General Assembly. By letting contracts for the execution of specific projects to the Specialized Agencies, which already provided some modest help to governments, EPTA was intended to enlarge and coordinate technical assistance in the whole UN system. Its approach sought economic development through upgrading the skills of national governmental service, through better administrative techniques and planning, and through the provision of experts for short periods to help solve specific problems. This programme met at least some of the demands of the poor countries for assistance and fitted well with post-colonial needs.

After unsuccessful exploration of a large capital grant agency, which the rich countries declined to fund, the General Assembly established the (first) UN Special Fund in 1958 to support longer-term projects that were expected to eventuate in investment. An inventory of natural resources or a training scheme for middle managers would be examples of such projects. The organization was merged with EPTA by the General Assembly in 1965 to form the UN Development Programme (UNDP) which is still a principal UN operational agency for development. It relies on voluntary contributions from member governments and, like its forerunners, engages other organizations in the UN system and the UN Secretariat as its contractors.

To a steady drumbeat of criticism from the developing countries, each year more numerous, about what they saw as inadequate funding, the level of contributions mounted. In 1950, EPTA began with $20 million. In 1988, contributions exceeded $900 million. Yet inflation and the growing needs of the developing countries and especially the poorest lands moderate the significance of this growth.

Although the size of UNDP, its omnipresence in the developing countries and the variety of projects undertaken represent a unique accomplishment, it is nevertheless only one of the intergovernmental agencies that now operate. The World Bank towers head and shoulders above limited UNDP grants by providing long-term, low-interest 'soft loans' for development as well as higher-interest, self-liquidating loans. The Bank also undertakes technical assistance projects, sometimes as a UNDP contractor, but more often on its own account. On technical assistance, it has outspent UNDP since 1982; its project lending, some of which grows out of technical assistance, exceeds $15 billion dollars annually. Furthermore, other multilateral sources of technical assistance, such as the European Community, also offer increasing shares of the total available aid.

Technical assistance, as it operates in the 1990s, aims at cooperative efforts and matching financing, although the poorest countries are excused from most local costs. Projects are mounted only after a formal request is made by the receiving government, which must have drawn up a definite plan that includes a training element. In principle, technical assistance projects can be divided into four categories:

1. Provision of foreign experts, some of whom are themselves from developing countries. They train local personnel to take over as soon as possible. An analogous function is the furnishing of short-term advisers on technical problems.
2. Scholarships to enable residents of developing countries to acquire needed skills, sometimes abroad, sometimes in regional or internationally-supported institutions.
3. Establishment of regional training centres where technicians can study common problems.
4. Organizing pre-investment projects of up to five years' duration to set out definite plans for investment: in addition, creating facilities and manpower resources to encourage outside investment. UNDP reports that a majority of the projects do in fact lead to investment, a large proportion of which relies on loans from the World Bank and its affiliates.

Aside from complaints that UNDP falls far short of the needs of developing countries, the organization has attracted both praise and criticism. Probably incontrovertible in some instances, this criticism can in part be understood as resulting from UNDP's reliance on developmental choices made by recipient countries. Added to this is the complexity of operating a field programme in a varied world. Furthermore, it has no foolproof doctrine for stimulating development, any more than do the recipient governments or the World Bank. In addition, it must counter the centrifugal force of intergovernmental agencies – its principal executing partners – that have their own mandates and limited willingness to submit to centralized control.

Cooperation among the UNDP offices under Resident Directors at the field level, representatives and staff of other organizations in the UN system, the World Bank and the IMF, and officials of the host governments, has not always been optimal. Moreover, donor governments acting on their own mount development projects. The different organizational bases encourage differing points of view about the same goals of development. Conflicts have to be ironed out in a negotiating process that sometimes causes great impatience among the officials of the host country. Sometimes also, technical experts cannot adapt to local conditions at their posts or act in ways that the local culture rejects. Sometimes they are insufficiently briefed or inappropriately trained. The central bureaucracy of UNDP was in fact organized without much expectation of the several waves of expansion that have taken place since the 1960s and has also been subject to the parsimonious financing provided to most international agencies.

The effective authority over general policy in UNDP was placed by the General Assembly in the hands of a Governing Council, made up of the representatives of 48 countries. The operations of UNDP are led by its Administrator, who is chief executive officer. Along with field offices in 116 developing countries, this structure, it was hoped, would contribute to the effectiveness of technical assistance throughout the UN system. It has indeed resulted in the expansion of services administered by the UN system and brought about cooperation on a larger scale with the World Bank. It nevertheless was neither intended as a centralized command post nor has it developed such a character. Consequently, its original complexity only increased with the larger scope of its programme.

In addition, the Governing Council, which functions under the authority of the Economic and Social Council and the General Assembly, also supervises the limited grant agency, the UN Capital Development Fund, set up in 1966; the UN Population Fund (UNFPA) (see below): the UN Volunteers, set up in 1970 (see below): the UN Sahelian Office, established in 1974; and some additional programmes, such as assistance in the fields of science and technology, and some trust funds for special purposes, such as the UN Development Fund for Women. UNDP Resident Directors also supervise the actual projects, report back on their programmes, represent the UN Disaster Relief Organization and the UN development system, take on occasional special assignments and try to help shape bilateral and multilateral projects into a coherent whole.

UN POPULATION FUND

Although the UN system has long shown an interest in demographic developments, for the first two decades its members could rarely agree on practical programmes affecting population growth; yet it was understood by all that such growth was intimately related to development. In 1966, the General Assembly began the construction of the UN Fund for Population Activities, which later became the present UN Population Fund. By 1990, it could credibly propose a budget, contributed mainly by governments, of more than $200 million. Its work reflects the links among population growth, development and deterioration of the global environment. Even though the concept of family planning finds increasing acceptance, the progress in reducing birth rates was reported as disappointing.

UNFPA supports national governments in collecting basic population data, in applying knowledge of population dynamics to training and development planning, family planning services, policies beyond family planning and information and education programmes. Ironically, the United States, a prime mover in establishing UNFPA, declined to contribute to the agency from 1985 to 1993 because of contested assertions that it supported abortions and coercive family planning in China.

UN CAPITAL DEVELOPMENT FUND (UNCDF)

The idea of a fund that could make financial grants to the developing countries is nearly as old as the United Nations itself: so is the chilly opposition from most donors. Yet the General Assembly in 1966 decided that existing sources of capital assistance, then rare, should be supplemented by a UN Capital Development Fund (UNCDF). It concentrates on grants and long, low-interest loans, especially for community development in the least developed countries. Initial contributions gradually grew until in 1991 annual voluntary contributions reached some $93 million.

UN VOLUNTEERS

This modest part of UNDP, set up in 1970, seeks to tap the vigour of youth in constructive opportunities to help with national development by means of international cooperation. In 1991, more than 2000 volunteers from every part of the world were serving. UNV is financed by voluntary contributions of less than $1 million.

UN CHILDREN'S FUND (UNICEF)

A veteran among the assistance mechanisms, UNICEF has always enjoyed the support and attention of member governments and of non-governmental organizations. It also has acquired a reputation as a well-administered, alert organization. UNICEF was established by the General Assembly in 1946 to provide special aid to children who had suffered from the Second World War. Its earliest tasks involved provision of supplies and services for direct relief, which eventually became less pressing. Its new tasks, reflecting what its staff had learned, included support to governments for developing long-term programmes for health improvement, social welfare and teaching, with special reference to children, pregnant women and nursing mothers. It frequently acts in cooperation with other agencies, especially WHO and UNDP. It was a primary international actor in bringing relief to the displaced people along the Thai border after the genocidal activities of the Khmer Rouge government in Cambodia in the late 1970s and has been active in other human disasters.

UNICEF operated on a budget of more than $590 million, most of it contributed by governments, at the beginning of the 1990s. Some 18 per cent of its budget is raised from private sources through sale of greetings cards and other collections managed by national UNICEF committees. Its policies are set by a 41-member Executive Board on which different regions of the world are represented.

UN CONFERENCE ON TRADE AND DEVELOPMENT

More than any other agency in the UN system, UNCTAD acts as the interest group for the Third World. Its original rationale included a distinctive analysis of underdevelopment associated with Raul Prebisch, who was Executive Secretary of the UN Economic Commission for Latin America (ECLA). His approach contended that advanced development takes place in certain economic centres, while countries on the periphery grow dependent. The periphery suffers from declines in the terms of trade, the price levels for their production as related to their imports. This dependency can be changed, said Prebisch, by changing the terms of trade in favour of the developing countries.

This view greatly appealed to developing countries with single major exports, such as Ghana with its cocoa crop. The Prebisch view made its way through the UN machinery and resulted in a three-month conference in Geneva in 1964, despite steady scepticism on the part of the developed countries. The conference sought a counterweight to the 'rich man's clubs', in and outside the UN system, as well as to the disappointment with the Economic and Social Council (see below). Consequently, the 1964 meeting was turned into a permanent organ of the General Assembly, to be called UNCTAD. It includes a Trade and Development Board and a permanent secretariat. Every three or four years, UNCTAD meets in a general conference, usually marked by sharp controversies between developing and developed countries. The board meets in the interim. The formal purposes are to:

- promote international trade so as to encourage development;
- formulate and give effect to policy principles on international trade;
- stimulate action in the UN system to reach multilateral agreements on trade, especially to stabilize commodity prices;
- serve as a centre for harmonizing trade and related policies of governments and regional groupings.

It would achieve its main goals by bargaining among three groups of UN members – the developed, the socialist countries and the developing countries. The device of dividing UNCTAD into negotiating units created the 'Group of 77', the original developing countries at UNCTAD 1 in Geneva.

The Group of 77 tries to present a common policy. This is not easy as its membership has grown by another 50 governments. Many of the G-77 differ in their interests, as a comparison of Nepal and Mexico would indicate at once. Furthermore, the group includes high-income oil producers and newly industrialized countries at various stages of development. The 30-odd poorest countries have gradually been singled out for special treatment. Despite differences, the Group gradually manifested strength in other international meetings. Its members tried to hang together because of the conviction that they must do so in order to achieve anything at all. Gradually, G-77 has lost much of its significance as individual developing countries form alignments that reflect their particular interests on an issue.

Even if few governments proclaim much satisfaction with the concrete results from UNCTAD, it has offered an institutional service to the developing countries. Its meetings encourage them to formulate their economic views more precisely. Moreover, the UNCTAD Secretariat has adapted to an 'interdependence' approach that gives attention to 'northern' interests. UNCTAD publications provide a basis for continuing interchanges between rich and poor countries and project a critical light on what the developing world regards as the orthodoxies of the IMF and the World Bank.

UNCTAD also presents critical opinions on the progress of negotiations on reductions of tariffs and obstacles to trade under the auspices of the General Agreement on Tariffs and Trade (GATT), which has drastically reduced customs duties since its foundation in 1948 under UN auspices. This critical function and other parts of the work of UNCTAD are regarded by some as healthy competition. UNCTAD has also promoted the drafting or revision of agreements among producer and consumer countries to regulate trade and price of cocoa, rubber, coffee, tin, olive oil, sugar, wheat and tropical timber. In 1980, after years of negotiations, both developing and developed countries agreed to establish a Common Fund for Commodities. It would finance buffer stocks of commodities in international trade during times of low demand. When demand increased, the stocks could be used, thus helping to stabilize price levels. In practice, its provisions operate only to a limited degree.

Meanwhile, the end of 1990 had a special significance for GATT. This agency, spun off from the abortive attempt in 1948 to create an international Trade Organization, had drastically lowered tariffs for most world trade and helped to control some non-tariff barriers. Its contracting parties, now more than 100, had been through seven rounds of negotiations in 1986, when a new one was launched in a session in Uruguay. In mid-1993, it had not yet been concluded. The Uruguay Round developed severe controversies over free trade for services, such as banking and insurance, and especially for agricultural products. As the issues are complex and the negotiating process in GATT slow and painstaking, with major traders such as the United States and the European Communities pitted against each other, prospects for a successful outcome were sombre as deadlines were passed over.

NEW INTERNATIONAL ECONOMIC ORDER

The UNCTAD approach to economic change begins with the assumption that the working of the world economy could be changed by deliberate governmental action. Even though GATT and the IMF programme look towards a world economy free of central direction, the notion of directed – or at least guided – change underlies other UN programmes. The first two 'Development Decades', proclaimed by the General Assembly, reflect the popularity of a global, directed approach to the world economy. The high point of this approach was reached during the aftermath of the oil embargo of 1973, when in the following year the sixth special session of the General Assembly demanded a New International Economic Order (NIEO).

While the oil crisis was an immediate cause, deeper reasons for this attempt to direct a vast change in the world economy could be found in the anguish of the developing countries and their increasing sophistication and solidarity. They pushed their programme of action, seeking NIEO, through a controversial Assembly session in which the developed countries repeatedly proclaimed their reservations. Essentially, the developing countries took the oil crisis as an opportunity to validate and advance their programme, which contained familiar elements: expansion of producers' associations (with the example of the Organization of Petroleum Exporting Countries [OPEC] in mind); linking prices of imports in developing countries to exports from them; reform of the international monetary system; and free exercise of full permanent sovereignty over natural resources (which implied a right of nationalization).

This was followed by a Mexican-sponsored proposal of a Charter of Economic Rights and Duties of States, which was adopted by a vote that showed overt opposition or significant abstention by almost all developed countries. This polarization moderated somewhat by September 1975, when both the developing countries and the United States and some of its friends came to the seventh special session of the General Assembly with a more cooperative attitude. This led to the adoption of a resolution covering a negotiating framework for application of NIEO measures in the UN system. The resolution also affirms a target of 0.7 per cent growth of gross national product of developed countries as their portion of assistance; this had long been sought by the poorer lands.

Yet, with the sombre international economic situation of the subsequent years and the rise of a strong free-market philosophy in the United States and other developed countries, the momentary grouping around the notion that common difficulties could be overcome with international cooperation soon drained away. NIEO had no vitality at the beginning of the 1990s. Several positive elements did, however, emerge. These include broader activities by the World Bank and the IMF, the creation of a general system of tariff preferences to benefit the developing countries, increased capitalization for the World Bank and IMF where the developing countries increased participation, and some parts of the not-yet-operative law of the sea convention.

THE GLOBAL ENVIRONMENT

The political differences between wealthy and poor countries that NIEO dramatized also play a part in the rise to prominence of environmental issues. While some of the leaders of the developing countries strove with endless zeal for industrialization, groups within the developed countries sought to rein in increasing use of energy and natural resources. The startling dispersal of radioactive material from the breakdown of a nuclear power reactor at Chernobyl in the USSR in 1986, the disclosure of unrestrained dumping of toxic wastes in Africa and other developing areas, the connection between population growth and desertification, and the rapid cutting of the tropical rain forest all contributed to the new understanding. So too did the evidence of the destruction of the ozone layer and the possibility of global warming as a result of the use of fossil fuels. The UN system was in various ways involved in all of this.

Gradually, governments of both developed and developing countries came to accept that the world environment was seriously threatened by despoliation of the natural environment. Yet considerable strife emanated from fears in developing countries that their efforts to lift their levels of well-being would be impaired. Although the UN system decided to make room for environmental considerations with the creation of the UNEP in 1972, it was only as the 1990s approached that the issue reached the top of the international agenda.

Even though UNEP is a dwarf agency compared with the World Bank or FAO, its staff of fewer than 400 people and its 58-country Governing Council adroitly took advantage of growing concern among many publics about threats to the environment. In 1988, it developed a six-year environmental programme which sets priorities for the whole UN system for the period 1990–95. Five years earlier, it had persuaded the General Assembly to establish a World Commission on Environment and Development, which was headed by the then Prime Minister of Norway, Gro Harlem Brundtland. Its report in 1987, titled *Our Common Future*, linked the environmental safeguards with a series of recommendations for 'a new era of economic growth' that is both socially and environmentally sustainable. The heads of all agencies in the UN system, plus the World Bank and the IMF, then gathered to emphasize that all development projects must help to sustain rather than harm the environment. This was followed by UNEP's own report to the General Assembly on how to proceed.

One outcome was the summoning of a UN Conference on the Human Environment, twenty years after the first environmental conference in 1972, to take place in Brazil. It was to take up climatic change; management of international traffic in dangerous wastes and products; protection of fresh water resources and of the oceans; combating deforestation, desertification and drought; preservation of biological diversity; integration of biological and developmental concerns to improve living standards; and protection of health.

The conference adopted the Rio Declaration on Environment and Development; a programme of action entitled 'Agenda 21'; and a statement of principles on the management, conservation and sustainable development of all types of forests. Two conventions were opened for signature at Rio. That on climatic changes aims at stabilizing omissions of carbon dioxide and other greenhouse gases to prevent the 'greenhouse effect'. The second convention deals with biological diversity and seeks 'sustainable use of all the earth's species and the ecosytems of which they are a part.'

REFUGEES AND DISASTERS

Organized international concern with refugees dates back to the early days of the League of Nations. Only after the Second World War, when millions of displaced persons in Europe and Asia roamed across the path of the victorious armies did the scope of assistance and protection operations reach a large scale. Since then, in several organizational forms, the United Nations has tried to cope with refugees.

The principal organizational instrument since 1951 has been the UNHCR, which was originally created by the General Assembly as a temporary agency. It rests on a renewable General Assembly resolution and the UN Convention on the Status of Refugees (1951), which has some 90 adherents. The sudden outflow of Hungarian refugees after the suppression of a rebellion against oppressive Communist rule in 1956 saw UNHCR assisting with the handling and eventual resettlement of some 200 000 people. With the passage of years, even the Hungarian government expressed its gratitude. Since then UNHCR has been on the scene, first to protect the human rights of people outside their own countries with a well-founded fear of persecution, and then to offer material assistance, wherever forced migrations occur. In 1990, it was responsible for aid to some four million refugees from Afghanistan, some two million from Ethiopia and other hundreds of thousands who appear in the wake of repression or violence elsewhere. Its estimates of refugees who could claim help, aside from displaced persons within their own countries, reached 18 million in the world in 1992. With its restricted budget and the constraints of working through national governments, it clearly could not reach every refugee.

In other humanitarian disasters too, the UN structure has responded. As a device to signal a humanitarian emergency, the system has the services of UNDRO. It has few resources of its own and must rely mainly on other UN agencies or bilateral responses. It has often been criticized for inadequate or slow responses in case of earthquakes, floods and other natural castastrophes.

Since 1987, the UN Secretary-General's office has been building up new capacity as a centre for early warning of humanitarian emergencies.

This helps to mobilize resources from many quarters and to back up UNHCR and UNDRO. And for extraordinary humanitarian emergencies, such as the droughts in Africa during the 1980s and the situation of the Cambodians who fled their country during the depredations of the Pol Pot government in the late 1970s, the UN has organized special operations to bring food, shelter and other services. The African emergency office was quickly phased out after efficient work (which could not, however, prevent new disasters in the long term), but the UN Border Relief Operation, which assists Cambodians, continued to operate in 1990, pending a political settlement of the future of their country. In all of these emergency operations, WFP has been a principal source of food aid. Originally conceived as a means to funnel surplus food so as to promote development, WFP planned for the 1991–92 biennium a $1.5 billion programme, about three-quarters of which would rely on commodities contributed by governments.

Although refugees and victims of man-made disasters, such as that of Cambodia, supposedly need only short-term attention, more than one incident has turned into a long-term concern. The fate of the refugees from the Arab–Israeli war of 1948 can be taken as a clear example of this transformation. By 1992, more than one-and-a-half million people, most of them children and grandchildren of the original refugees, now were receiving some sort of assistance from the UN Relief and Works Agency for Palestine Refugees (UNRWA). It was organized to care for refugees until they could return to what is now Israel. Most of the UNRWA employees are drawn from the refugee ranks, while the organizational headquarters was removed to Vienna after fighting engulfed Beirut in the early 1980s. The necessary political settlement appeared as distant in 1993 as in 1950. The Israeli government recently has used force to cope with riotous situations, which Arabs call *Intifada*, in UNRWA-assisted camps in the territory it occupied after the 1967 war. Elsewhere in the Arab countries where other refugees live, governments have usually avoided merely absorbing them. Most of the budget for UNRWA camps, schools and other services is covered by contributions from the Western countries, including never less than 25 per cent from the United States.

NARCOTIC DRUGS CONTROL

Control of the traffic in narcotic drugs is one of the oldest items on the international agenda. An interlocking system of international conventions and control organs dates back to before the First World War.

The League of Nations supervised the system and developed it further. The United Nations took over the League's tasks and formed a narcotic drugs commission under the wings of the Economic and Social Council. These bodies have led several phases of revisions of existing laws and the establishment of expert organs, including research laboratories located in Vienna. WHO joins the effort by identifying substances that need control. A voluntary UN Fund for Drug Abuse Control offers technical assistance to 49 countries on projects intended to reduce the demand for controlled drugs, their supply and distribution. Application of the rules, however, remains in the hands of national authorities. National efforts to reduce the illicit traffic range from negligible to strenuous.

The burgeoning international trade in narcotics dramatically came into the spotlight when the President of Colombia, whose country is a principal source of illicit cocaine, received a standing ovation in the General Assembly in 1989, for a speech demanding new measures. The Assembly called a special session on narcotics for early 1990, where an action programme was approved and governments were asked to adhere to the latest UN Convention Against Illicit Traffic in Narcotic Drugs and Psychotropic Substances, which had been sent to them in 1988. The years 1991–2000 were proclaimed the UN Decade Against Drug Abuse, and explorations of the possibility of an international criminal court for drug traffickers were undertaken.

AIDS

The main source of international leadership to cope with the growing spread of AIDS (Acquired Immune Deficiency Syndrome), as might be expected, is WHO. By 1990, it had mounted a programme of assistance to more than 125 countries and worked with national committees in 155 lands. The General Assembly gave strong endorsement to the programme in 1987, when for the first time it urged support on a health issue, and has since then discussed sombre reports from WHO. UNDP and the World Bank have adjusted their projects to support WHO's Global Programme on AIDS, which by 1990 had available more than $100 million in voluntary funds. Meanwhile, even with the gross under-reporting of cases characteristic in some countries, there was evidence that more and more people had begun to understand the sexual nature of the transmission of the disease and to respond to preventive information made available via WHO through national governments.

CONVENTIONAL ECONOMIC, SOCIAL AND CULTURAL COOPERATION

The mushrooming growth of UN operations to support economic and social development and to promote the general welfare combine improvisation, imagination, dire need, political compromise and a shortage of resources. These programmes derive from older forms of organized international activity. These continue to be applied, day-in and day-out, and ultimately affect the newer programmes.

For all its shortcomings and futile ambition, the NIEO demonstrates how old forms can still be used to express ideas that only three decades ago would hardly have come to the surface. It had a basis in the familiar form of a recommendation by an international deliberative body. All members of the United Nations are pledged to take joint and separate action to effect to recommended plans for promoting the general welfare [Art. 56, UN Charter]. Because the majority of governments vote for a recommendation, it is a reasonable assumption (that often fails to become actual) that the governments will follow policies that they approve at the international level.

Relying on national governments to cooperate by giving practical effect to agreed policies is a method that reaches back through the League of Nations to the middle of the nineteenth century. It starts with the assumption that some problems, such as the spread of an epidemic disease or the use of the telegraph, affect all states and that their cooperation is obviously in their self-interest. Each cooperating country carries out the general international policy with its own resources. This basic notion gradually grew more sophisticated and came to include the drafting of a long series of international conventions on specific subjects, such as the international trade in narcotics. Scholars, too, elaborated theoretical concepts to explain the increasing practical international cooperation.

The conceptual line that has had the most influence on the creation of international institutions and their programmes was developed by the 'functionalist' writers. A leading inspiration to some of the theorists of our time was David Mitrany, an English academic and adviser to multilateral business. He wrote his best-known book, *A Working Peace System*, at the formative stage of the post-Second World War institutions. Mitrany argued that transnational cooperation springs out of technological development. Conventional politicians may impede or distort such cooperation, but they do not manage it. The web of technical cooperation, which was illustrated by the highly successful collaboration during both the world wars among the civil servants, engineers and scientists of the victors, eventually becomes so dense that it delimits the action of the state. Technical experts can agree, no matter what conventional politicians think. Therefore, the real world is shaped by technological imperatives. The cooperation thus bred eventually will 'spill over' into what are now regarded as political areas.

The functionalist argument has served as an important justification for separating the functions of the specialized agencies in the UN system from the central organization, at least for day-to-day operations and technical recommendations. It also supported additional attention to technical cooperation, especially as its worth in several fields had been proved during the days of the League of Nations.

The notion that an efficient international system requires cooperation on technical subjects has found expression in the complex organizational structure of the United Nations. The set of agencies and deliberative bodies, some of which are discussed earlier in this chapter, develops policy recommendations covering an endless series of topics with respect to economic, social, cultural, educational, health, and related problems, as set out in Article 55 of the Charter. The UN Secretary-General and his staff prepare studies for the system and make proposals, either on their own initiative or with the cooperation of governmental representatives. The Economic and Social Council, discussed in Chapter 2, has the formal assignment of giving central direction.

In the hope of assembling the best technical advice, ECOSOC has created a series of commissions, composed of specialists nominated by their governments. A few similar commissions existed under the League of Nations, where, however, specialists were appointed in their personal capacities, not as governmental nominees. The ECOSOC commissions cover such subjects as statistics, population, the status of women and development planning, as well as human rights and narcotic drugs, mentioned earlier. In addition, a long list of even more specialized advisory bodies, such as the Committee on Crime Prevention and Control, offer their advice.

Along with promoting cooperation on specific topics, ECOSOC has also set up a more decentralized system along regional lines. A set of commissions offers advice to governments and limited services to governments in their regions. These bodies include the UN Economic Commission for Africa (headquarters in Addis Ababa), the Economic Commission for Asia and the Western Pacific (Bangkok), the Economic Commission for Europe (Geneva), the Economic Commission for Latin America (Santiago, Chile) and the Economic Commission for Western Asia (Baghdad). Assisted by small staffs, drawn mostly from their own regions, these deliberative organs have scored some success but remain the subject of debate, both in regard to the validity of the regional principle and their claims to speak for regions. Yet they sometimes help stimulate economic and foster regional standards. At the height of the Cold War in Europe, the Economic Commission for Europe was one of the few places where a few cooperative and constructive relationships between the two sides could carry on.

Despite the elaborate institutional structures and the early welcome accorded to functionalist ideas, many member governments complain that the UN system lacks both sharpness and responsiveness. The specialized agencies and the World Bank and IMF duly submit reports to ECOSOC, the formal coordinator, but then tend to go their own ways. ECOSOC and its system of developing general policy recommendations remains what it has been: it is secondary in immediate impact, as compared with the practical programmes and ambitious aspirations encouraged by an unprecedented degree of international organization.

8 The 1990s: A Changing UN

As the world changes, so does the United Nations. At the start of the last decade of the twentieth century, the United Nations was experiencing a revival both in use and in general appreciation.

Gone were the days when the United Nations was facilely denounced as simply a bureaucratic, useless, spendthrift organization. The memory had dimmed of the moment in 1983 when a departing deputy representative of the United States talked of moving the United Nations headquarters from New York, while the American delegation stood 'down at the dockside, waving a fond farewell as [it] sailed into the sunset'. That was the time of the Kassebaum Amendment, originating in the US Senate, that ordered a cutback of American contributions to the UN budget from 25 to 20 per cent unless a system of weighted voting was introduced for financial decisions. A series of economy measures that still affected the UN system years later followed from Washington. That was also the time when the ultra-conservative Heritage Foundation, claiming in 1984 that 'a world without a United Nations could be a better one', reached its greatest influence on the Reagan White House. That same year, the United States, later followed by the United Kingdom and Singapore, withdrew from UNESCO, criticizing it for mismanagement and 'politicization'. It seemed then only a matter of time before the United States would depart from the United Nations itself.

In the first part of the 1990s, all of this had either undergone a marked change or seemed to be on the way there. The United States government had obviously revised its attitude, especially where the Security Council was concerned. Also at the United Nations itself, overall morale had greatly improved. A renewed faith in the future of the organization as it neared its fiftieth anniversary appeared in the remarks of government leaders. In the crucial issues of international peace and security, the UN was employed as never before. A remarkable signal of the intention to do so in the future was the Security Council meeting attended by heads of governments of states early in 1991 and its request to the Secretary-General to analyze and recommend ways to strengthen the UN capacity for preventive diplomacy, peace-making and peace-keeping. His report, *An Agenda for Peace*, was published in July 1992. (See Chapter 4.)

The services of the Secretary-General once again took on special significance. He had a crucial role in ending the eight-year war between Iraq and Iran. He and his agents negotiated the departure of Soviet troops from Afghanistan. Through UNTAG, the organization supervised the decolonization of Namibia. By 1993, he had under his direction more than 10 peace-keeping forces.

Iraq was the centre of a second, more important burst of activity in 1990–91, after President Saddam Hussein ordered his troops to invade Kuwait (see Chapter 4). For the first time in a dispute that had nothing to do with colonialism, the Security Council ordered economic sanctions. Although these measures put great pressure on Iraq, its government continued unperturbed to annex Kuwait, loot the country, threaten to spread the war and generally to menace lives and peace. To that point, non-violent sanctions to give effect to a system of collective security proved untenable. They were not tested further. Rather, the Security Council authorized members to use military action. This was a severe trial for the UN security system. Whether the system emerged solid enough to undergo another such test remained unclear during the next two years. Nevertheless, it was obvious that among the governments of the world, gobbling up a neighbour was regarded as supremely objectionable and ripe for a coercive response. Equally clear was the fact that a heavy military force was needed to repel a determined aggressor. In the case of Kuwait, the nucleus of such a force was available because of decisions in Washington. Afforded extra prestige by the United Nations, those American decisions also attracted very wide support and encouraged an active role for the Security Council.

The smooth working relationship of the permanent members of the Council, as well as the widespread support for turning back what almost all governments perceived as an unacceptable violation of the Charter by Iraq, formed an extraordinary backdrop to the adoption of a series of resolutions. Improved relations between the Soviet Union and the United States provided an essential foundation for decision-making. In general, this loose, increasingly uneven partnership continued to function even after Russia succeeded the dissolved Soviet Union. Unlike the days of the Cold War when their rivalry paralyzed the Council, now they were not only cooperating closely but doing so in regard to a variety of issues, with support from France and the United Kingdom, that formed a nucleus from which decisions could emerge, although it was not a guarantee of eternal harmony either between the two former antagonists or the other members of the Council.

THE SOVIET UNION

For many years, the Soviet Union took a reserved or negative attitude towards the United Nations. While carefully protecting its autonomy of action, it refrained from constructive initiatives that others could accept. Its position was symbolized by the nickname 'Mr Nyet', given longtime Foreign Minister Andrei A. Gromyko, who cast many vetoes in the Security Council in the course of a few years. The Soviet Union usually opposed expanding UN activities and, like the United States, was critical of the expenditures and the level of salaries paid to UN staff members. It consistently opposed the use of peace-keeping forces and refused to pay part of its obligatory, assessed contributions. It eventually boycotted the first two Secretaries-General, Lie and Hammarskjöld, and provokingly proposed weakening the office by turning it into a 'troika', named after a three-horse Russian carriage.

With Mikhail Gorbachev's ascent to power, the Soviet approach changed drastically. In 1987, he published a major article in the Soviet press on his views about the UN and followed it with a similar speech to the General Assembly. He pleaded for closer multilateral cooperation within the UN framework. One proposal urged establishing a UN centre to lessen the danger of war. Wider use should be made of UN military observers and peace-keeping forces in disengaging warring troops and observing ceasefire and armistice arrangements. States should be encouraged to cooperate within the UN framework in combating international terrorism.

Other proposals by Gorbachev referred to closer cooperation among states to establish both economic and ecological security. The UN role in the field of human rights should be strengthened and a special fund for humanitarian cooperation should be created. The role of the ICJ should be upgraded and the international community should encourage the Secretary-General to undertake good offices, mediation and reconciliation.

Even if Gorbachev's proposals were hardly original or revolutionary and echoed the provisions of the UN Charter, they were put forward as a comprehensive package by the leader of a major power. Moreover, it was a power that had shown little enthusiasm for an active United Nations and had opposed some of the very programmes, such as genuine promotion of human rights, that now were praised. Soviet participation in UN bodies promptly turned from reserve to staunch defence of the UN. Its representatives began making numerous proposals to strengthen the organization. Even after Boris Yeltsin's Russian government took over the Soviet position in the United Nations, it generally followed the approach laid out by Gorbachev.

THE FIVE POLICEMEN

What was happening at the United Nations at the beginning of the 1990s looked much like the application of the concept of the four, or rather five, great power 'policemen' patrolling the world scene, as Franklin Roosevelt originally conceived it. That concept requires the kind of close co-operation among the great powers in order to maintain international peace and security that became visible in a series of Security Council actions after the Gorbachev-led change of atmosphere.

All the same, the UN security system operates under serious structural limitations that have been understood from the beginning, for nothing can be done if one of the permanent members behaves cynically or casts the veto for irrelevant or selfish purposes or uses force. Furthermore, under the veto-protected Charter, to change the rigid composition of the permanent members would be possible only under exceptional circumstances. Besides that, the system has never had the standing military forces foreseen in the Charter, so that even an agreed response to a breach of the peace still demands much unpredictable improvising.

A possibly even greater political drawback of the system began to surface after the revival of the Security Council. Elected members and all of the rest of the UN membership may chafe under the governance of the Big Five. Some grumbling became audible, especially from the middle powers, such as Canada, that normally furnish peace-keeping components.

The participation and services of the middle powers in the UN has a rather special character. Even without permanent places at the Security Council table, some of them, such as Germany and Japan, have used their financial resources to bolster peace-keeping operations. By 1993, Germany and Japan had begun to campaign for upgrading their participation to permanent membership on the Security Council. The United States supported them. Their success would almost certainly complicate decision-making in the Council and perhaps would induce other governments to seek similar status. Among Third-World powers, India and Pakistan have made considerable military contributions to peacekeeping. Middle powers also contributed to the force used against Iraq.

Echoing the restiveness among the middle powers, other smaller powers also have more than once indicated that their interests were not sufficiently taken into account. Apprehension about domination by the great powers dates back to the San Francisco Conference, when the unanimity rule was discussed and the smaller powers lost the fight to eliminate it. Thus, while an application of the concept of the five policemen may help to maintain international peace and security, it may eventually involve costs in terms of international consensus.

The concept of peace-keeping, to which the middle powers had contributed so much, began to show signs of new elasticity. Once it was used successfully, the idea was applied for quite different purposes, ranging from the original task of supervising truce agreements to the observation of elections in such countries as Namibia, Nicaragua, and El Salvador. In Cambodia, peace-keeping was understood as an essential element in forming a completely new government. In Somalia and Yugoslavia, it was understood as an adjunct to aid to victims of political disaster and civil war. In the latter three places, as well, frequent demands were made to edge the peace-keepers towards armed enforcement.

THE THIRD WORLD

Most of the governments of the poor countries of Africa and Asia probably place the abolition of poverty and the need to catch up with the economic level of the major industrialized lands ahead of maintaining international peace and security in distant locations. For the countries of the South, the new cooperation in the Security Council and among the rich and powerful does not necessarily rank as stunning progress. On the contrary: it arouses some fear that a new world order, referred to by President Bush in a speech to the General Assembly in 1990, may be established at the expense of the low-income countries. Development funds from rich countries that used to be destined for the Third World may now be used to help the development of post-communist Eastern Europe. Third World countries would no longer be able to use East–West competition for footholds in Africa and Asia to their own advantage: it would no longer be possible to play off the United States against the Soviet Union. The New International Economic Order (NIEO) glimmered farther away than ever.

Despite these fears and suspicions, the Afro-Asian majority in the 1990s still regarded the United Nations as one route to their goals, even if at times it served only a symbolic purpose and a means of keeping issues alive. The organization retained utility for them as a means of contact, a channel for assistance, an opening for political influence and as a tug on the conscience of the great and the rich.

THE UNITED STATES

From the point of view of the United States as the 1990s began, much had changed to its advantage both within and without the United Nations. Most of the countries in Eastern Europe had rejected central planning and state socialism and were in the process of installing market economies of the Western type – as the United States had always advocated. The unification of Germany was widely understood as a victory for the West and for democracy. The disappearance of the Soviet state had disposed of an adversary and left in its place a weaker but frequent partner.

The immediate worldwide response to the Iraqi invasion of Kuwait took the form of overall support for US-led political and military measures. In the autumn of 1990, the United States found itself heading an unlikely alliance, consisting of its NATO partners, its former Soviet enemies and a sizable group of Arab and other Third World countries. As this alliance was founded partly on the basis of resolutions adopted by the Security Council, the overall approach of the United States to the UN became much more favourable than in the recent past. The government in Washington clearly intended to channel more of its international activities through UN bodies. Congress began to release funds to pay up the delinquent American contributions to the United Nations. At the same time, as the Bush administration departed, the Department of State still declined to urge a return to UNESCO. It seemed likely that some years must pass and that the United Nations would need to post a series of successes prized in Washington before the favourable attitudes of the Hammarskjöld period would be restored.

COLLECTIVE LEGITIMIZATION

Creation of a broad consensus about permissible behaviour for governments constitutes a primary task for any diplomacy and especially of the procedures in multilateral organizations. As the variety of situations bearing on peace and security reaches towards the infinite, the constant reinterpretation and adaptation of the basic norms of the UN Charter is necessary. Once a consensus – or even a near-consensus – is reached, it can be used to give the actions of a government an explicit stamp of legitimacy, or general acceptance by what diplomats call the world community.

'Collective legitimization' is what Inis Claude has called this function. It sets the conditions under which violence in international relations may be acceptable. For example, the military operations of the United States to help South Korea after the attack by North Korea in 1950 received broad approval in the UN. Although the United States had the military power to carry on by itself, that government thought it prudent to garner international recognition that its actions were permissible and worthy of general support. It seemed likely in 1990 that the international reaction to Iraq's seizure of Kuwait would be another case in point; and so it proved.

Collective legitimization depends entirely on whether the UN member governments form opinions on a particular issue that add up to something near unanimity. When there is wide division, seeking legitimization is hopeless; this is another way of saying that the government that arbitrarily embarks on violent actions, or other hurtful practices, cannot expect automatic or any approval at all from the rest of the world. A clear example can be found in the Vietnam War of the 1960s and the early 1970s. The United States made no real effort to seek support from the UN, as it would have been in vain.

In the recent past, Afro-Asian states often have been in a better position than Western countries to recruit support from the majority of the United Nations for their independently-decided military actions. To some extent, this explains the backing given by a majority of the General Assembly to 'wars of liberation' in such places as the Portuguese African colonies, Rhodesia/Zimbabwe and Namibia. It also relates to the support given the Palestine Liberation Organization (PLO). The definition of aggression adopted by the General Assembly in 1974 [UN Res. 3314 (XXIX)] explicitly excludes such wars. Cuba claimed in 1975 that among the justifications for its intervention in Angola was its intention to 'execute the resolutions of the General Assembly'.

Thus, the United Nations can be used to produce some judgement as to the permissibility of military operations that probably could not have been stopped in any case. Actions that some governments view as aggression can thus also sometimes be turned into operations with collective legitimization.

THE SECRETARY-GENERAL

The role of the Secretary-General was particularly braced by the new attitude of support for the United Nations as the 1990s began.

Secretary-General Hammarskjöld once enunciated a conception of his office that clearly demonstrated how the divisions of opinion about the place of the UN in world politics restrict the functioning of the organization. He declared that the United Nations should rely on, and give voice to, the policies of the small powers that had little ability to resist the actions of the great. He viewed his office as the protector of the 'general interest'. The great powers, especially the Soviet Union, understood this notion as reducing their influence. The smaller powers, bound by their own nationalistic notions, were hardly eager to surrender their policies to an activist secretary-general, even if he claimed to be impartial. U Thant and Kurt Waldheim both tried to stand as persuasive presences in international politics, but U Thant failed to dissuade the United States from its policies in Vietnam and Waldheim found no way to project his organization into a durable centrality in the Middle East, the 1973 oil crisis or the hostage-taking of US embassy personnel in Iran in 1979–80.

During the second term of Javier Pérez de Cuéllar, as the 1990s opened, the office seemed to have regained some of its former influence in international affairs, especially with regard to peace and security. He made skilful use of the opportunities offered by the international context that now included support from the permanent members of the Security Council. His good offices, either in person or through personal representatives, contributed to the resolution of such already-mentioned issues as the war between Iraq and Iran and the independence of Namibia. In the last hours of his tenure, he was able to persuade the government and insurgents in El Salvador finally to move convincingly on the way to a UN-assisted peace.

Whether the end of Pérez's term marked a permanent reversal of fortunes for the office of Secretary-General was not immediately obvious. His successor, Boutros Boutros-Ghali, paved the way for an active policy by announcing he would not be a candidate for a second term. Like most of his predecessors, Boutros-Ghali gave priority to issues of peace and security over economic and social cooperation and management. He did, however, reshuffle the senior level of the Secretariat and brought in some new people. He has repeatedly offered his views on aspects of the most serious conflicts, including Cambodia, Iraq and Yugoslavia. Furthermore, he has publicly advocated strengthening some of the ongoing peace-keeping missions and has not hesitated to criticize some of the policies of the permanent members. His success in such ventures will, of course, much influence the future of the office. Moreover, the future of the office will continue to be shaped by whether enough highly motivated and able staff can be appointed. In the recent past, the prestige of the office suffered from the fact that recruitment to the UN Secretariat gave priority to 'as wide a geographical basis as possible' over 'the highest standards of efficiency, competence, and integrity', reversing the order set out in the Charter [Article 101(3)]. This practice arises from pressure from the member governments to obtain appointments for their nationals and also from electoral campaigning by candidates for the office. As the middle of Boutros-Ghali's term approached, there was little sign that such pressures had abated or that the financial difficulties and budgetary constraints imposed on the organization by member governments would encourage outstanding appointments.

THE SPECIALIZED AGENCIES

Along with the United Nations as the central organization, the various other agencies of the UN family also make up an active, probably indispensable, element in organized international relations. The several technical and operational agencies associated in the UN system formed a varied picture at the outset of the 1990s. Some of the smaller organizations go about their daily activities in a quiet, disciplined and quite effective manner. Little is heard of political controversy at the Universal Postal Union (UPU), the International Civil Aviation Organization (ICAO), the International Telecommunication Union (ITU), the World Meteorological Organization (WMO), the International Maritime Organization (IMO) and the World Intellectual Property Organization (WIPO). Their useful function in today's world comes close to what David Mitrany once called 'technical self-determination'. At the same time, their utility is no guarantee that the winds of political controversy can never disturb them.

The two big financial agencies, the World Bank and its daughters, and the IMF, remain strong, independent and generally respected institutions. Because their system of weighted voting allows the main capital-contributing governments to set the tone of the discussions in these Washington-based agencies, they have avoided the peril of 'politicization'. As Kaufmann and Schrijver have pointed out, the management of the Bank and Fund remains highly technocratic, with a strong reliance on market forces and, compared to other agencies, relatively little democratic control. Their staff policies are primarily based on qualitative considerations rather than geographical distribution. The skills of these organizations, however, do not protect them from the accusation, especially from the poor countries, that they have too conservative an attitude. This implies that they allow a preference for financially sound economic policies to override those of a social and humanitarian nature. This criticism poses a dilemma, for without practices acceptable to the international banking community they could not raise the funds needed for their operation; but with them they leave their member-clients unsatisfied.

The 'Big Four' specialized agencies, UNESCO, WHO, FAO and ILO, all have felt the lash of criticism, culminating in accusations of mismanagement and 'politicization'. The latter term is used mostly by Western governments when they find the fora of the specialized agencies used for controversial proposals not to their liking. Applications for membership by the PLO offer a case in point. As membership in the United

Nations itself remains unattainable for the PLO because of the likelihood that the United States and perhaps others would veto the application in the Security Council, Arab governments have tried on several occasions to open seats for the PLO in UNESCO, WHO and FAO. These attempts set off bitter political debates, with the United States announcing that it would cut off its considerable financial contributions to these organizations and thus threaten their very existence. Through 1990, the threats succeeded, usually by 'postponing' decisions for a year. Yet there is little doubt that this is an issue of 'politicization' with a long life.

The United States not only withdrew from UNESCO, as mentioned, but from the ILO in the 1970s. It returned to the latter soon afterward, but neither the United States nor Singapore and the United Kingdom were convinced by mid-1993 that reforms in UNESCO under a new Director-General had resolved difficulties which included mismanagement by the long-time executive head, Mokhtar M'Bow, and political pressures on management decisions. The United States and some other governments levied similar charges against FAO, but withdrawals did not follow at once.

Some of the difficulties have a structural origin, given the powerful and secure positions held by the chief executives of most of the specialized agencies. They can act as if they were princes in their own fiefdoms with little outside control over their activities and positive support from their own constituencies within national governments. Neither ECOSOC nor the General Assembly effectively can direct what the agencies do. Given the variety of motives that play in the selection of the chief executives of the specialized agencies and even some of the organizations, such as UNICEF and UNCTAD, that report to the General Assembly, the difficulty of coordinating the system seems likely to persist.

Yet these difficulties should not be overdramatized, no matter what impression an occasional crisis produces for the headline readers of the international press. The specialized agencies serve and are likely to continue to serve as a bedrock of information, skills and cooperation in their fields. They offer genuine services in such activities as the combat by WHO against transmissible diseases, including AIDS; the search for an end to hunger in the world by FAO; the setting of labour standards by ILO; and the promotion of literacy and scientific networks by UNESCO. Even IAEA, usually routinely occupied with inspection of nuclear installations, emerged as key operator on the ground in controlling and dismantling of armaments in Iraq during 1992. It would indeed be hard to imagine a world that would not be worse off without them.

THE UN IN THE 1990S

One-third into the 1990s, the United Nations clearly was changing in the way it operated internally, in the support from its members, and in the expectations it met and the functions it served. Striking as this was, it owed little to the manifold proposals for structural reform that had been discussed for years and almost never put into practice. Members of the organization were far from agreement on proposals for such changes as weighted voting in the General Assembly, associate membership for micro-states, expansion of the permanent membership of the Security Council, abolition of the veto or the establishment of a stable financial basis for the UN. Nevertheless, nearly 50 years after its founding, the United Nations not only existed but had revived its appeal and at least for a time gained new strength.

Whether the new role of the UN could be made permanent, or whether its rediscovery had only a shaky foundation, was not immediately clear. Some observers talked of an organisation 'over its head in expansion', while others viewed the high rate of activity as evidence of success and an irreversible tendency. Clearly, the next few years in the middle of the 1990s will be crucial.

Fifty national governments founded the United Nations in 1945. Since then, 130 more have joined the organization, most of them one-time colonies that are now independent. With very few exceptions, all governments in the world consider it important to belong to the United Nations. They find uses for the organization to satisfy some of their policy needs and in seeking international cooperation and peaceful negotiation of differences. Most of them complain of its shortcomings, as well, and sometimes with good cause, as this volume has tried to point out. Despite that, there is every reason to expect that the United Nations will continue as a serious and indispensable factor in the international politics of the twenty-first century.

Appendix:
Charter of the United Nations

WE THE PEOPLES OF THE UNITED NATIONS DETERMINED

to save succeeding generations from the scourge of war, which twice in our lifetime has brought untold sorrow to mankind, and

to reaffirm faith in fundamental human rights, in the dignity and worth of the human person, in the equal rights of men and women and of nations large and small, and

to establish conditions under which justice and respect for the obligations arising from treaties and other sources of international law can be maintained, and

to promote social progress and better standards of life in larger freedom,

AND FOR THESE ENDS

to practice tolerance and live together in peace with one another as good neighbours, and

to unite our strength to maintain international peace and security, and

to ensure by the acceptance of principles and the institution of methods, that armed force shall not be used, save in the common interest, and

to employ international machinery for the promotion of the economic and social advancement of all peoples,

HAVE RESOLVED TO COMBINE OUR EFFORTS TO ACCOMPLISH THESE AIMS

Accordingly, our respective Governments, through representatives assembled in the city of San Francisco, who have exhibited their full powers found to be in good and due form, have agreed to the present Charter of the United Nations and do hereby establish an international organization to be known as the United Nations.

Chapter I

PURPOSES AND PRINCIPLES

Article 1

The Purposes of the United Nations are:

1.   To maintain international peace and security, and to that end: to take effective collective measures for the prevention and removal of threats to the peace, and for the suppression of acts of aggression or other breaches of the peace and to bring about by peaceful methods, and in conformity with the principles of justice and international law, adjustment or settlement of international disputes or situations which might lead to a breach of the peace.

2.   To develop friendly relations among nations based on respect for the principle of equal rights and self-determination of peoples, and to take other appropriate measures to strengthen universal peace;

3.   To achieve international co-operation in solving international problems of an economic, social, cultural, or humanitarian character, and in promoting and encouraging respect for human rights and for fundamental freedoms for all without distinction as to race, sex, language, or religion; and

4.   To be a centre for harmonizing the actions of nations in the attainment of these common ends.

Article 2

The organization and its Members, in pursuit of the Purposes stated in Article 1 shall act in accordance with the following Principles.

1.   The Organization is based on the principle of the sovereign equality of all its members.

2.   All members, in order to ensure to all of them the rights and benefits resulting from membership, shall fulfil in good faith the obligations assumed by them in accordance with the present Charter.

3.   All Members shall settle their international disputes by peaceful means in such a manner that international peace and security, and justice, are not endangered.

4.   All members shall refrain in their international relations from the threat or use of force against the territorial integrity or political independence of any state, or in any other manner inconsistent with the Purposes of the United Nations.

5.   All Members shall give the United Nations every assistance in any action it takes in accordance with the present Charter, and shall refrain from giving assistance to any state against which the United Nations is taking preventive or enforcement action.

6.   The Organization shall ensure that states which are not Members of the United Nations act in accordance with these Principles so far as may be necessary for the maintenance of international peace and security.

7.   Nothing contained in the present Charter shall authorize the United Nations to intervene in matters which are essentially within the domestic jurisdiction of any state or shall require the Members to submit such matters to settlement under the present Charter; but this principle shall not prejudice the application of enforcement measures under Chapter VII.

Chapter II

MEMBERSHIP

Article 3

The original Members of the United Nations shall be the states which, having participated in the United Nations Conference on International Organization at San Francisco, or having previously signed the Declaration by United Nations of 1 January 1942, sign the present Charter and ratify it in accordance with Article 110.

Article 4

1. Membership in the United Nations is open to all other peace-loving states which accept the obligations contained in the present Charter and, in the judgement of the Organization, are able and willing to carry out these obligations.
2. The admission of any such state to membership in the United Nations will be effected by a decision of the General Assembly upon the recommendation of the Security Council.

Article 5

A Member of the United Nations against which preventive or enforcement action has been taken by the Security Council may be suspended from the exercise of the rights and privileges of membership by the General Assembly upon the recommendation of the Security Council. The exercise of these rights and privileges may be restored by the Security Council.

Article 6

A Member of the United Nations which has persistently violated the Principles contained in the present Charter may be expelled from the Organization by the General Assembly upon the recommendation of the Security Council.

Chapter III

ORGANS

Article 7

1. There are established as the principal organs of the United Nations: a General Assembly, a Security Council, an Economic and Social Council, a Trusteeship Council, an International Court of Justice, and a Secretariat.
2. Such subsidiary organs as may be found necessary may be established in accordance with the present Charter.

Article 8

The United Nations shall place no restrictions on the eligibility of men and women to participate in any capacity and under conditions of equality in its principal and subsidiary organs.

Chapter IV

THE GENERAL ASSEMBLY

Composition

Article 9

1.   The General Assembly shall consist of all the Members of the United Nations.
2.   Each Member shall not have more than five representatives in the General Assembly.

Functions and Powers

Article 10

The General Assembly may discuss any questions or any matters within the scope of the present Charter or relating to the powers and functions of any organs provided for in the present Charter, and, except as provided in Article 12, may make recommendations to the Members of the United Nations or to the Security Council or to both on any such questions or matters.

Article 11

1.   The General Assembly may consider the general principles of co-operation in the maintenance of international peace and security, including the principles governing disarmament and the regulation of armaments, and may make recommendations with regard to such principles to the Members or to the Security Council or to both.
2   The General Assembly may discuss any questions relating to the maintenance of international peace and security brought before it by any Member of the United Nations, or by the Security Council, or by a state which is not a Member of the United Nations in accordance with Article 35, paragraph 2, and, except as provided in Article 12, may make recommendations with regard to any such questions to the state or states concerned or to the Security Council or to both. Any such question on which action is necessary shall be referred to the Security Council by the General Assembly either before or after discussion.
3.   The General Assembly may call the attention of the Security Council to situations which are likely to endanger international peace and security.
4.   The powers of the General Assembly set forth in this Article shall not limit the general scope of Article 10.

Article 12

1.   While the Security Council is exercising in respect of any dispute or situation the functions assigned to it in the present Charter, the General Assembly shall not make any recommendation with regard to that dispute or situation unless the Security Council so requests.
2.   The Secretary-General, with the consent of the Security Council, shall notify the General Assembly at each session of any matters relative to the maintenance of international peace and security which are being dealt with by the

Security Council and shall similarly notify the General Assembly, or the Members of the United Nations if the General Assembly is not in session, immediately the Security Council ceases to deal with such matters.

Article 13

1. The General Assembly shall initiate studies and make recommendations for the purpose of:

a. promoting international co-operation in the political field and encouraging the progressive development of international law and its codification;

b. promoting international co-operation in the economic, social, cultural, education, and health fields, and assisting in the realization of human rights and fundamental freedoms for all without distinction as to race, sex, language, or religion.

2. The further responsibilities, functions and powers of the General Assembly with respect to matters mentioned in paragraph 1(b) above are set forth in Chapters IX and X.

Article 14

Subject to the provisions of Article 12, the General Assembly may recommend measures for the peaceful adjustment of any situation, regardless of origin, which it deems likely to impair the general welfare or friendly relations among nations, including situations resulting from a violation of the provisions of the present Charter setting forth the Purposes and Principles of the United Nations.

Article 15

1. The General Assembly shall receive and consider annual and special reports from the Security Council: these reports shall include an account of the measures that the Security Council has decided upon or taken to maintain international peace and security.

2. The General Assembly shall receive and consider reports from the other organs of the United Nations.

Article 16

The General Assembly shall perform such functions with respect to the international trusteeship system as are assigned to it under Chapters XII and XIII, including the approval of the trusteeship agreements for areas not designated as strategic.

Article 17

1. The General Assembly shall consider and approve the budget of the Organization.

2. The expenses of the Organization shall be borne by the Members as apportioned by the General Assembly.

3. The General Assembly shall consider and approve any financial and budgetary arrangements with specialized agencies referred to in Article 57 and shall examine the administrative budgets of such specialized agencies with a view to making recommendations to the agencies concerned.

Voting

Article 18

1. Each member of the General Assembly shall have one vote.
2. Decisions of the General Assembly on important questions shall be made by a two-thirds majority of the members present and voting. These questions shall include: recommendations with respect to the maintenance of international peace and security, the election of the non-permanent members of the Security Council, the election of the members of the Economic and Social Council, the election of members of the Trusteeship Council in accordance with paragraph 1(c) of Article 86, the admission of new Members to the United Nations, the suspension of the rights and privileges of membership, the expulsion of Members, questions relating to the operation of the trusteeship system, and budgetary questions.
3. Decisions on other questions, including the determination of additional categories of questions to be decided by a two-thirds majority, shall be made by a majority of the members present and voting.

Article 19

A Member of the United Nations which is in arrears in the payment of its financial contributions to the Organization shall have no vote in the General Assembly if the amount of its arrears equals or exceeds the amount of the contributions due from it for the preceding two full years. The General Assembly may, nevertheless, permit such a Member to vote if it is satisfied that the failure to pay is due to conditions beyond the control of the Member.

Procedure

Article 20

The General Assembly shall meet in regular annual sessions and in such special sessions as occasion may require. Special sessions shall be convoked by the Secretary-General at the request of the Security Council or of a majority of the Members of the United Nations.

Article 21

The General Assembly shall adopt its own rules of procedure. It shall elect its President for each session.

Article 22

The General Assembly may establish such subsidiary organs as it deems necessary for the performance of its functions.

Chapter V

THE SECURITY COUNCIL

Composition

Article 23

1.   The Security Council shall consist of fifteen Members of the United Nations. The Republic of China, France, the Union of Soviet Socialist Republics, the United Kingdom of Great Britain and Northern Ireland, and the United States of America shall be permanent members of the Security Council. The General Assembly shall elect ten other Members of the United Nations to be non-permanent members of the Security Council, due regard being specially paid, in the first instance to the contribution of Members of the United Nations to the maintenance of international peace and security and to the other purposes of the Organization, and also to equitable geographical distribution.

2.   The non-permanent members of the Security Council shall be elected for a term of two years. In the first election of the non-permanent members after the increase of the membership of the Security Council from eleven to fifteen, two of the four additional members shall be chosen for a term of one year. A retiring member shall not be eligible for immediate re-election.

3.   Each member of the Security Council shall have one representative.

Functions and Powers

Article 24

1.   In order to ensure prompt and effective action by the United Nations, its Members confer on the Security Council primary responsibility for the maintenance of international peace and security, and agree that in carrying out its duties under this responsibility the Security Council acts on their behalf.

2.   In discharging these duties the Security Council shall act in accordance with the Purposes and Principles of the United Nations. The specific powers granted to the Security Council for the discharge of these duties are laid down in Chapters VI, VII, VIII, and XII.

3.   The Security Council shall submit annual and, when necessary, special reports to the General Assembly for its consideration.

Article 25

The Members of the United Nations agree to accept and carry out the decisions of the Security Council in accordance with the present Charter.

Article 26

In order to promote the establishment and maintenance of international peace and security with the least diversion for armaments of the world's human and economic resources, the Security Council shall be responsible for formulating, with the assistance of the Military Staff Committee referred to in Article 47, plans to be submitted to the Members of the United Nations for the establishment of a system for the regulation of armaments.

Voting

Article 27

1. Each member of the Security Council shall have one vote.
2. Decisions of the Security Council on procedural matters shall be made by an affirmative vote of nine members.
3. Decisions of the Security Council on all other matters shall be made by an affirmative vote of nine members including the concurring votes of the permanent members; provided that, in decisions under Chapter VI, and under paragraph 3 of Article 52, a party to a dispute shall abstain from voting.

Procedure

Article 28

1. The Security Council shall be so organized as to be able to function continuously. Each member of the Security Council shall for this purpose be represented at all times at the seat of the Organization.
2. The Security Council shall hold periodic meetings at which each of its members may, if it so desires, be represented by a member of the government or by some other specially designated representative.
3. The Security Council may hold meetings at such places other than the seat of the Organization as in its judgement will best facilitate its work.

Article 29

The Security Council may establish such subsidiary organs as it deems necessary for the performance of its functions.

Article 30

The Security Council shall adopt its own rules of procedure, including the method of selecting its President.

Article 31

Any member of the United Nations which is not a member of the Security Council may participate, without vote, in the discussion of any question brought before the Security Council whenever the latter considers that the interests of that Member are specially affected.

Article 32

Any Member of the United Nations which is not a member of the Security Council or any state which is not a Member of the United Nations, if it is a party to a dispute under consideration by the Security Council, shall be invited to participate, without vote, in the discussion relating to the dispute. The Security Council shall lay down such conditions as it deems just for the participation of a state which is not a Member of the United Nations.

Chapter VI

PACIFIC SETTLEMENT OF DISPUTES

Article 33

1. The parties to any dispute, the continuance of which is likely to endanger the maintenance of international peace and security, shall, first of all, seek a solution by negotiation, enquiry, mediation, conciliation, arbitration, judicial settlement, resort to regional agencies or arrangements, or other peaceful means of their own choice.

2. The Security Council shall, when it deems necessary, call upon the parties to settle their dispute by such means.

Article 34

The Security Council may investigate any dispute, or any situation which might lead to international friction or give rise to a dispute, in order to determine whether the continuance of the dispute or situation is likely to endanger the maintenance of international peace and security.

Article 35

1. Any Member of the United Nations may bring any dispute, or any situation of the nature referred to in Article 34, to the attention of the Security Council or of the General Assembly.

2. A state which is not a Member of the United Nations may bring to the attention of the Security Council or of the General Assembly any dispute to which it is a party if it accepts in advance, for the purposes of the dispute, the obligations of pacific settlement provided in the present Charter.

3. The proceedings of the General Assembly in respect of matters brought to its attention under this Article will be subject to the provisions of Articles 11 and 12.

Article 36

1. The Security Council may, at any stage of a dispute of the nature referred to in Article 33 or of a situation of like nature, recommend appropriate procedures or methods of adjustment.

2. The Security Council should take into consideration any procedures for the settlement of the dispute which have already been adopted by the parties.

3. In making recommendations under this Article the Security Council should also take into consideration that legal disputes should as a general rule be referred

by the parties to the International Court of Justice in accordance with the provisions of the Statute of the Court.

Article 37

1. Should the parties to a dispute of the nature referred to in Article 33 fail to settle it by the means indicated in that Article, they shall refer it to the Security Council.

2. If the Security Council deems that the continuance of the dispute is in fact likely to endanger the maintenance of international peace and security, it shall decide whether to take action under Article 36 or to recommend such terms of settlement as it may consider appropriate.

Article 38

Without prejudice to the provisions of Articles 33 to 37, the Security Council may, if all the parties to any disputes request, make recommendations to the parties with a view to a pacific settlement of the dispute.

Chapter VII

ACTION WITH RESPECT TO THREATS TO THE PEACE, BREACHES OF THE PEACE, AND ACTS OF AGGRESSION

Article 39

The Security Council shall determine the existence of any threat to the peace, breach of the peace, or act of aggression and shall make recommendations, or decide what measures shall be taken in accordance with Articles 41 and 42, to maintain or restore international peace and security.

Article 40

In order to prevent an aggravation of the situation, the Security Council may, before making the recommendations or deciding upon the measures provided for in Article 39, call upon the parties concerned to comply with such provisional measures as it deems necessary or desirable. Such provisional measures shall be without prejudice to the rights, claims, or position of the parties concerned. The Security Council shall duly take account of failure to comply with such provisional measures.

Article 41

The Security Council may decide what measures not involving the use of armed force are to be employed to give effect to its decisions, and it may call upon the Members of the United Nations to apply such measures. These may include complete or partial interruption of economic relations and of rail, sea, air, postal, telegraphic, radio, and other means of communication, and the severance of diplomatic relations.

Article 42

Should the Security Council consider that measures provided for in Article 41 would be inadequate or have proved to be inadequate, it may take such action by air, sea, or land forces as may be necessary to maintain or restore international peace and security. Such action may include demonstrations, blockade, and other operations by air, sea, or land forces of Members of the United Nations.

Article 43

1. All Members of the United Nations, in order to contribute to the maintenance of international peace and security, undertake to make available to the Security Council, on its call and in accordance with a special agreement or agreements, armed forces, assistance, and facilities, including rights of passage, necessary for the purpose of maintaining international peace and security.

2. Such agreement or agreements shall govern the numbers and types of forces, their degree of readiness and general location, and the nature of the facilities and assistance to be provided.

3. The agreement or agreements shall be negotiated as soon as possible on the initiative of the Security Council. They shall be concluded between the Security Council and Members or between the Security Council and groups of Members, and shall be subject to ratification by the signatory states in accordance with their respective constitutional processes.

Article 44

When the Security Council has decided to use force it shall, before calling upon a Member not represented on it to provide armed forces in fulfilment of the obligations assumed under Article 43, invite that Member, if the Member so desires, to participate in the decisions of the Security Council concerning the employment of contingents of that Member's armed forces.

Article 45

In order to enable the United Nations to take urgent military measures, Members shall hold immediately available national air-force contingents for combined international enforcement action. The strength and degree of readiness of these contingents and plans for their combined action shall be determined, within the limits laid down in the special agreement or agreements referred to in Article 43, by the Security Council with the assistance of the Military Staff Committee.

Article 46

Plans for the application of armed force shall be made by the Security Council with the assistance of the Military Staff Committee.

Article 47

1. There shall be established a Military Staff Committee to advise and assist the Security Control on all questions relating to the Security Council's military requirements for the maintenance of peace and security, the employment and command of forces placed at its disposal, the regulation of armaments, and possible disarmament.

2. The Military Staff Committee shall consist of the Chiefs of Staff of the permanent members of the Security Council or their representatives. Any Member of the United Nations not permanently represented on the Committee shall be

invited by the committee to be associated with it when the efficient discharge of the Committee's responsibilities requires the participation of that Member in its work.

3. The Military Staff Committee shall be responsible under the Security Council for the strategic direction of any armed forces placed at the disposal of the Security Council. Questions relating to the command of such forces shall be worked out subsequently.

4. The Military Staff Committee, with the authorization of the Security Council and after consultation with appropriate regional agencies, may establish regional sub-committees.

Article 48

1. The action required to carry out the decisions of the Security Council for the maintenance of international peace and security shall be taken by all the Members of the United Nations or by some of them, as the Securi y Council may determine.

2. Such decisions shall be carried out by the Members of the United Nations directly and through their action in the appropriate international agencies of which they are members.

Article 49

The Members of the United Nations shall join in affording mutual assistance in carrying out the measures decided upon by the Security Council.

Article 50

If preventive or enforcement measures against any state are taken by the Security Council, any other state, whether a Member of the United Nations or not, which finds itself controlled with special economic problems arising from the carrying out of those measures shall have the right to consult the Security Council with regard to a solution of those problems.

Article 51

Nothing in the present Charter shall impair the inherent right of individual or collective self-defence if an armed attack occurs against a Member of the United Nations, until the Security Council has taken measures necessary to maintain international peace and security. Measures taken by Members in the exercise of this right of self-defence shall be immediately reported to the Security Council and shall not in any way affect the authority and responsibility of the Security Council under the present Charter to take at any time such action as it deems necessary in order to maintain or restore international peace and security.

Chapter VIII

REGIONAL REQUIREMENTS

Article 52

1. Nothing in the present Charter precludes the existence of regional arrangements or agencies dealing with such matters relating to the maintenance of international peace and security as are appropriate for regional action, provided that

such arrangements or agencies and their activities are consistent with the Purposes and Principles of the United Nations.

2.   The Members of the United Nations entering into such arrangements or constituting such agencies shall make every effort to achieve pacific settlement of local disputes through such regional arrangements or by such regional agencies before referring them to the Security Council.

3.   The Security Council shall encourage the development of pacific settlement of local disputes through such regional arrangements or by such regional agencies either on the initiative of the states concerned or by reference from the Security Council.

4.   This Article in no way impairs the application of Articles 34 and 35.

Article 53

1.   The Security Council shall, where appropriate, utilize such regional arrangements or agencies for enforcement action under its authority. But no enforcement action shall be taken under regional arrangements or by regional agencies without the authorization of the Security Council, with the exception of measures against any enemy state, as defined in paragraph 2 of this Article, provided for pursuant to Article 107 or in regional arrangements directed against renewal of aggressive policy on the part of any such state, until such time as the Organization may, on request of the Governments concerned, be charged with the responsibility for preventing further aggression by such a state.

2.   The term enemy state as used in paragraph 1 of this Article applies to any state which during the Second World War has been an enemy of any signatory of the present Charter.

Article 54

The Security Council shall at all times be kept fully informed of activities undertaken or in contemplation under regional arrangements or by regional agencies for the maintenance of international peace and security.

Chapter IX

INTERNATIONAL ECONOMIC AND SOCIAL CO-OPERATION

Article 55

With a view to the creation of conditions of stability and well-being which are necessary for peaceful and friendly relations based on respect for the principle of equal rights and self-determination of peoples, the United Nations shall promote:

a.   higher standards of living, full employment, and conditions of economic and social progress and development:

b.   solutions of international economic, social, health, and related problems; and international cultural and educational co-operation; and

c.   universal respect for, and observance of, human rights and fundamental freedoms for all without distinction as to race, sex, language, or religion.

Article 56

All Members pledge themselves to take joint and separate action in co-operation with the Organization for the achievement of the purposes set forth in Article 55.

Article 57

1.   The various specialized agencies, established by intergovernmental agreement and having wide international responsibilities, as defined in their basic

instruments, in economic, social, cultural, educational, health, and related fields, shall be brought into relationship with the United Nations in accordance with the provisions of Article 63.

2.   Such agencies thus brought into relationship with the United Nations are hereinafter referred to as specialized agencies.

Article 58

The Organization shall make recommendations for the co-ordination of the policies and activities of the specialized agencies.

Article 59

The Organization shall, where appropriate, initiate negotiations among the states concerned for the creation of any new specialized agencies required for the accomplishment of the purposes set forth in Article 55.

Article 60

Responsibility of the discharge of the functions of the Organization set forth in this Chapter shall be vested in the General Assembly and, under the authority of the General Assembly, in the Economic and Social Council, which shall have for this purpose the powers set forth in Chapter X.

Chapter X

THE ECONOMIC AND SOCIAL COUNCIL

Composition

Article 61

1.   The Economic and Social Council shall consist of fifty-four Members of the United Nations elected by the General Assembly.

2.   Subject to the provisions of paragraph 3, eighteen members of the Economic and Social Council shall be elected each year for a term of three years. A retiring member shall be eligible for immediate re-election.

3.   At the first election after the increase in the membership of the Economic and Social Council from twenty-seven to fifty-four members, in addition to the members elected in place of the nine members whose term of office expires at the end of the year, twenty-seven additional members shall be elected. Of these twenty-seven additional members, the term of office of nine members so elected shall expire at the end of one year, and of nine other members at the end of two years, in accordance with arrangements made by the General Assembly.

4.   Each member of the Economic and Social Council shall have one representative.

Functions and Powers

Article 62

1.   The Economic and Social Council may make or initiate studies and reports with respect to international economic, social, cultural, educational, health, and

related matters and may make recommendations with respect to the specialized agencies concerned.

2. It may make recommendations for the purpose of promoting respect for, and observance of, human rights and fundamental freedoms for all.

3. It may prepare draft conventions for submission to the General Assembly, with respect to matters falling within its competence.

4. It may call, in accordance with the rules prescribed by the United Nations, international conferences on matters falling within its competence.

Article 63

1. The Economic and Social Council may enter into agreements with any of the agencies referred to in Article 57, defining the terms on which the agency concerned shall be brought into relationship with the United Nations. Such agreements shall be subject to approval by the General Assembly.

2. It may co-ordinate the activities of the specialized agencies through consultation with and recommendations to such agencies and through recommendations to the General Assembly and to the Members of the United Nations.

Article 64

1. The Economic and Social Council may take appropriate steps to obtain regular reports from the specialized agencies. It may make arrangements with the Members of the United Nations and with the specialized agencies to obtain reports on the steps taken to give effect to its own recommendations and to recommendations on matters falling within its competence made by the General Assembly.

2. It may communicate its observations on these reports to the General Assembly.

Article 65

The Economic and Social Council may furnish information to the Security Council and shall assist the Security Council upon its request.

Article 66

1. The Economic and Social Council shall perform such functions as fall within its competence in connexion with the carrying out of the recommendations of the General Assembly.

2. It may, with the approval of the General Assembly, perform services at the request of Members of the United Nations and at the request of specialized agencies.

3 It shall perform such other functions as are specified elsewhere in the present Charter or as may be assigned to it by the General Assembly.

Voting

Article 67

1. Each member of the Economic and Social Council shall have one vote.

2. Decisions of the Economic and Social Council shall be made by a majority of the members present and voting.

Procedure

Article 68

The Economic and Social Council shall set up commissions in economic and social fields and for the promotion of human rights, and such other commissions as may be required for the performance of its functions.

Article 69

The Economic and Social Council shall invite any Member of the United Nations to participate, without vote, in its deliberations on any matter of particular concern to that Member.

Article 70

The Economic and Social Council may make arrangements for representatives of the specialized agencies to participate, without vote, in its deliberations and in those of the commissions established by it, and for representatives to participate in the deliberations of the specialized agencies.

Article 71

The Economic and Social Council may make suitable arrangements for consultation with non-governmental organizations which are concerned with matters within its competence. Such arrangements may be made with international organizations and, where appropriate, with national organizations after consultation with the Member of the United Nations concerned.

Article 72

1.   The Economic and Social Council shall adopt its own rules of procedure, including the method of selecting its President.
2.   The Economic and Social Council shall meet as required in accordance with its rules, which shall include provision for the convening of meetings on the request of a majority of its members.

Chapter XI

DECLARATION REGARDING NON-SELF-GOVERNING TERRITORIES

Article 73

Members of the United Nations which have or assume responsibilities for the administration of territories whose peoples have not yet attained a full measure of self-government recognize the principle that the interests of the inhabitants of these territories are paramount, and accept as a sacred trust the obligation to promote to the upmost, within the system of international peace and security established by the present Charter, the well-being of the inhabitants of these territories, and, to this end:

a.   ensure, with due respect for the culture of the peoples concerned, their political, economic, social, and educational advancement, their just treatment, and their protection against abuses;

b.   to develop self-government, to take due account of the political aspirations of the peoples, and to assist them in the progressive development of their free political institutions, according to the particular circumstances of each territory and its peoples and their varying stages of advancement;

c.   to further international peace and security;

d.   to promote constructive measures of development, to encourage research, and to co-operate with one another and, when and where appropriate, with specialized international bodies with a view to the practical achievement of the social, economic, and scientific purposes set forth in this Article; and

e.   to transmit regularly to the Secretary-General for information purposes, subject to such limitation as security and constitutional considerations may require, statistical and other information of a technical nature relating to economic, social, and educational conditions in the territories for which they are respectively responsible other than those territories to which Chapters XII and XIII apply.

Article 74

Members of the United Nations also agree that their policy in respect of the territories to which this Chapter applies, no less than in respect of their metropolitan areas, must be based on the general principle of good-neighbourliness, due account being taken of the interests and well-being of the rest of the world, in social, economic, and commercial matters.

Chapter XII

INTERNATIONAL TRUSTEESHIP SYSTEM

Article 75

The United Nations shall establish under its authority an international trusteeship system for the administration and supervision of such territories as may be placed thereunder by subsequent individual agreements. These territories are hereafter referred to as trust territories.

Article 76

The basic objectives of the trusteeship system, in accordance with the Purposes of the United Nations laid down in Article 1 of the present Charter, shall be:

a.   to further international peace and security;

b.   to promote the political, economic, social, and educational advancement of the inhabitants of the trust territories, and their progressive development towards self-government or independence as may be appropriate to the particular circumstances of each territory and its peoples and the freely expressed wishes of the peoples concerned, and as may be provided by the terms of each trusteeship agreement;

c. to encourage respect for human rights and for fundamental freedoms for all without distinction as to race, sex, language, or religion, and to encourage recognition of the interdependence of the peoples of the world; and

d. to ensure equal treatment in social, economic, and commercial matters for all Members of the United Nations and their nationals, and also equal treatment for the latter in the administration of justice, without prejudice to the attainment of the foregoing objectives and subject to the provisions of Article 80.

Article 77

1. The trusteeship system shall apply to such territories in the following categories as may be placed thereunder by means of trusteeship agreements:

a. territories now held under mandate;

b. territories which may be detached from enemy states as a result of the Second World War; and

c. territories voluntarily placed under the system by states responsible for their administration.

2. It will be a matter for subsequent agreement as to which territories in the foregoing categories will be brought under the trusteeship system and upon what terms.

Article 78

The trusteeship system shall not apply to territories which have become Members of the United Nations, relationship among which shall be based on respect for the principle of sovereign equality.

Article 79

The terms of trusteeship for each territory to be placed under the trusteeship system, including any alteration or amendment, shall be agreed upon by the states directly concerned, including the mandatory power in the case of territories held under mandate by a Member of the United Nations, and shall be approved as provided for in Articles 83 and 85.

Article 80

1. Except as may be agreed upon in individual trusteeship agreements, made under Articles 77, 79, and 81, placing each territory under the trusteeship system, and until such agreements have been concluded, nothing in this Chapter shall be construed in or itself to alter in any manner the rights whatsoever of any states or any peoples or the terms of existing international instruments to which Members of the United Nations may respectively be parties.

2. Paragraph 1 of this Article shall not be interpreted as giving grounds for delay or postponement of the negotiation and conclusion of agreements for placing mandated and other territories under the trusteeship system as provided for in Article 77.

Article 81

The trusteeship agreement shall in each case include the terms under which the trust territory will be administered and designate the authority which will exercise the administration of the trust territory. Such authority, hereinafter called the administering authority, may be one or more states or the Organization itself.

Article 82

There may be designated, in any trusteeship agreement, a strategic area or areas which may include part or all of the trust territory to which the agreement applies, without the prejudice to any special agreement or agreements made under Article 43.

Article 83

1.   All functions of the United Nations relating to strategic areas, including the approval of the terms of the trusteeship agreements and of their alteration or amendment, shall be exercised by the Security Council.
2   The basic objectives set forth in Article 76 shall be applicable to the people of each strategic area.
3.   The Security Council shall, subject to the provisions of the trusteeship agreements and without prejudice to security considerations, avail itself of the assistance of the Trusteeship Council to perform those functions of the United Nations under the trusteeship system relating to political, economic, social, and educational matters in the strategic areas.

Article 84

It shall be the duty of the administering authority to ensure that the trust territory shall play its part in the maintenance of international peace and security. To this end the administering authority may make use of volunteer forces, facilities, and assistance from the trust territory in carrying out the obligations towards the Security Council undertaken in this regard by the administering authority, as well as for local defence and the maintenance of law and order within the trust territory.

Article 85

1.   The functions of the United Nations with regard to trusteeship agreements for all areas not designated as strategic, including the approval of the terms of the trusteeship agreements and of their alteration or amendment, shall be exercised by the General Assembly.
2.   The Trusteeship Council, operating under the authority of the General Assembly, shall assist the General Assembly in carrying out these functions.

Chapter XIII

THE TRUSTEESHIP COUNCIL

Composition

Article 86

1.   The Trusteeship Council shall consist of the following Members of the United Nations:
a.   those Members administering trust territories;

b.   such of those Members mentioned by name in Article 23 as are not administering trust territories; and

c.   as many other Members elected for three-year terms by the General Assembly as may be necessary to ensure that the total number of members of the Trusteeship Council is equally divided between those Members of the United Nations which administer trust territories and those which do not.

2.   Each member of the Trusteeship Council shall designate one specially qualified person to represent it therein.

Functions and Powers

Article 87

The General Assembly and, under its authority, the Trusteeship Council, in carrying out their functions, may:

a.   consider reports submitted by the administering authority;

b.   accept petitions and examine them in consultation with the administering authority;

c.   provide for periodic visits to the respective trust territories at times agreed upon with the administering authority; and

d.   take these and other actions in conformity with the terms of the trusteeship agreements.

Article 88

The Trusteeship Council shall formulate a questionnaire on the political, economic, social, and educational advancement of the inhabitants of each trust territory, and the administering authority for each trust territory within the competence of the General Assembly shall make an annual report to the General Assembly upon the basis of such questionnaire.

Voting

Article 89

1.   Each member of the Trusteeship Council shall have one vote.

2   Decisions of the Trusteeship Council shall be made by a majority of the members present and voting.

Procedure

Article 90

1.   The Trusteeship Council shall adopt its own rules of procedure, including the method of selecting its President.

2.   The Trusteeship Council shall meet as required in accordance with its rule, which shall include provision for the convening of meetings on the request of a majority of its members.

Article 91

The Trusteeship Council shall, when appropriate, avail itself of the assistance of the Economic and Social Council and of the specialized agencies in regard to matters with which they are respectively concerned.

Chapter XIV

THE INTERNATIONAL COURT OF JUSTICE

Article 92

The International Court of Justice shall be the principal judicial organ of the United Nations. It shall function in accordance with the annexed Statute, which is based upon the Statute of the Permanent Court of International Justice and forms an integral part of the present Charter.

Article 93

1. All Members of the United Nations are *ipso facto* parties to the Statute of the International Court of Justice.
2. A state which is not a Member of the United Nations may become a party to the Statute of the International Court of Justice on conditions to be determined in each case by the General Assembly upon the recommendation of the Security Council.

Article 94

1. Each Member of the United Nations undertakes to comply with the decision of the International Court of Justice in any case to which it is a party.
2. If any party to a case fails to perform the obligations incumbent upon it under a judgement rendered by the Court, the other party may have recourse to the Security Council, which may, if it deems necessary, make recommendations or decide upon measures to be taken to give effect to the judgement.

Article 95

Nothing in the present Charter shall prevent Members of the United Nations from entrusting the solution of their differences to other tribunals by virtue of agreements already in existence or which may be concluded in the future.

Article 96

1. The General Assembly of the Security Council may request the International Court of Justice to give an advisory opinion on any legal question.
2. Other organs of the United Nations and specialized agencies, which may at any time be so authorized by the General Assembly, may also request advisory opinions of the Court on legal actions arising within the scope of their activities.

Chapter XV

THE SECRETARIAT

Article 97

The Secretariat shall comprise a Secretary-General and such staff as the Organization may require. The Secretary-General shall be appointed by the General Assembly upon the recommendation of the Security Council. He shall be the chief administrative officer of the Organization.

Article 98

The Secretary-General shall act in that capacity in all meetings of the General Assembly, of the Secretary Council, of the Economic and Social Council, and of the Trusteeship Council, and shall perform such other functions as are entrusted to him by these organs. The Secretary-General shall make an annual report to the General Assembly on the work of the Organization.

Article 99

The Secretary-General may bring to the attention of the Security Council any matter which in his opinion may threaten the maintenance of international peace and security.

Article 100

1. In the performance of their duties the Secretary-General and the staff shall not seek or receive instructions from any government or from any other authority external to the Organization. They shall refrain from any action which might reflect on their position as international officials responsible only to the Organization.
2. Each Member of the United Nations undertakes to respect the exclusively international character of the responsibilities of the Secretary-General and the staff and not to seek to influence them in the discharge of their responsibilities.

Article 101

1. The staff shall be appointed by the Secretary-General under regulations established by the General Assembly.
2. Appropriate staffs shall be permanently assigned to the Economic and Social Council, the Trusteeship Council, and, as required, to other organs of the United Nations. These staffs shall form a part of the Secretariat.
3. The paramount consideration in the employment of the staff and in the determination of the conditions of service shall be the necessity of securing the highest standards of efficiency, competence, and integrity. Due regard shall be paid to the importance of recruiting staff on as wide a geographical basis as possible.

Chapter XVI

MISCELLANEOUS PROVISIONS

Article 102

1.   Every treaty and every international agreement entered into by any Member of the United Nations after the present Charter comes into force shall as soon as possible be registered with the Secretariat and published by it.

2.   No party to any such treaty or international agreement which has not been registered in accordance with the provisions of paragraph 1 of this Article may invoke that treaty or agreement before any organ of the United Nations.

Article 103

In the event of a conflict between the obligations of the Members of the United Nations under the present Charter and their obligations under any other international agreement, their obligations under the present Charter shall prevail.

Article 104

The Organization shall enjoy in the territory of each of its Members such legal capacity as may be necessary for the exercise of its functions and the fulfilment of its purposes.

Article 105

1.   The Organization shall enjoy in the territory of each of its Members such privileges and immunities as are necessary for the fulfilment of its purposes.

2.   Representatives of the Members of the United Nations and officials of the Organization shall similarly enjoy such privileges and immunities as are necessary for the independent exercise of their functions in connexion with the Organization.

3.   The General Assembly may make recommendations with a view to determining the details of the application of paragraphs 1 and 2 of this Article or may propose conventions to the Members of the United Nations for this purpose.

Chapter XVII

TRANSITIONAL SECURITY ARRANGEMENTS

Article 106

Pending the coming into force of such special agreements referred to in Article 43 as in the opinion of the Security Council enable it to begin the exercise of its responsibilities under Article 42, the parties to the Four-Nation Declaration, signed at Moscow, 30 October 1943, and France, shall, in accordance with the provisions of paragraph 5 of that Declaration, consult with one another and as occasion requires with other Members of the United Nations with a view to such joint action on behalf of the Organization as may be necessary for the purpose of maintaining international peace and security.

Article 107

Nothing in the present Charter shall invalidate or preclude action, in relation to any state which during the Second World War has been an enemy of any signatory to the present Charter, taken or authorized as a result of that war by the Governments having responsibility for such action.

Chapter XVIII

AMENDMENTS

Article 108

Amendments to the present Charter shall come into force for all Members of the United Nations when they have been adopted by a vote of two thirds of the members of the General Assembly and ratified in accordance with their respective constitutional processes by two-thirds of the Members of the United Nations, including all the permanent members of the Security Council.

Article 109

1.   A General Conference of the Members of the United Nations for the purpose of reviewing the present Charter may be held at a date and place to be fixed by a two-thirds vote of the members of the General Assembly and by a vote of any nine members of the Security Council. Each Member of the United Nations shall have one vote in the conference.

2.   Any alteration of the present Charter recommended by a two-thirds vote of the conference shall take effect when ratified in accordance with their respective constitutional processes by two-thirds of the Members of the United Nations including all the permanent members of the Security Council.

3.   If such a conference has not been held before the tenth annual session of the General Assembly following the coming into force of the present Charter, the proposal to call such a conference shall be placed on the agenda of that session of the General Assembly, and the conference shall be held if so decided by a majority vote of the members of the General Assembly and by a vote of any seven members of the Security Council.

Chapter XIX

RATIFICATION AND SIGNATURE

Article 110

1.   The present Charter shall be ratified by the signatory states in accordance with their respective constitutional processes.

2.   The ratifications shall be deposited with the Government of the United States of America, which shall notify all the signatory states of each deposit as well as the Secretary-General of the Organization when he has been appointed.

3.   The present Charter shall come into force upon the deposit of ratification by the Republic of China, France, the Union of Soviet Socialist Republics, the United Kingdom of Great Britain and Northern Ireland, and the United States of America,

and by a majority of the other signatory states. A protocol of the ratifications deposited shall thereupon be drawn up by the Government of the United States of America which shall communicate copies thereof to all signatory states.

4. The states signatory to the present Charter which ratify it after it has come into force will become original Members of the United Nations on the date of the deposit of their respective ratifications.

Article 111

The present Charter, of which the Chinese, French, Russian, English, and Spanish texts are equally authentic, shall remain deposited in the archives of the Government of the United States of America. Duly certified copies thereof shall be transmitted by that Government to the Governments of the other signatory states.

IN FAITH WHEREOF the representatives of the Governments of the United Nations have signed the present Charter.

DONE at the city of San Francisco the twenty-sixth day of June, one thousand nine hundred and forty-five.

Note: Amendments to Articles 23, 27 and 61 of the Charter were adopted by the General Assembly on 17 December 1963 and came into force on 31 August 1965. A further amendment to Article 61 was adopted by the General Assembly on 20 December 1971, and came into force on 24 September 1973. An amendment to Article 109, adopted by the General Assembly on 20 December 1965, came into force on 12 June 1968.

The amendment to Article 23 enlarges the membership of the Security Council from eleven to fifteen. The amendment to Article 27 provides that decisions of the Security Council on procedural matters shall be made by a affirmative vote of nine members (formerly seven) and on all other matters by an affirmative vote of nine members (formerly seven), including the concurring votes of the five permanent members of the Security Council.

The amendment to Article 61, which entered into force on 31 August 1965, enlarged the membership of the Economic and Social Council from eighteen to twenty-seven. The subsequent amendment to that Article, which entered into force on 24 September 1973, further increased the membership of the Council from twenty-seven to fifty-four.

The amendment to Article 109, which relates to the first paragraph of that Article, provides that a General Conference of Member States for the purpose of reviewing the Charter may be held at a date and place to be fixed by a two-thirds vote of the members of the General Assembly and by a vote of any nine members (formerly seven) of the Security Council. Paragraph 3 of Article 109, which deals with the consideration of a possible review conference during the tenth regular session of the General Assembly, has been retained in its original form in its reference to a 'vote, of any seven members of the Security Council', the paragraph having been acted upon in 1955 by the General Assembly, at its tenth regular session, and by the Security Council.

Bibliography

A vast quantity of official documentation and secondary writing is available to anyone wanting to know more about the work of the United Nations. Most of the work of deliberative organs is recorded in the Official Records series, which is arranged under the name of the main organs, such as the Security Council or General Assembly, that is responsible for the work. Official documents are available in UN-appointed depository libraries, many of which are in universities and research institutions, as well as in official government installations in most member countries. Official publications eventually appear in six official languages: Arabic, Chinese, English, French, Russian and Spanish. In addition, the UN Secretariat publishes official reports and unofficial public information materials. These materials, available in UN Information Centres in many parts of the world, include statistical publications and guides to, and summaries of the work of the organization.

A useful survey of the work of the United Nations can be found in the *Yearbook of the United Nations*, published annually by the UN Department of Public Information but lagging some years behind. The yearbooks, which are standard items in reference libraries all over the world, contain the texts of the most important resolutions adopted by the deliberative organs, as well as brief versions of debates and a summary of the earlier treatment of the topics by the several organizational agencies. A briefer reference source, which includes few verbatim texts, is *Everyman's United Nations*, for the period 1945–65. Its companion volume, *Everyone's United Nations*, deals with the period 1965–1977/8. Both sets of volumes were published by the UN Department of Public Information, as is the quarterly journal, *United Nations Chronicle*, which contains current information on the work of the United Nations and briefer treatment of other organizations in the UN system.

A more independent reference source on current activities is the annual volume, *Issues before the...th General Assembly of the United Nations*, prepared by the United Nations Association of the United States of America. It appears each September at the opening of the General Assembly and is now published by Lexington Books. Another source on current activities are the essays on UN documentary sources, published by the Academic Council on the United Nations System, whose office is at Watson Institute for International Studies, Box 1970, Brown University, Providence, RI 02912–1970.

GENERAL REFERENCES

A careful collection of documentary materials is Louis B. Sohn (ed.), *International Organization and Integration: Annotated Basic Documents of International Organizations and Arrangements* (Dordrecht: Martinus Nijhoff, 1986). For an authoritative legal and historical commentary on the structure and intended operation of the United Nations, see Leland M. Goodrich, Edvard Hambro, and Anne Patricia Simons, *Charter of the United Nations. Commentary and Documents*, 3rd rev. edn (New York: Columbia University Press, 1969). See also D. W. Bowett, *The Law of International Institutions*, 2nd edn (London: Stevens, 1970); Henry G. Schermers, *International Institutional Law*, 3 vols (Leyden: Sijthoff, 1972); Robert C. R. Siekmann, *Basic Documents on United Nations and Related Peace-Keeping Forces*, 2nd enlarged edn (Dordrecht: Martinus Nijhoff, 1989); Bruno Simma (ed.), *The Charter of the United Nations: Commentary* (Oxford: Oxford University Press, 1993).

Many general accounts of the United Nations for general audiences and for university study are available. Among the most helpful of these are: Inis L. Claude, Jr, *Swords into Plowshares*, 4th edn (New York: Random House, 1971); H. G. Nicholas, *The United Nations as Political Institution*, 5th edn (London: Oxford University Press, 1975); A. LeRoy Bennett, *International Organizations*, 2nd edn (Englewood Cliffs NJ: Prentice-Hall, 1980): Harold K. Jacobson, 2nd edn, *Networks of Interdependence* (New York: Knopf, 1984): Adam Roberts and Benedict Kingsbury (eds), *United Nations, Divided World: The UN's Roles in International Relations* (Oxford: Clarendon Press, 1988): Lawrence S. Finkelstein (ed.), *Politics in the United Nations System* (Durham and London: Duke University Press, 1988).

1. INTRODUCTION

Luard, Evan, *A History of the United Nations: The Years of Western Domination* (London: Macmillan, 1982).

Mangone, Gerard J., *A Short History of the United Nations Charter* (New York: McGraw-Hill, 1954).

Russell, Ruth B., *A History of the United Nations Charter. The Role of the United States* (Washington, DC: Brookings Institution, 1958).

Walters, Frank P. *A History of the League of Nations*, 2 vols (London: Oxford University Press, 1952)

2. CHARTER AND STRUCTURE OF THE UNITED NATIONS

Bailey, Sydney D., *The Procedure of the UN Security Council* (Oxford: Oxford University Press, 1975).

Bloed, A. and van Dijk, P., *Forty Years International Court of Justice: Jurisdiction, Equity and Equality* (Utrecht: Europa Instituut, 1988).

Finkelstein, Lawrence S. (ed.), *Politics in the United Nations System* (Durham and London: Duke University Press, 1988).

Franck, Thomas M., 'The Good Offices Function of the UN Secretary-General', in Roberts and Kingsbury, op.cit., pp. 79–94.

Goodrich, Leland M., Edvard Hambro and A. P. Simons, *Charter of the United Nations. Commentary and Documents*, 3rd. rev. edn (New York: Columbia University Press, 1969).

Meron, Theodor, *The United Nations Secretariat* (Lexington, Mass.: D. C. Heath, 1977).

Nichol, Davidson, *et al.*, *The United Nations Security Council: Towards Greater Effectiveness* (New York: UN Institute for Training and Research, 1982).

Pérez de Cuéllar, Javier, 'The Role of the UN Secretary-General', in Roberts and Kingsbury, op.cit., pp. 61–77.

Peterson, M. J., *The General Assembly in World Politics* (Boston, Mass.: Allen & Unwin, 1986).

Urquhart, Brian, *Hammarskjöld* (New York: Knopf, 1972).

3. MEMBERSHIP AND DECISION-MAKING

Baehr, Peter R. and Castermans, Monique C. (eds), *The Netherlands and the United Nations: Selected Issues* (The Hague: I. M. Asser Institute, 1990).

Groom, A. J. R., Paul Taylor and Andrew Williams, *The Study of International Organisation: British Experiences* (Hanover, NH: Academic Council on the United Nations System, 1990).

Kaufmann, Johan, *United Nations Decision-Making* (Alphen aan den Rijn: Sijthoff & Noordhoff, 1980).

Kaufmann, Johan, *Conference Diplomacy: An Introductory Analysis*, 2nd rev. edn (Dordrecht: Martinus Nijhoff, 1988).

Kay, David A., *The New Nations in the United Nations 1960–1967*. (New York: Columbia University Press, 1970).

Kirkpatrick, Jeane J., *The Reagan Phenomenon and other Speeches on Foreign Policy* (Washington, DC: American Enterprise Institute for Public Policy Research, 1983).

Morphet, Sally, 'Resolutions and Vetoes in the UN Security Council: Their Relevance and Significance', *Review of International Studies* 16 (1990), pp. 341–59.

Stokman, Frans N., *Roll Calls and Sponsorship* (Leyden: Sijthoff, 1977).

4. THE MAINTENANCE OF PEACE AND SECURITY

Abi-Saab, Georges, *The United Nations Operation in the Congo 1960–1964* (New York: Oxford University Press, 1978).

Berridge, G. R., *Return to the UN: UN Diplomacy in Regional Conflicts* (London: Macmillan, 1991).

Boutros-Ghali, Boutros, *An Agenda for Peace: Preventive Diplomacy, Peacemaking and Peace-keeping* (New York: United Nations, 1992).

Claude, Inis L. Jr, *Power and International Relations* (New York: Random House, 1964).

Goodrich, Leland M., *Korea: A Study of U.S. Policy* (New York: Council on Foreign Relations, 1956).

Gordenker, Leon, *The U.N. Secretary-General and the Maintenance of Peace* (New York: Columbia University Press, 1967).

Gordenker, Leon and Weiss, Thomas G., *Soldiers, Peacekeepers and Disasters* (London: Macmillan, 1992).

Haas, Ernst, 'Regime Decay: Conflict Management and International Organizations, 1945–1981', *International Organization*, 37:2 (Spring 1983), pp. 189–235.

Higgins, Rosalyn, *United Nations Peacekeeping* 1946–1967. *Documents and Commentary* (New York: Oxford University Press, 1980).

Howard, Michael, 'The United Nations and International Security', in Roberts and Kingsbury, op.cit., pp. 31–45.

James, Alan, 'The Security Council: Paying for Peacekeeping', in David P. Forsythe (ed.), *The United Nations in the World Political Economy: Essays in Honour of Leon Gordenker* (London: Macmillan, 1989), pp. 13–35.

Murphy, John F., *The United Nations and the Control of International Violence* (Totowa, NJ: Allanheld, Osmun, 1983).

Norton, Augustus Richard and Thomas G. Weiss, 'UN Peacekeepers: Soldiers with a Difference', *Headline Series*, No. 292 (Spring 1990).

Rikhye, Indar Jit, *The Future of Peacekeeping* (New York: International Peace Academy, 1989).

Stegenga, James A., *The United Nations Force in Cyprus* (Columbus, Ohio State University Press, 1968).

United Nations, *The Blue Helmets: A Review of United Nations Peace-keeping*, 2nd edn (New York: Department of Public Information, 1990).

Weiss, Thomas G. (ed.), *Collective Security in a Changing World* (Boulder, CO and London: Lynne Rienner Publishers, 1993).

White, N. D., *The United Nations and the Maintenance of International Peace and Security* (Manchester: Manchester University Press, 1990).

5. HUMAN RIGHTS

Alston, Philip (ed.), *The United Nations and Human Rights: a Critical Reappraisal* (Oxford: Clarendon Press, 1992).

Donnelly, Jack, 'Human Rights at the United Nations, 1955–1985: The Question of Bias', *International Studies Quarterly* 32 (1988), pp. 275–303.

Farer, Tom J., 'The United Nations and Human Rights: More than a Whimper, Less than a Roar', in Roberts and Kingsbury, op.cit., pp. 95–138.

Forsythe, David P., *Human Rights and World Politics*. 2nd edn (Lincoln: University of Nebraska Press, 1989).

Humphrey, John P., *Human Rights and the United Nations: A Great Adventure* (Dobbs Ferry, NY: Transnational, 1983).

McColdrick, Dominic, *The Human Rights Committee: Its Role in the Development of International Covenant on Civil and Political Rights* (Oxford, Clarendon Press, 1991).

Morphet, Sally, 'Economic, Social and Cultural Rights: The Development of Governments' Views, 1971–88', in Ralph Bedard and Dilys Hill (eds), *Economic, Social and Cultural Rights: Progress and Achievement* (London: Macmillan, 1992), pp. 74–92.

Mower, Glenn A., *The United States, the United Nations and Human Rights* (Westport, Conn.: Greenwood Press, 1979).

Ramcharan, B. G., *Humanitarian Good Offices in International Law: The Good Offices of the United Nations Secretary-General in the Field of Human Rights* (The Hague: Martinus Nijhoff, 1982).

Rodley, Nigel S., 'The Development of United Nations Activities in the Field of Human Rights and the Role of Non-Governmental Organizations', in Toby I.

Gati (ed.), *The US, the UN, and the Management of Global Change* (New York: New York University Press, 1983).

Stenson Clark, Roger, *A United Nations Commissioner for Human Rights* (The Hague: Martinus Nijhoff, 1972).

Tolley, Howard Jr, *The U.N. Commission on Human Rights* (Boulder and London: Westview Press, 1987).

United Nations, *Human Rights: A Compilation of International Instruments* (New York: United Nations, 1993).

Van Boven, Theo, *People Matter: Views on International Human Rights Policy* (Amsterdam: Meulenhoff, 1982).

6.   FROM COLONIALISM TO INDEPENDENCE

Dale, Richard, 'The UN and Decolonization in Namibia', in Forsythe, op.cit., (1989), pp. 165–96.

Dore, Isaak I., *The International Mandate System and Namibia* (Boulder, CO.: Westview Press, 1985).

Dugard, John (ed.), *The South-West Africa/Namibia Dispute* (Berkeley: University of California Press, 1973).

El-Ayouty, Yassin, *The United Nations and Decolonization: The Role of Afro-Asia* (The Hague: Martinus Nijhoff, 1971).

Emerson, Rupert, *From Empire to Nation: The Rise to Self-Assertion of Asian and African Peoples* (Cambridge, Mass.: Harvard University Press, 1960).

Gowlland-Debbas, Vera, *Collective Responses to Illegal Acts in International Law: United Nations Action in the Question of Southern Rhodesia* (Dordrecht: Martinus Nijhoff, 1990).

Jessup, Philip C., *The Birth of Nations* (New York and London: Columbia University Press, 1974).

Nkala, Jericho, *The United Nations, International Law and the Rhodesian Independence Crisis* (Oxford: Clarendon Press, 1985).

Rotberg, Robert I. (ed.), *Namibia: Political and Economic Perspectives* (Lexington, MA.: Lexington Books, 1983).

Sears, Mason, *Years of High Purpose: from Trusteeship to Nationhood* (Washington, DC: University Press of America, 1980).

Slonim, Solomon, *South West Africa and the United Nations: An International Mandate in Dispute* (Baltimore: Johns Hopkins University Press, 1973).

Totemeyer, Gerhard, Kandetu, Vesera and Werner, Wolfgang, *Namibia in Perspective* (Windhoek: Council of Churches in Namibia, 1987).

Toussaint, Charmian E., *The Trusteeship System of the United Nations* (Westport, Conn.: Greenwood Press, 1976).

7.   COOPERATION FOR ECONOMIC AND SOCIAL PROGRESS

Camps, Miriam, with Catherine Gwin, *Collective Management: The Reform of Global Economic Organization* (New York: McGraw-Hill, 1981).

Cox, Robert W., Harold K. Jacobson, *et al.*, *The Anatomy of Influence: Decision Making in International Organization* (New Haven: Yale University Press, 1973).

Dadzie, Kenneth, 'The United Nations and the Problem of Economic Development', in Roberts and Kingsbury, op.cit., pp. 139–57.

Finkelstein, Lawrence S., 'The Political Role of the Director-General of UNESCO', in Finkelstein, op.cit., pp. 385–423.

Forsythe, David P., 'The Political Economy of UN Refugee Programmes', in Forsythe, op.cit. (1989), pp. 131–43.

Friedheim, Robert L., 'Value Allocation and North–South Conflict in the Third United Nations Law of the Sea Conference', in Finkelstein, op.cit., pp. 175–213.

Gordenker, Leon, *International Aid and National Decisions* (Princeton, NJ: Princeton University Press, 1976).

Gordenker, Leon, *Refugees in International Politics* (London: Croom Helm, 1989).

Harrod, Jeffrey and Nico Schrijver (eds), *The UN Under Attack* (Aldershot: Gower, 1988).

Jackson, Robert, *A Study of the Capacity of the UN Development System* (New York: United Nations, 1969).

Kaufmann, Johan, 'The Economic and Social Council and the New International Economic Order', in Forsythe, op.cit. (1989), pp. 54–66.

Kaufmann, Johan and Nico Schrijver, *Changing Global Needs: Expanding Roles for the United Nations System* (Hanover, NH: Academic Council on the United Nations System, 1990).

Marchisio, Sergio and DiBiase, Antonietta, *The Food and Agriculture Organization* (Rome: Martinus Nijhoff, 1991).

Michalak, Stanley J., 'UNCTAD as an Agent of Change', in Forsythe, op.cit, (1989), pp. 69–85.

Mitrany, David, *A Working Peace System* (Chicago: Quadrangle Books, 1966).

Rothstein, Robert L., *Global Bargaining: UNCTAD and the Quest for a New International Economic Order* (Princeton, NJ: Princeton University Press, 1979).

Sauvant, Karl P., *The Group of 77. Evolution, Structure, Organization* (New York: Oceana Publications, 1981).

Williams, Douglas, *The Specialized Agencies and the United Nations: The System in Crisis* (London: C. Hurst & Co., 1987).

8. THE 1990S: A CHANGING UN

Bertrand, Maurice, *The Third Generation World Organization*. (Dordrecht: Martinus Nijhoff, 1989).

Coate, Roger, *Unilateralism, Ideology and United States Foreign Policy: The US In and Out of UNESCO* (Boulder: Lynne Rienner, 1988).

Falk, Richard A., *A Study of Future Worlds* (New York: The Free Press, 1975).

Finger, Seymour Maxwell, *Your Man at the UN* (New York: New York University Press, 1980).

Franck, Thomas M., *Nation against Nation: What Happened to the U.N. Dream and what the U.S. Can Do about It* (New York and Oxford: Oxford University Press, 1985).

Fromuth, Peter, *A Successor Vision: The United Nations of Tomorrow* (Lanham, Md: University Press of America, 1988).

Gati, Toby Trister (ed.), *The US, the UN, and the Management of Global Change* (New York: New York University Press, 1983).

Gorbachev, Mikhail, *Realities and Guarantees for a Secure World* (Moscow: Novosti Press, 1987).

Gordenker, Leon (ed.), *The United Nations in International Politics* (Princeton, NJ: Princeton University Press, 1971).

Kaufman, Johan and Schrijver, Nico, *Changing Global Needs: Expanding Roles for the United Nations System* (Hanover, NH: Academic Council on the United Nations System, 1990).

Kaufman, Johan, Leurdijk, Dick, and Schrijver, Nico, *The World in Turmoil: Towards a Renaissance of the United Nations?* (Hanover, NH: Academic Council on the United Nations System, 1991).

Luard, Evan, 'Conclusion: The Contemporary Role of the United Nations', in Roberts and Kingsbury, op.cit., pp. 209–30.

Moynihan, Daniel Patrick, *A Dangerous Place* (New York: Berkley Books, 1980).

Müller, Joachim W., *The Reform of the United Nations* (New York, London : Oceana , 1992).

Müller, Joachim W., *The Reform of the United Nations* (New York/London/ Rome: Oceana Publications, 1992).

Puchala, Donald J. and Roger A. Coate, *The State of the United Nations, 1988* (Hanover, NH: The Academic Council on the United Nations System, 1988).

Puchala, Donald J. and Roger A. Coate, *The Challenge of Relevance: The United Nations in a Changing World Environment* (Hanover, NH: The Academic Council on the United Nations System, 1989).

Renninger, John P. (ed.), *The Future Role of the United Nations in an Interdependent World* (Dordrecht: Martinus Nijhoff, 1989).

Rivlin, Benjamin and Leon Gordenker (eds), *The Challenging Role of the UN Secretary-General: Making 'The Most Impossible Job in the World' Possible* (Westport, CT: Praeger, 1993).

Urquhart, Brian and Erskine Childers, *A World in Need of Leadership: Tomorrow's United Nations* (Uppsala: Dag Hammarskjöld Foundation, 1990).

Index